Football and the English

A *Social History of* Association *Football* in *England*, 1863–1995

Dave Russell

Carnegie Publishing 1997

First published in 1997 by
Carnegie Publishing Ltd, 18 Maynard Street, Preston PR2 2AL

ISBN 1-85936-038-6

Typeset by Carnegie Publishing, 18 Maynard St, Preston
Printed and bound by Bookcraft (Bath) Ltd

To the memory of my parents

Norah Russell (1922–1980)
Raymond Russell (1925–1996)

Contents

Acknowledgements

Many people have given invaluable assistance at various stages of this project. Staff at a number of libraries, particularly those at the British Library, provided excellent service in not always easy circumstances, while Lorna Parnell and her colleagues at the Football League and David Barber and Aileen Wood at the Football Association provided informed and prompt help. David Barber's generous help with illustrations was greatly appreciated as was that of journalists and library staff at the *Bradford Telegraph and Argus*, *Halifax Courier*, *Huddersfield Examiner* and *Lancashire Evening Post*. Gillian Lonergar complied an index with great speed and efficiency at short notice. A number of friends and colleagues looked at draft material and criticised it with greater or lesser degrees of tact, but always with great purpose and effect. Tony Mason gave support at a crucial time to another scholar on the loose in territory he has done so much to open up. I am especially grateful to Rex Pope for supporting my application for the study leave which allowed this book to be written and for helpful comments on chapters three and four, Chris Riley for comments and help with sources and to Jan Bentley whose patient eye allowed me to remove innumerable inaccuracies and grammatical errors from the first draft. Any remaining errors and inaccuracies are unquestionably my responsibility. I am grateful to Alistair Hodge and Alan Crosby at Carnegie Publishing for suggesting that I write this book and to the staff at Carnegie for their help and courtesy. Finally, Veronica Russell encouraged and supported me throughout the trials and tribulations that befall all authors, especially those with a propensity to over-enthusiastic use of the 'delete' key on their word-processor.

Dave Russell
Summer, 1996

Introduction

One day in the late 1960s my history teacher – a brilliant practitioner despite a firm belief in the pedagogical value of public ridicule – caused much merriment when returning exam essays on the social and economic importance of the railway by pouring scorn upon a classmate's claim that one of its key functions was to bring northern football supporters to Wembley cup finals. We all guffawed dutifully, and none louder than I; fancy bringing football into the 'O' level syllabus. (I am ashamed to admit that a similar cynicism struck when, as a first-year undergraduate at York University in 1971, I heard that the Sociology Department was offering a 'football option'.) Sadly, I suspect that my schoolfriend was, as our teacher claimed, struggling desperately to fill paper rather than demonstrating original historical insight, but the incident has often returned to me over the years on encountering a similar point, albeit probably expressed rather more subtly, in numerous scholarly books and articles. If only the social history explosion had taken place a few years earlier, he might have been spared a re-sit.

It is still possible to meet the unconverted who deem football too trivial a topic for academic consideration, while in the wider world the conjunction of academia and football is still a fertile source of lazy journalistic humour. My own involvement in an exhibition on the history of the Football League in 1988, for example, led to an article in a local paper noting that, on visiting my office, the careful observer could see football boots peeping out from under my gown. However, despite these mild tribulations, the case for the value of sports history has largely been won. A beneficiary of social history's rise to prominence from the 1970s, the history of sport in general, and football in particular, has became an important aspect of the academic terrain, losing much of its pariah status *en route*.

Although a small body of serious writing on football's history existed before the 1970s – the game's lack of social cachet denying it a literature of similar size to that enjoyed by cricket – the *academic* community had almost completely ignored it.[1] The turning point came in 1975 with the publication of James Walvin's *The People's Game*. Inevitably, given the state of research at that time, it was only a relatively brief overview of the British game (and its transposition to Europe and the rest of the world) from the mid-nineteenth century to the 1970s, but it nevertheless served a vital function in identifying the history of football as valid territory for academic exploration and raising a number of central issues for subsequent consideration.[2] Walvin's introductory work was fairly soon followed by an ever growing body of specialist monographs and articles too numerous to list here. Among their number, however, were several books to which this work owes a particular debt and which will remain central to all studies of the game for the foreseeable future. Most important here are Tony Mason, *Association Football and English Society, 1863–1915* (1980); Stephen Wagg, *The Football World. A Contemporary Social History* (1984); Wray Vamplew, *Pay up and Play the Game* (1988); Richard Holt, *Sport and the British* (1989); and Nicholas Fishwick, *English Football and Society, 1910–1950* (1989). The growing interest in sport and soccer among historians has been parallelled in other disciplines, especially sociology, while recent years have also witnessed the rise of a vigorous tradition of serious football literature from outside the academic establishment by writers and journalists such as Simon Inglis and John Harding.[3] The very existence of this tradition of 'popular' sports history is suggestive of a more secure place for football within British society after the problems of the 1970s and 1980s.

It was the increasingly healthy state of football's scholarly literature that led to the decision to write this book, ultimately a work of synthesis, which has the dual aim of guiding the new reader through the increasingly full shelves, while offering more seasoned students the chance to reflect and to place specialist interests in a wider context. The focus is on *English* rather than British football, simply because I do not possess the space, and more honestly, the knowledge, required to do justice to the history of the Irish, Scottish or Welsh games.[4] Professional soccer as played in the Football League and various domestic cup competitions forms the heart of this study, although other aspects including amateur football, the women's game and international football are dealt with where relevant. Within that context, geographical accident, in the form of my recent occupational and domestic location, has meant that one or two clubs feature rather more than others: close readers of early drafts commented on the relative frequency of references to Preston North End and Bradford City. Coverage has obviously not been exhaustive: indeed, a secondary aim of the book is to identify (I suspect sometimes unwittingly) some of the many gaps which remain to be filled by future research. The problem of content choice is particularly problematic in regard to very recent events. Much of this book was written during the 1995–96 season when a number of issues, most notably the whole future of the transfer system, were being debated. Rather than risk disguising provisional outcome as definite historical record, such issues have been conveniently ignored or dealt with only cursorily. I hope that any disadvantages of this approach are outweighed by the opportunity to consider the game's development over the widest possible chronological sweep.

Above all, this is a social and cultural history of football. This is *not* to suggest that the game itself will be ignored, for most sections include at least a brief discussion of tactics, strategy, style and rule changes. Social historians do not always concern themselves with the actual mechanics and laws of sport, but it is helpful to pay them some attention. Apart from the intrinsic interest in studying the evolution of a game, shifts in patterns of play and major rule changes, although often the product of an autonomous sporting context, can also be valuable indicators of shifting social currents and attitudes. The main intention, however, is to examine the relationship between football, defined here to embrace players, managers, administrators and spectators, and the wider English society. This allows for the coverage of numerous topics including the relationship between sport and the media; the impact of economic change upon the fortunes of both the game and individual clubs; the players' long battle against the retain and transfer system; and the nature of crowd culture and behaviour. The particular emphasis is upon the role that football has played in reflecting, constructing and representing debates and conflicts relating to the issues of class and class conflict, local, regional and national identity and gender. Indeed, a central premise of this study is that association football has been shaped by, and has in turn shaped, the power relations that have existed between different social groups in English society.

What follows is aimed at both an academic readership and what publishers' blurbs usually describe as 'an intelligent lay audience'. This is a balancing trick fraught with difficulty. At the first hint of anecdote some of the former will demand greater rigour while at the first sight of a three-syllable sociological term, some of the latter will fax 'Pseud's Corner'. I only hope that both audiences, thus equally insulted, are equally satisfied.

1

Association Football and the Men Who Made It, 1863–1885

Association football formally originates from a series of meetings held in London in 1863. The main function of this chapter is to examine how the game moved from being the property of a small number of young men educated at public and grammar schools to become a far more broadly rooted game, poised to become the national winter sport. It is necessary to precede this, however, with a brief exploration of the relationship between association football and the 'folk' and public school games that preceded it. This 'story' is well known, so well known in fact that it is often compressed into a rather simplified version, roughly as follows. A primitive type of football had existed for centuries, but in the early and mid-nineteenth century this rowdy, ill-disciplined folk game was suppressed by a propertied class anxious to preserve law and order. Various versions of the game were kept alive and 'civilised' by public school masters seeking to promote discipline and 'muscular Christianity'. Public schoolboys keen to enjoy football on leaving school then developed agreed, codified versions of the game in the form of association football and rugby football (1871), which those with a social conscience then 'took out' to the urban working class. There is, of course, a great deal of truth in this bald outline, but research over the last two decades has revealed complexities which dispel the more simplistic notions about the rise of the game.

'Folk' football

Football certainly has deep roots in England, although exactly how deep will always be a matter for speculation. The first written records of so-called 'folk' football in England date from the fourteenth century when successive governments attempted to ban it as both a threat to law and order and a distraction from vital practice for military pursuits, especially archery. However, it is perfectly possible that the game pre-dates this period.[1] There was, of course, no single game called football from this point, rather a family of related games played in different parts of the country. It is the vision of the large-scale, set-piece games usually coincident with village feasts, fairs and wakes, or national holidays such as Shrove Tuesday, that is most commonly evoked by the term 'folk' football. Such games were probably played mainly by men from the lower social orders, although some historians claim the presence of gentry and other elite elements, and women certainly took part in some games. The popular view is of a game that was little more than a free-for-all involving unlimited numbers, few rules and 'pitches' that might encompass a whole town. The famed Shrove Tuesday game between (nominally) the parishes of All Saints and St Peter's in Derby, which could feature 'teams' of 500–1,000, and which often involved the use of the river Derwent for periods of a game that regularly took six hours to complete, fits this picture well.[2] Others, however, such as the unusually well-documented Cornish variant termed 'hurling' had quite well-established sets of rules, relatively confined playing areas and featured balanced sides of 15, 20 or 30 players. While all games involved some degree of physical violence (the Welsh 'knappan' or 'cnappan' which, according to one early seventeenth-century account, could feature 2,000 players including cudgel-wielding horsemen), they were perhaps not always as ill-disciplined as is sometimes implied.[3]

By the third and fourth decades of the nineteenth century, these various games were either extinct or under serious and usually terminal threat, victims of the cluster of social and economic forces that were to reshape so many elements of pre- and early industrial recreation. Some fell victim to the loss of space associated with both the enclosure of common ground and the accelerating pace of urbanisation, others were challenged by pressure from evangelical groups who saw football as a decidedly 'worldly' and unsuitable pastime. Crucially, football was also seen as a threat to the social and political order. Its sometimes carnivalesque element – unpopular or merely well-dressed people were sometimes 'dusted' with soot or powder during the Shrovetide Derby game – and its habit of bringing the younger element of the lower orders into public spaces in large numbers were increasingly seen as inappropriate and, indeed, positively dangerous in an age of mass political radicalism and subsequent fear for public order. It should be noted, however, that while much of the active opposition to folk football came from the propertied classes, local elites provided protection for the game in some areas, while it was sections of the working classes who actually opposed the game on occasions. Evangelicalism fuelled their dislike in perhaps the majority of cases, but industrial and political radicalism could also stimulate criticism. Striking trade unionists in Derby in 1833–34, for example, saw the local game as 'barbarous recklessness and supreme folly', promoted by the local elite in a display of de-radicalising paternalism which encouraged workers to behave in a demeaning manner.[4] As was often the case in the decades ahead, the lines of social fissure that football created were not always neatly drawn along the boundaries of social class.

As a result of these influences, often acting in subtle concert rather than individually, games fell into desuetude or were suppressed. The suppression of folk football was often vigorously contested by players and supporters. Varying degrees of threat and force were used to end the games at several locations in Middlesex and Surrey, for example, including Richmond (1840), East Molesey and Hampton Wick (1857), Hampton (1864) and Kingston-upon-Thames (1867) while in Derby in 1846 the Riot Act had to be read and a troop of cavalry used to disperse the players. One or two games managed to carry on into the late nineteenth century, and the Ashbourne Shrove Tuesday game, almost outlawed in the early 1860s, still persists, protected in the late nineteenth century by a gloss of 'tradition' and a local pride which turned social problem into celebrated idiosyncrasy.[5] In general, however, the great set-piece games did not survive into the second half of the nineteenth century.

Folk football of this type was obviously important as a fertile source of raw material for the codified games of soccer and rugby that were to develop in the later nineteenth century, and as a generator of local rivalries that the later professional game was able to feed on. Beyond that, however, the significance of the *set-piece* games for the later development of mass team sports is not particularly clear. Few of the late nineteenth-century soccer enthusiasts will have known much of the traditional game, which had largely died by 1850, while many of the late survivals such as those in Surrey and Middlesex noted above were in areas which were not central to soccer's take-off in the 1870s and '80s. It was in fact, as Richard Holt has suggested, informal *street* football that provided rather more continuity between folk football and the later mass participatory game, keeping at least some element of popular interest in the game alive and providing a base upon which to build in the more propitious climate of the 1870s and 1880s.[6] Rather less well known to historians than the set-piece game, perhaps because rather less dramatic in design and outcome, street football was not a separate game, merely a more informal, more spontaneous (and probably more frequent) version of the various games described above. It was certainly open to suppression like all forms of the folk game and for the same reasons. The 1835 Highways Act provided for a fine of 40*s*. for 'playing at football or any other game on any part of the said Highways, to the Annoyance of any Passenger', a piece of legislation backed up by numerous local by-laws. Doubtless the level of street football activity declined considerably as a result, but it almost certainly continued to some degree. The *Morning Chronicle*'s survey of popular recreation in mid-century Birmingham, while stressing the decline of the game as a whole, noted its continued existence, presumably at street level, 'among young boys and lads'.[7] While close local research based on the local press and on police records is needed in order to explore this point further, future historians of football's roots might be advised to concentrate attention on the micro-culture of the street rather than the macro-culture of the village feast.

Public schools, codification and the establishment of the 'Association game'

It is within the realms of the public school that altogether more obvious connections between the primitive and the modern games can be located. Football existed at Eton from at least 1747, at Westminster from 1749 and was well established at Harrow, Shrewsbury, Winchester and Charterhouse by more or less the same period.[8] In general, the games seem to have been run by the boys, sometimes in the face of quite strenuous opposition from the masters, and they mirrored power relationships within the student community. While senior boys adopted the more active, attacking roles, younger pupils fulfilled defensive tasks, such as lining up along goal-lines to form a human barricade designed to prevent the opposition from scoring. Such activities were revealingly referred to at a number of schools as 'fagging' at football. Boys would sometimes play against youths from the local town, which could further exacerbate the often troubled relationship between the school and the local community.[9]

It was not until about 1830, when headmasters such as Arnold at Rugby set out to reform schools that were increasingly seen as providing an inadequate education for the nation's future male elite, that staff (often junior members) began to consider the educative value of football and games in general.[10] Initially, games were used as a mechanism for encouraging senior boys to exercise responsible authority on behalf of the staff, with the expectation that they would run games in a manner which provided discipline but avoided bullying. This establishment of a properly constituted layer of command had the dual benefit of constraining the senior boys who had posed the greatest threat to the teachers' control and improving discipline among the younger pupils. Team sports were also increasingly viewed as preferable to the various bloodsports that many schoolboys had hitherto enjoyed. By the 1840s and 1850s, the so-called 'cult of games' began to take hold in the public schools: games were no longer viewed as simply a useful stratagem for establishing control, but as a formidable vehicle for character building. Daily sports became a feature of the curriculum in many schools, and football had a central place in this process.

A major outcome of this was the emergence of codified games governed by defined rules and regulations. Each school had its own set of rules and style of game: some such as Rugby, Marlborough and Cheltenham fostered what was essentially a handling game while others, including Eton, Shrewsbury, Westminster and Charterhouse, adopted kicking games.[11] The great problem facing schoolboys when they chose to continue their sporting activities after leaving school was the consequent lack of agreed rules. In the late 1830s, in 1846 and again in 1848, attempts were made by students at Cambridge University to marry elements of the handling and kicking games; the 1848 'Cambridge rules' (modified again in 1856) were indeed adopted by a number of the first generation of formally constituted football clubs that began to emerge from the later 1850s. However, specific school-based variants remained popular; Sheffield FC, established in October 1857 and the country's first football club, played a Harrow-style kicking game learnt by many of the founder members at Sheffield Collegiate School, whereas the Blackheath Club, founded in 1858, chose to play according to Rugby School rules.[12]

Successful agreement as to adoption of rules was probably easier to reach in localities where only a limited number of the game's variants were on offer and/or where one club swiftly attained authority. Some sixteen teams, for example, were established in the Sheffield area by the early 1860s, mainly playing under Sheffield club rules.[13] However, in other places where rival codes were in contention, partisan commitment to specific school games, fuelled by the status battles between different schools, rendered the process a great deal more complicated, as was to be proven by the events of late 1863. On 26 October 1863 the first of a series of six meetings was held involving, initially, eleven London football clubs anxious to agree rules which would allow unproblematic contests between them. Taking for themselves the title of the Football Association, they first proposed a set of twenty-three rules which included a number of the regulations associated with the more robust forms of the catching game. These included provision for running with the ball in the hands if a catch had been taken 'on the full' or on the first bounce, as well as for players to be 'hacked on the front of the leg' while running with the ball and for limited use of tripping. This is perhaps a little surprising, for at almost the same time the fairly influential 'Cambridge rules' were being revised yet again in favour of the minimal use of hands and physical contact. Considerable debate ensued within the nascent Football Association over these points, and particularly over the role of hacking, deemed by some to be the essence of masculine toughness and the basis of British martial spirit, but by others as a degrading and uncivilised habit which would turn any sensible adult away from the game. Eventually those clubs in support of minimal handling and the abolition of hacking proved victorious by 13 votes to 4, and their preferences were subsequently enshrined in the rules agreed a week later on 8 December 1863.[14] Blackheath Club, the most vocal exponents of hacking, seceded from the FA and were to be instrumental in setting up the rival Rugby Football Union in 1871 (where, interestingly, hacking was speedily outlawed). Whatever Blackheath and others' objections, the 'Association game' – 'association' quickly abbreviated to 'soccer' or 'socker' in public school slang – and its ruling body had emerged.

The popular game

In the period immediately following the establishment of the Football Association, soccer retained the appearance of a fledgling sport. The rules, not to mention the size of teams, were fluid and subject to dispute. The game remained very much the preserve of ex-public and grammar schoolboys, and involved only a relatively small number of largely southern-based clubs playing a relatively small number of games. Membership of the FA, although growing steadily from the late 1860s, still stood at only 50 in 1871 and only 15 clubs entered the FA Challenge Cup, inspired by public school 'cock house' trophies, inaugurated in that year.[15] The dominant teams of the 1860s and 1870s were mainly 'old boys' sides notably the Old Etonians (1865) and the Wanderers (1864), a side only open to men who had attended the leading public schools and Oxbridge, and which won the FA Cup on five occasions between 1871 and 1878. The FA also failed to exert anything resembling total control over the administration and laws of the game. The 26-member Sheffield Association kept its distance from the FA until as late as 1877, when it agreed to abandon its own version of the offside rule and affiliate to the national body, while a number of clubs continued to play under a variety of rules in order to participate in particular games, with the captains agreeing procedures beforehand. The habit of two clubs playing one match under Rugby rules and the return under Association, or even of using one code for one half of a match and then swapping codes at half-time, was common well into the 1870s.[16]

From the early 1870s the picture began to alter. Until this point to be a footballer was to be a 'gentleman', visible evidence of attendance at either public school or grammar school and thus of membership of at least the local and perhaps the national male elite. From then on, however, the game began to exhibit a very different social ambience as it was adopted by a whole range of people, from entrepreneurs to members of the semi-skilled working class, who were previously excluded by educational and social considerations. Evidence of the 'democratisation' of soccer comes in many forms. One obvious sign was simply the growth in number of clubs from the early 1870s. Of those members of the Sheffield Football Association listed in the 1880 *Football Annual* whose foundation date is known, 16 were founded before 1870, while 34 emerged between 1870 and 1880. Similarly, while only one club affiliated to the Birmingham FA in 1880 was in existence before 1870, nine had been founded between 1870 and 1875, and all 40 clubs affiliated to the Lancashire FA in 1880 had been founded in the previous ten years.[17] Moreover, clubs that joined associations tell only part of the story at this stage. As Alan Metcalfe has pointed out in an important study, many clubs were often very short-lived and did not always survive long enough to join a local association. The 1870s and early 1880s saw a plethora of such clubs, including the exquisitely named east Lancashire trio of Flash Ramblers, Accrington Heroes and Helmshore Young Tipplers, short-lived but indicative of the new popular enthusiasm for football.[18] As will be seen later, the game's geography was fairly complex and by the early 1880s there were still areas of the country that were virtually untouched by interest in soccer or indeed any other form of mass sporting culture. However, a clear momentum had been established. The expansion in the game's appeal was also demonstrated by the growth in crowd size. While only 2,000 people attended the 1872 FA Cup final, 8,000 attended Sheffield's Cromwell Cup final in 1877 and 9,000 witnessed the first Lancashire Cup final in 1880.[19] From the early 1880s and probably before, a small number of successful sides in Lancashire and the midlands were becoming 'gate-taking' clubs, drawing large enough crowds to make it worth charging admission and erecting the stands and enclosures that were to evolve into the first generation of football stadiums in the next decade.

Above all else, football's balance of power, at least on the pitch, was swinging away from the mainly southern old boys sides towards the more popularly based teams of textile Lancashire, and the north and west midlands. This shift was firmly underlined in 1883 when Blackburn Olympic, founded as recently as 1878, beat the Old Etonians in the FA Cup final, the winning goal scored by Jimmy Costley, a cotton spinner by trade.[20] No old boys side was ever to win the cup again and it is from this point that the record books have begun to take on a reassuringly 'modern' look for the generation of youngsters coming to the game's history for the first time, baffled by the presence of the Royal Engineers and the Old Carthusians and wondering when Wanderers had added the name Bolton, Wolverhampton or Wycombe.

As Costley's appearance in the FA Cup final suggests, soccer's growth from the early 1870s owed much to its adoption by sections of the male working class. The issue of the game's social structure will be examined in detail in the next chapter but it does require some attention here. Obviously the extent of working-class involvement should not be exaggerated to the point of arguing that football had become a 'working-class' sport by the early 1880s. At least with regard to the leading clubs, formal control rarely, if ever, passed out of the hands of local elites; middle-class spectators continued to attend in significant numbers and at least until the early 1880s, teams, although increasingly comprised of players from working-class backgrounds, were socially mixed to at least some degree. As late as 1888 Preston North End's FA Cup final side included a surgeon, a master at the local Catholic grammar school and a solicitor's clerk among the ex-miners and tradesmen who made up the bulk of the team.[21] Clerks and other lower-middle-class occupational groups played a central role in some locations, notably Birmingham. However, the growth in the game's popularity could simply not have occurred without major commitment from within the working class. The immediate concern here must be to isolate the social and economic changes that facilitated this involvement.

Many of the developments which took place in the field of communications in mid-century were to prove crucial to the game's long-term growth. Football could not have developed a mass base without the emergence of the rail network, rising literacy levels, an expanding press and a cheap postal system. However, two factors, the introduction of the Saturday half-holiday and the concomitant rise in real incomes, were especially important. The Saturday holiday was, of course, utterly essential to the growth not merely of soccer, but of all sports. While it did not always amount to an *increase* in leisure time – indeed, workers in a number of industries traded the half-holiday for more regular attendance at other times of the week – it was vital in creating clear blocks of free time into which new activities could spread. It was gained over the course of the second half of the nineteenth century by ever larger numbers of workers. Some won it via Parliamentary legislation, such as textile workers who were granted a 56½-hour week with a one o'clock Saturday finish under legislation passed in 1874 (completing a process of Saturday reduction begun in 1847), others as a result of individual agreements between employers and workers. Some had to fight bitterly for the privilege, others gained it without even asking. The most dramatic increases in the growth of the holiday took place between 1872 and 1874 during which period a 'general and comprehensive reduction of normal hours [took place] in nearly all unionised trades'.[22] Although at any time in the period after 1850 there were always likely to be groups of working men with free time from Saturday lunchtime, only from the early 1870s were numbers large enough to facilitate the emergence of a viable and sustained popular sporting culture. That culture was, of course, particularly likely to root itself in communities where substantial elements of the male working population enjoyed the half-holiday and it is, therefore, hardly surprising that the Lancashire textile area was to be a major early focus of working-class soccer. The importance of the Saturday half-holiday is further exemplified by the sporting experience of towns where its arrival was delayed. In Liverpool for example, a city with a high proportion of non-unionised, casual workers of exactly the type that did not benefit from the events of the early 1870s, the game grew only slowly. Detailed local research shows that while Birmingham newspapers recorded 811 soccer matches in 1879–80, their Liverpool counterparts noted only two. The Liverpool and District Football Association was not founded until 1882. Similar factors may well have retarded the growth of soccer in London.[23]

Free time without money, of course, is of little value and the second major factor underpinning the growth of the game was the rise in real wages that many workers experienced in the later nineteenth century. The best general estimate is that real wages rose by approximately one third between 1875 and 1900. This is a notoriously dangerous topic about which to make glib generalisations. The pattern of real wage rises was erratic, complicated by endless occupational and regional variations and was prone to reversal. Above all else, even in the trades and areas which witnessed rising living standards, many did not benefit as a result of illness, injury, unemployment and old age. Nevertheless, while allowing for all this and for the fact that perhaps the most significant rises of all were not to come until the 1890s, soccer's growth owed much to this rise in purchasing power.[24] Some areas enjoyed further financial advantages. Lancashire's peculiarly advanced role in the emergent football culture (and indeed in other areas of popular culture including the seaside holiday, the music hall and the fish and chip trade) owed much to the relative economic stability and prosperity of working-class life, which was rooted in wages levels which were at least reasonable and regular, and the relatively high employment rates for single and recently married women. The 'family wage' did much to underpin soccer's growth in the textile districts.[25]

While these socio-economic changes *facilitated* the growth of the game beyond its previously narrow base within the middle and upper classes, they do not account for its actual growth or the mechanisms of that growth. How did soccer reach the working and lower-middle classes and what was the basis of its appeal? In essence, they entered the game as players and as spectators either by attaching themselves to those existing clubs which were prepared to allow a degree of open social contact, or, more commonly, by founding new ones. The new clubs had many roots. A significant number grew from existing sports clubs, especially cricket clubs, members seeing soccer as a way of keeping friendship groups together over the winter, and, as the commercial value of soccer became clear, as providing a useful subsidy for the summer game. Sheffield Wednesday and Preston North End (originally a rugby club), both founded in 1867, originated in this way. It is likely, however, that such teams were, at least initially, rooted in the middle class, and the more overtly working-class sides came mainly from four other sources; church and chapel, the pub, the workplace and the street or neighbourhood. (It is, of course, often extremely hard to tell the exact origins of a club from names alone, our most common source of evidence, and these 'categories' are obviously loose and overlapping.) The churches were certainly fertile sponsors of football teams, with perhaps 25 per cent of early clubs enjoying clear church or chapel connections. A number of football sides grew from this initial root including Barnsley, Blackpool, Bolton, Everton and Southampton.[26] The workplace was another key source with Stoke City, West Bromwich Albion, Manchester United and Arsenal among the numerous League sides originating in this way. The public house in its turn was such a central feature of working-class life that it would have been strange indeed if it had not played a major role in soccer's early growth. The Rising Sun (Blackburn) and the Stars and Stripes (Clitheroe) are indicative of the public house roots of many early junior sides. Many sides, even those whose origins lay elsewhere, used pubs as changing rooms, further evidence of the astonishingly rich range of services that the pub supplied in this period. Pub sides, of course, merge into the final category, that of the 'neighbourhood' club, based on friendship groups within districts or streets of particular towns. Richard Holt has suggested that, at least by about 1890, this was indeed the most common root of all.[27] Again, useful findings await the game's patient local historians.

Many early histories of football suggested that the game had effectively been brought to the working class by sections of the middle and upper class anxious to provide useful, directed recreations in order to occupy the new blocks of leisure time that might otherwise be filled in less 'suitable' ways. As sharp an observer as Stephen Wagg has talked of the game being spread among the working class 'principally by priests'.[28] There is, of course, plentiful evidence of just this type of motivation. The football club was often yet another manifestation of the 'rational recreation' that was such a feature of British society from the 1820s and 1830s, a phenomenon fired by a diversity of social, economic and political motives and which helped to generate such diverse cultural products as the mechanic's institute, the workingmen's club, the public park and the coffee tavern.[29] Early soccer clubs formed for the working class were frequently the product of 'muscular Christianity', a web of ideas prevalent from the 1850s which married a sense of respect for the body as a sacred duty with a concern for the problems of urban degeneracy. Many young ministers, themselves products of this ideology when at school, undoubtedly took the game to young working men in an attempt to Christianise them, although some probably viewed football simply as a bait designed to attract otherwise reluctant young men into the churches' ambit. Other clubs were the product of another (albeit often interrelated) strand of rational recreation which stressed the belief that leisure could be a site for the construction of harmonious industrial and political relations. A good example here, albeit one drawn from the 1890s, was Thames Iron-works, founded by entrepreneur Arnold F. Hills as part a wider apparatus of company leisure institutions which included a string band, a drama group and a temperance organisation. The club was reformed as West Ham United in 1900.[30]

Much recent writing, however, has demonstrated three main dangers inherent in an excessive concentration on the notion of sport as externally imposed, or as a tool of elite control. First, as has been demonstrated above, many, and indeed perhaps most, soccer teams grew from *within* the community with absolutely no help from or attachment to agencies such as the church. Alongside this, it is dangerous to assume that even church or works teams were always based on an initiative from above, for many almost certainly resulted from grass roots approaches to local community leaders for facilities. Tottenham Hotspur's association with the YMCA is a good case in point.[31] Finally, there is plentiful evidence that once middle- or upper-class sponsors imposed what were deemed unacceptable ideological demands upon a team, then their relationship was either re-negotiated or ended. Christ Church FC, eventually to evolve into Bolton Wanderers, split from the church in 1877 when the vicar attempted to impose some level of church attendance upon the players in return for his continued support. St Mark's FC, West Gorton, known from 1894 as Manchester City, parted company from the host church in 1881 when church officials objected to the team bringing in players from outside the local community in order to improve its performances.[32] At the very least, players with church sides often had the wit to maintain as wide a range of sponsors and patrons as possible, the Wesleyan Bible scholars of Aston Villa, for example, taking their playing field from a butcher and their changing room from a publican.[33] As such examples show (and they can be multiplied many times, and with reference to many leisure pursuits besides football) working-class culture could be extremely resistant, capable of utilising those aspects of elite provision which suited it but rejecting many of the accompanying ideological accoutrements. Whether, as some go on to argue, all this points to a genuine level of popular 'control' over leisure in general and football in particular remains to be debated later.

Ultimately football developed a mass base not because of any externally imposed set of social values, but because it offered so many rewards, emotional, social, aesthetic and, for some, economic. At its worst it was 'something to do' in the new Saturday half-holiday, but it could also offer colour, spectacle, excitement, humour and much else beside. Crucially, it had considerable novelty value, while at the same time slotting comfortably into existing patterns of popular culture. Again, it is Holt who has pointed out that historians, quite rightly anxious to stress the newness of much sporting development in the period 1860–1880, have ignored the many *continuities* that it drew upon.[34] If, as has been argued, street football had retained some purchase within the working-class community, soccer was a novelty which was at least rooted in a pastime that they could relate to. It was, too, a new topic for conversation in the traditional meeting places of pub and street, it provided an opportunity for modest gambling and it allowed for the expression of loyalty to street, neighbourhood and town. Much of the popular recreation of the eighteenth and earlier nineteenth century was based to some degree upon territorial rivalry, parish against parish in some ball games, town or county against others in cockfighting, and so on, and the appeal of soccer was rooted in these traditional rivalries as well as encouraging new ones. As much as it introduced vital new elements into British life, the sporting revolution of the nineteenth century grew out of well-established social and cultural practices.

Soccer and rugby

One of the most intriguing aspects of the history of Victorian team games concerns the idiosyncratic geographical pattern of sporting preference that emerged in the third quarter of the nineteenth century.[35] A *Times* article of 1880 on the development of rugby and soccer observed that:

> the distribution of the game is sporadic and curious. The seed of the one or the other game has, for no visible reason, settled in some districts and been wholly driven out in others. In Nottingham and Sheffield the Rugby game is regarded with contempt but nothing else is played round most of the large towns in Yorkshire, while the same game again, is largely predominant in Lancashire. In Berkshire and Buckinghamshire there is a cup for Association clubs, while next to nothing is heard of the Rugby game.[36]

The differential spread of the two games at first sight certainly was 'curious' and no single causal factor can be identified. Some early attempts at explanation were rooted in analysis of occupational structure. In particular, it was argued that rugby became 'firmly rooted in mining towns and other areas where the occupational base encouraged the retention of standards of masculinity in which physical toughness, strength and courage were emphasised.'[37] Such an analysis, however, apart from reducing both working-class male culture and concepts of masculinity to rather simple stereotypes, also fails to explain why many male workers (including miners) in jobs demanding both strength and courage adopted soccer in preference to rugby. A better explanation for this aspect of nineteenth-century sporting geography is perhaps afforded by consideration of the educational backgrounds of local male elites. While, as argued above, many *teams* owed their origins to popular rather than elite aspiration, ex-public and grammar schoolboys were usually responsible for the establishment of a particular *code*, as they took their games into the wider world for adoption and imitation. This might explain the initial dominance of rugby. A 'kicking game' only appears to have developed in a relatively small number of high status public schools, such as Eton and Harrow. Hardly surprisingly therefore, only the limited number of clubs which had contact with ex-pupils of such schools were likely to take up soccer. The most obvious evidence here is provided by the exploits of Old Harrovians. To give just two brief examples, Lancashire's first soccer club, Turton FC, was part-founded by Harrow old boy J. T. Kay in 1872, while the establishment of neighbouring Darwen FC owed much to three Old Harrovian brothers. Similarly, the under-development of the game in much of Yorkshire noted earlier might well be explained by educational patterns. Tentative research suggests that boys from leading families in Yorkshire in the 1840s and 1850s did not usually go to high status public schools, and thus an opportunity for experiencing 'kicking games' was denied. A lot more research across a far greater geographical base is needed on this issue, but this evidence is certainly suggestive.

While the patterns of local difference provide much interest, they are secondary to a far more important change: the supersession of rugby by soccer as the national winter game. Such an outcome was by no means inevitable, and was indeed perhaps even unlikely at first sight. As has already been suggested, rugby had enjoyed a headstart, *The Times* claiming as late as 1880 that 'the players of the Rugby Union game are probably twice as numerous as those of the Association.'[38] Moreover, many of the points made above concerning the social and economic reasons for soccer's growth and the nature of its appeal obviously also applied to rugby union. Soccer's eventual 'victory' over its rival code, albeit one which was never total, was ultimately secured the late nineteenth and early twentieth centuries as exposure given to the game by the press and the state education system combined to elevate soccer to its place as the national game. These issues will be returned to in the next chapter. However, even in the 1870s and early 1880s, before these twin forces had had much time to exert an influence, soccer was often able to displace rugby in the local affections, in some cases almost totally. As ever, more local research is required before we grasp fully the social mechanics of these changes, but the east and south-east Lancashire experience is perhaps indicative of the wider processes beginning to take hold. Association football first emerged in only a very limited part of the county. When the Lancashire FA was founded in 1878 all 28 founder clubs came from just six neighbouring east Lancashire towns, Blackburn, Bolton, Church, Darwen, Haslingden and Rawtenstall.[39] Rugby predominated everywhere else in the county. However, by the early 1880s other parts of Lancashire had been significantly penetrated by soccer. Preston, for example, was virtually exclusively a rugby town until about 1879, when a relatively minor rugby side, Preston North End, began to experiment with the association game. By 1882 soccer had effectively colonised a 25-mile band stretching eastwards from Preston to Burnley, with many existing rugby sides turning to soccer and most new sides taking up the game. The experience of changing codes was often painful, Preston losing 16–0 to Blackburn Rovers in 1881 and Burnley Rovers, soon to be simple Burnley FC, suffering some similar indignities in their first soccer season of 1882–83.[40] Nevertheless, the game rapidly took firm hold, a point underlined at the end of the decade when the Lancashire Rugby Football Union, deciding to set up a federal structure, did not even bother to form a section in the east of the county.[41]

Two factors appear to have exerted a particular influence here. One was the failure of the highly conservative Lancashire Rugby Union to establish a cup competition; 'pot-hunting', they claimed, was likely to introduce an 'unseemly' air into the game. The Lancashire Football Association, however, had no such scruples, and the Lancashire Cup, founded in 1879, along with local involvement in the FA Cup, did much to encourage interest in soccer. As was so often the case, a competitive edge, especially when allied to the expression of local pride and hostility to rival local communities, lay at the heart of sporting development. It is surely instructive in this regard that in Yorkshire, where a rugby cup competition *was* instigated in 1876, soccer was much less successful in gaining a foothold, remaining almost unknown outside of the Sheffield area until the mid-1890s.[42] Rugby was indeed the 'people's game' in most of Yorkshire until the early twentieth century. The second factor is perhaps more contentious, but soccer's rapid spread at rugby's cost would suggest that the former had certain structural and aesthetic qualities which made it, in the eyes of both players and spectators, quite simply a superior game.[43]

Association and rugby football had grown from the same roots and contained overlaps even after 1863. Soccer initially allowed limited handling by outfield players, for example, and it was not until the early 1870s that this privilege was restricted to the goalkeeper. By 1880, however, *The Times* could assert that 'people now regard the games as both good of their kind, but quite distinct.'[44] The governing bodies of both games made good progress in clarifying existing rules and establishing new ones. Obviously, soccer matches were marked by arguments over the interpretation and implementation of the rules, but by 1880, as the jurisdiction of the Football Association and its regional affiliated bodies spread, at least teams were usually sure about the rules they were playing under when a game started. Incidents such as that in 1876 when a game between Lancashire sides Darwen and Turton was almost called off because the two clubs could not agree on an aspect of the 'handball' rule became ever less frequent. The introduction of the crossbar and of touchlines in 1882 removed another source of dispute which had sometimes bedevilled games.[45] Crucially, though, soccer remained a simpler game in the sense that it possessed fewer rules – 14 in 1863 as opposed to rugby's 59 in 1871 – making it both easier to play and to follow.

Above all, the game took on a style and structure that enhanced its appeal with both players and spectators alike, evolving into a rather more varied, open and fluent game than its rival code. To a large degree this resulted from the supersession of the 'dribbling' by the 'passing' game. Association football in the 1860s was in many ways a highly individual game built around dribbling skills; indeed, well into the 1880s, and particularly in areas where the game was not played extensively, it was often referred to as the 'dribbling code'. Sides quite often contained seven forwards who tended to run with the ball until losing it, at which point colleagues were expected to follow up and begin the dribbling sequence anew. However, by the late 1870s and early 1880s, a passing game involving far less individual forward play, greater team-work and variety of tactics had become the norm.

The growth of the passing game is so central to soccer's development that a slight detour to consider its origins is merited here. Primary sources reveal rather contradictory versions of the emergence of the passing game. Charles Alcock, highly involved in the game's early development as a player, administrator and journalist, stated that the 'passing-on' game was 'first introduced in any degree of perfection by the Northerners in the early matches between London and Sheffield' in the late 1860s. He claimed that two rather distinctive variants then evolved from the early 1870s, the short passing game associated with the highly influential Scottish sides Queen's Park and Vale of Leven, and the 'alternation of long passing and vigorous rushes', which was associated in particular with the 1883 Blackburn Olympic side, 'as far as I can remember, the first English team to give any exhibition of a systematic passing game in London.' Alcock's implication in this last statement that southern football was still dominated by dribbling in the early 1880s is interesting but probably misleading, given that as early as 1880 he had been arguing that the balance in the game had generally moved too far against dribbling.[46]

Alcock's version is to some extent contradicted by the autobiography of Frederick Wall, Alcock's replacement as secretary of the Football Association in 1894. Wall suggested that 'the advantages of combination', by which he presumably meant the passing game, 'over the old style of individualism' was first developed in England by the Royal Engineers side of the early 1870s and taken out into the provinces, including Sheffield, in 1873.[47] Wall's tendency to celebrate the virtues of the amateur ideal coupled with his loyalty to London football might have led him to construct a picture which minimised the role of Scotsmen and Northerners, many of whom were proto-professionals, in inaugurating crucial developments in playing style. If Wall's view of the importance of the Royal Engineers is correct, it does cast doubt on those social interpretations of the game's development which suggest that the growth of team-work and the passing game may have resulted from the arrival in the game of working men who had not enjoyed the benefit of learning dribbling skills at school, and for whom passing represented a translation of the values of community and mutual support into the sporting arena.[48]

Whatever the history and motivation, the passing game quickly became the norm, introducing a new repertoire of skills and tactics that increased its appeal. There were, too, other innovations which enhanced the game and its allure in relationship to rugby. Especially important here was the abolition in 1877 of the rule which demanded that 'the throw in from touch' must be at right angles, a change (not initially adopted in Scotland) which Charles Alcock saw as a key innovation as it 'tended to make the game so much faster'.[49] Heading appears to have become a frequent addition to the range of options by the later 1870s, and was deemed an essential skill by the mid-1880s, albeit one which some critics thought was being demonstrated 'to excess'.[50] Growing heading skills also led to far greater accuracy in crossing from the wings, a tactic used very effectively by the Preston North End sides of the 1880s. All these various changes probably helped promote soccer above rugby in those areas where the two codes were rivals, at least as regards spectator appeal. The outlawing of the forward pass in rugby denied the game some of the 'three-dimensionality' of soccer and the abolishing of hacking in 1871, previously an effective tactic for breaking up scrimmages, slowed the game down considerably.[51] Lengthy scrums might have been a source of pleasure to those familiar with the code, but they did lead to a rather static game in comparison with soccer. A number of rule changes were introduced from the late 1870s in order to inject more pace into the game, but it is highly significant that throughout the next century both rugby codes continued to devote much time to improving the game's spectator appeal. The crucial battle with soccer, however, was perhaps lost at a very early stage. A final but not inconsequential factor in the battle between rugby and soccer was the fact that, although soccer remained an extremely physical and, indeed, downright dangerous game for certain players, especially goalkeepers – until 1892, they could be challenged even when they did not have the ball – it ultimately required less sheer physical presence than rugby.[52] Soccer has always been a game where even the smallest players can have a major influence.

Professionals and amateurs

The period between the game's foundation in 1863 and the early 1880s had seen what was in many ways a revolution in footballing culture, with both the game itself and its social structure and context transformed. 1884–85 saw events which in many ways completed that transformation and secured the future stability and growth of the game at elite level. The central issue was, of course, the growth of professionalism. It has been claimed that Peter Andrews of Sheffield's Heeley club and J. J. Lang of rivals The Wednesday became the first professionals in 1876–77. However, it is impossible to date the origins of 'professionalism' exactly, given the illegality of much of this activity and the very looseness of the term. Lang, who on retirement was discovered to be blind in one eye, was certainly a very early example of the breed, being attracted from Scotland and given a sinecure in a knife-making works by the club.[53] It would have been strange indeed if some form of professionalism had not begun to feature in the game as it gained a popular following from the 1870s. There was a long history of professionalism in most spectator sports and indeed in some other areas of popular culture which placed a high premium upon competition: brass bands, for example, often employed specialist trainers and soloists. Similarly, paid entertainers were an ever more frequent feature of popular culture as the century progressed, as music halls, seaside piers and so forth became an established part of contemporary social life. The problem with professionalism in football arose essentially from the offence that the development caused to those mainly upper-middle and upper-class individuals, especially those with public school educations, for whom the threat to the amateur game carried a social and political challenge as much as a sporting one.

The battle was not actually over payment of money for playing. There never was a 'pure' amateur game in the sense that playing the game overrode all financial considerations. Old boys sides on provincial tours expected expenses: the Corinthians reputedly requested £150 per match by the 1880s. The FA's rule 16, introduced in 1882, allowed for the payment of expenses, including broken time payments, for those involved in FA Cup ties.[54] Rather, disputes centred on various abuses of the rules. 'Professionalism' in the 1870s and 1880s covered a multitude of 'offensive practices' including simply paying above the regulation rates for broken time, hiring players for specific matches and, above all, offering a whole series of inducements relating to off the field activities, in particular the provision of employment opportunities. The use of such inducements was clearly common by the early 1880s, at least in Lancashire, as was demonstrated by the flood of leading Scottish players into the county's premier sides from around 1882–83. By 1883 Burnley could field a side including ten Scotsmen and Preston North End regularly fielded nine in the 1884–85 season. Local talent was also poached from rival clubs, North End luring George Wilson from Blackburn Olympic by offering him the tenancy of the Black-a-Moor-Head public house.[55]

Upper- and middle-class opposition to the various practices, both real and imagined, that came under the label of 'professionalism' were numerous, and had already been well rehearsed in a number of other sporting contexts.[56] Some were clustered around the game itself or its organisation and structure. It was argued for example that working men, with their daily experience of hard, physical labour, would have a natural advantage over their white-collar counterparts. Other critics stressed the danger of a few wealthy clubs coming to dominate the game. Opposition was more frequently directed at the moral and social dimension. Professionalism, it was believed, would encourage gambling, partisanship and the will to win at all costs; turn what should be a source of pleasure and moral virtue into a mere job of work and, by leaving the professional sportsman with too much spare time on his hands, render him a highly unsuitable role model for the young working classes. Some of these concerns did spring from a genuine concern for the future of the game, but often they were no more than thinly veiled statements of class prejudice from individuals disturbed that football was losing its connotations of social exclusiveness, or was otherwise challenging accepted notions of social hierarchy and political power. Indeed, the 'veil' was sometimes non-existent, as when a contributor to the *Athlete* claimed that the, 'employment of the scum of the Scottish villages has tended, in no small degree, to brutalise the game.'[57]

It must be acknowledged that not all opposition was rooted in what might broadly be characterised as social and political conservatism. The Liberal *Manchester Guardian* was not alone in lamenting the loss of social integration which it foresaw as an inevitable consequence of professionalism. 'The idea has been to bring together all classes in football and athletics on terms of perfect equality. With the introduction of professionals a new departure is taken . . . Again a fresh excuse will be given for a tendency to exclusiveness.'[58] It is possible too that some members of the working class who had been exposed to currents of political radicalism might have had their objections. Certainly, in the next decade, a member of Reading's Co-operative movement was to express fundamental reservations about a plan for a professional club in the town, arguing that such bodies were dominated by small groups which thus prevented the sports club from becoming a participatory democracy.[59] Nevertheless, it is the conservative voice that seems to loom loudest in the historical record.

Interestingly, much of the dominant contemporary discourse of amateurism posited an idealised division between amateur and professional sporting culture that was not necessarily reflected in actual behaviour. At the very least, whether for reasons relating to sporting pride or social and political position, amateurs were by no means as gracious and free of the taint of competitiveness as they would have liked others to have believed. While they could show a sporting spirit towards opponents – the Old Etonians gave Darwen £5 to help with special training before a cup tie between the two sides in 1879 – unexpected defeat was not always taken well. Even FA secretary Charles Alcock, a conciliatory voice in the professionalism debate, betrayed a slightly less than stiff upper lip when describing Blackburn Olympic's 1883 defeat of the Old Etonians.

> The final produced a very stubborn contest, but the superior condition of the Northern team, who had systematically trained for some time before, gave them a rather lucky victory in an extra half hour's play, the Etonians having to play with only ten men, owing to injury to A. T. B. Dunn, one of their best forwards.[60]

Again, the play of amateur sides could be extremely intimidating and robust. H. A. Goodhart of the Old Etonians was remembered by a contemporary as 'a very heavy and very big man [who] simply ran over anyone who came in his way.' The *Preston Herald* in December 1885, admittedly not necessarily a totally objective source in the circumstances, termed the visiting amateur Corinthians side the 'roughest' seen at Preston all season. On a further visit in 1889 it commented with surprise on their adoption of the passing game and the absence of their usual 'kick and run tactics, with its accompanying heavy charging . . . rushing and not very gentle style of play.'[61] Win at all costs it might not have been, but manliness and competitiveness certainly overlapped in a most helpful manner.

A full-blown crisis finally occurred in January 1884 when the London side Upton Park complained to the FA that the Preston North End side they had just met in an FA Cup tie was to all intents and purposes a professional one. North End's secretary Major William Sudell, a mill manager by profession, acknowledged that the club imported players and found them work but argued that this was common practice and did not breach regulations. The FA nevertheless expelled North End from the tournament and Burnley and Great Lever followed by the beginning of the next season.[62] An aggressive response was inevitable and at the end of October a group of 31 leading clubs, including not only most of the leading Lancashire clubs but also Aston Villa, Walsall Swifts and Sunderland, threatened to form a break-away British Football Association. The FA decided to pursue a more cautious policy and set up a sub-committee which included Sudell among its number. Eventually, on 20 July 1885, the FA agreed that 'it is now expedient in the interests of Association Football, to legalise the employment of professional football players, but only under certain restrictions.'[63] Clubs were allowed to pay players provided that they had either been born or had lived for two years within a

N. L. 'Pa' Jackson. Founder of the Corinthians in 1882, Jackson was a leading supporter of the amateur game. (*Football Association*)

six-mile radius of the ground. In addition, professionals had to be registered annually. The decision was partly a response to pressure from the nascent professional clubs and their supporters in the press, and partly, to use Tischler's phrase, 'sheer weariness'. Ultimately, it represented a realisation among the game's ruling body that 'professionalism properly managed' represented the best way of them maintaining control of the game and of coating it with the cultural values that they believed in.[64] It was also very much in the interests of the clubs. In the early 1880s, leading players were in an extremely strong bargaining position, able to move clubs whenever they wished according to the (usually illegal) deal offered. As a result of the July 1885 decision they had lost some of their power, and clubs were quick to cement this, for them, more suitable master-servant relationship via the introduction of the maximum wage and the retain and transfer system.

As for the FA, they were quick to ensure that the newly legalised professional knew his place. Although professional footballers were never to be submitted to quite the regime of social apartheid experienced by their counterparts in county cricket, key symbolic and practical devices were soon in place.[65] In 1886 the first acknowledged professional to play international football for England found himself in a blue shirt, his amateur colleagues playing in the standard white, while in the same year, a Gentlemen versus Players fixture was established, further underlining the newly acknowledged hierarchy within the game.[66] Perhaps more importantly, in 1885 professionals and ex-professionals were effectively prevented from being allowed to shape the game's administrative development by a ruling which barred them from sitting on FA committees.[67] Some local FAs, most notably London, Middlesex and Surrey, still refused to accept professional clubs into membership, a policy which was to lead to a dramatic confrontation with the parent body in 1907.

We do not yet have the evidence which would allow for detailed analysis of the social and geographical basis of support or opposition on the issue of professionalism, but from what is known, it is clearly unhelpful to reduce the debate simply to a matter of conflict between antagonistic social classes. It is perhaps possible to see the debate in terms of an intra-middle-class conflict, with the provincial, non-public school educated business and commercial classes uniting with the working classes in support of professionalism, against the public school elite. However, as Mason has pointed out, public schoolboys were to be found on both sides of the divide and it was probably often simply personal preference that led individuals from such a background to decide whether or not to support the changes.[68] There was probably something of a north–south element here, as there so often was in sporting issues at this time. Lancastrians for example, almost irrespective of class, rallied to support their local clubs against what was often portrayed, at least in the county's press, as southern and/or metropolitan bias. Even then, Blackburn Rovers (despite paying players) did not back the October 1884 rebellion, while in Yorkshire, the Sheffield FA opposed professionalism in 1885.[69]

Blackburn Rovers, FA Cup winners in 1884–86, and the first northern side to dominate English football. (*Blackburn Public Library*)

Whatever the sociological groupings that emerged, soccer was at least able to reach a settlement without the formal rift that led to rugby's division into two rival organisations (and, eventually, two rival codes), the Rugby Union and the Northern Union, in 1895. As has been suggested by a number of commentators, most notably Dunning and Sheard in their pioneering study of rugby's formative years, perhaps the FA's leading administrators, drawn as some of them were from the upper echelons of British society, were so confident of their social position that they were able to compromise on such a large issue without loss of face, a compromise not so easily made by the slightly less socially secure elites who ran the Rugby Football Union.[70] Certainly Old Harrovian Charles Alcock and Old Etonian Lord Kinnaird were vital figures in the establishment of a compromise settlement. Similarly, as again Dunning and Sheard note, the football authorities faced an issue which did to some extent involve concession to working-class elements in the game during a period of relatively stable political and industrial relations, whereas their counterparts in the RFU were faced by the same issues in the 1890s after a period of considerable popular militancy, exemplified by the rise of the 'new unionism' of the unskilled workers, which may well have shaped their ultimate response.[71]

The debate over amateurism and professionalism had, of course, not been closed. The Edwardian period was to see further problems leading to a amateur break-away in 1907 and the FA worked continuously to maintain control over professionalism, defend amateur ideals and limit the commercialisation of the game until the Second World War and beyond. However, a compromise had been reached which helped lay the basis for future developments and especially the establishment of the Football League in 1888. Just as many within the ruling elite had been willing to reform the political system in the later nineteenth century in order to maintain influence, so they showed a willingness for accommodation and compromise in the sporting arena. Given the centrality of sporting culture in many parts of England by 1885, it is surely not fanciful to suggest that evidence of this spirit of compromise in such an important public arena played a part in maintaining popular faith in the essential goodwill of the nation's ruling class.

2

The Making of the National Game, 1888–1914

SOCCER HAD ESTABLISHED ITSELF as a major element of sporting culture in the decade after 1875, but even its most optimistic advocates would have been surprised by its dramatic growth over the next quarter century. The number of clubs affiliated to the Football Association rose from 1,000 in 1888, to 10,000 in 1905 and 12,000 by 1910. Attendance at the FA Cup final rose from 17,000 in 1888 to 120,081 in 1913, the event having moved from the Oval to the Crystal Palace. Similarly, while the twelve-strong Football League drew a total of some 600,000 spectators in the 1888–89 inaugural season, 5 million attended the games played in its twenty-strong First Division in 1905–6. By 1913–14, the figure had risen to 8,778,000.[1] Leading clubs could often attract crowds of over 5,000 to reserve team matches. At the same time, a modest but expanding service industry grew up around the game, as entrepreneurs adapted local skills and trade networks to the new opportunities it presented. The advertisement pages of the *Sports Trader* demonstrated, for example, that, by 1912, two representatives of the twine and yarn industry of Bridport, Dorset had diversified into the production of goal nets, at least two midlands hosiery factories were now specialists in athletic garments and that at least one firm in the shoe town of Kettering was now concentrating heavily on the production of football boots.[2]

Perhaps the most striking example of the game's impact can be seen in the nature and content of the press. The ½*d.* or 1*d.* Saturday night football special that had emerged in the early 1880s was a feature of most 'towns of any size' by the 1890s, while the amount of space dedicated to football in the press in general grew enormously.[3] Overall, it really is difficult to exaggerate the impact of soccer on the contemporary social, cultural and economic environment. In 1875, it was still largely a game for a leisured elite; by 1914, it lay at the heart of much English male culture.

The game and its organisation

The game itself was shaped by a series of rule changes, the most important of which further widened spectator appeal, either by rendering play more open or by making the officials' rulings less open to doubt. The goal nets that added to Bridport's prosperity, and which had first been tried in a North *v.* South game in 1891, became compulsory in 1892. This much reduced the incidence of disputes as to whether the ball had crossed the goal-line or passed between the posts.[4] Alongside this, a highly significant series of decisions redefined the specific roles of match officials. In football's infancy, each side had appointed an umpire to whom players appealed about incidents on the pitch: the referee had begun life in 1871 when 'neutrals' were introduced to resolve disputes between umpires in later rounds of the FA Cup. In 1891, the referee moved from his previous position on the touchline onto the pitch, although umpires still gave decisions in their part of the field. Finally, in 1894, the referee was given complete control of the game, the umpires effectively becoming linesmen. These alterations ended the delays, and the accompanying irritation among spectators and players alike, which had resulted from the old system of appeal and arbitration; the game could now move at a far faster pace.[5] Other significant rule changes punctuated the period. 1891 saw the introduction of the penalty kick, a device which bitterly upset many amateurs, who argued that the new legislation assumed that footballers could be capable of cheating.[6] Some old boys teams were still refusing to acknowledge penalties in the early twentieth century. From 1912 the goalkeeper, previously allowed to touch the ball anywhere within his own half, could now handle only inside the penalty area.[7] In terms of tactics, by the late 1880s all sides had adopted a basic formation comprising 2 full backs, 3 half backs and 5 forwards. Some of those who had learnt the game in the 1860s and 70s believed that it now lacked robustness – Alcock, probably referring to the protection increasingly afforded to goalkeepers, derided 'grandmotherly legislation' which made soccer 'ultra scientific' and 'ineffective' – but it was still a highly physical game.[8] By 1914, however, it was undoubtedly one which a modern observer would recognise.

A modern observer would also recognise the organisational structures that emerged. The establishment of the Football League in 1888 was obviously of the utmost importance to the development of the professional game.[9] The League was basically a mechanism designed by leading clubs to protect their considerable investment in terms of both capital and labour costs. The typical fixture list before 1888 consisted of various cup tournaments and a large number of 'friendlies', hardly a secure basis for the future. Cup competitions could lead to unexpectedly early and thus financially disastrous exits, and also often resulted in one-sided fixtures which were unattractive to spectators. Preston North End's 26–0 FA Cup defeat of Hyde in 1887 was a particularly acute case in point and, indeed, served as a catalyst for the discussion of new approaches. At the same time, clubs were prone to cancel friendlies at short notice if a more lucrative fixture arose.

In March 1888, William MacGregor, a Birmingham draper and Aston Villa committee member, called an exploratory meeting of leading clubs to discuss the formation of a competitive league with an established pool of guaranteed fixtures between well-matched sides. The 'Football League' was established at a further meeting in Manchester on 17 April. Its founders were much exercised by what would now be termed 'quality

William McGregor, whose initiative led to the founding of the Football League. (*Football Association*)

control', and the clubs chosen to participate were certainly among the best in the country. However, the need for financial security dictated that the League was also anxious to elect those clubs capable of drawing the largest gates. This worked to the obvious disadvantage of teams like Halliwell, a highly successful club, but situated in a small community in uneconomically close proximity to Bolton. The twelve founder members in order of their placing at the end of the first season were Preston, Aston Villa, Wolverhampton Wanderers, Blackburn Rovers, Bolton Wanderers, West Bromwich Albion, Accrington, Everton (deemed by many extremely lucky to have been preferred ahead of neighbours Bootle), Burnley, Derby County, Notts County and Stoke. The geographical distribution clearly reflected the role of textile Lancashire and the midlands in the early history of the game.

The first five games were played on 8 September. The competition enjoyed its share of early teething troubles. Accrington arrived an hour late for their first ever game (at Everton), while Stoke reached Preston's Deepdale ground in October 1888 with only nine players, one having missed the train, another having signed for a new club during the journey.[10]

Preston North End, 1888–89. The 'Invincibles' with the hugely influential (and later disgraced) secretary, William Sudell, standing third from right. (*Preston North End F.C.*)

However, despite such tribulations, and the fact that, at least initially, the FA Cup was still seen as 'the championship of English football', the League system was seen as a considerable success.[11] Preston's dominance – the 'Invincibles' had won the championship by early January and eventually finished with an eleven-point lead – took some of the excitement out of events, but, by the same token, their achievement of winning the League without losing any of their 22 matches gave a certain cachet to the new competition. Not surprisingly, other leagues followed almost immediately. The poorly organised Second Combination League had actually started at the same time as the Football League but survived only one season. 1889 saw the foundation of both the Northern and Midland Counties Leagues, and, more importantly, the Football Alliance, soon dubbed the 'Second League' and absorbed by the Football League as its Second Division in 1892. This was the first major step in an expansion programme that saw the League grow to embrace 40 clubs by 1905.[12] The Southern League was founded in 1894 and, by the end of the century, the country was criss-crossed by a network of leagues professional, semi-professional and amateur, providing the competitive structure that proved such a vital dynamic in the game's expansion.

Relationships between the Football League and their counterparts were not always good, the latters' clubs often attracting League players with offers of high wages accompanied by a refusal to pay transfer fees. From 1890–96 the League operated a boycott against clubs which behaved thus, and indeed it was the threat of losing key fixtures which was partially responsible for Millwall taking the lead in establishing the Southern League as the focus for London and southern professional sides.[13] Here, as in many areas, the determined attitude that typified the League's behaviour in its early days is well demonstrated. The League's history should not be rendered too triumphantly. Ten clubs, mainly, although not exclusively, from small towns, resigned from it before 1915 due to monetary problems. Most of these resignations took place in the 1890s when constructing the necessary financial infrastructure was clearly still a very delicate business. However, both Burslem Port Vale and Stoke were forced to resign as late as 1907 and 1908 respectively, the pottery towns being unable to sustain large enough crowds for the clubs to remain viable.[14] A number of other clubs also struggled dreadfully at times, both at the bank and on the field. Overall, however, a viable and credible structure had been created.

The national game: the geography of soccer

There were two striking features of soccer's changing spatial distribution between 1885 and 1914: its increased penetration of previous rugby strongholds, especially but not exclusively in the north of England, and the growth of the professional game in the south. A striking example of the first process is provided by the changing patterns of sporting preference in the West Yorkshire textile district. As late as 1894 a Bradford newspaper could argue that while 'prophecy is unsafe . . . there seems little likelihood that the dribbling game will ever prove a formidable rival here to rugby as it has done in Lancashire.'[15] A West Riding League was founded in 1895, but its ambitious title disguised a geographical base largely restricted to the mining towns south-east of Leeds. A number of Northern Union clubs including Batley, Bradford, Halifax, Huddersfield and Leeds, formed soccer sections in order to reach an accommodation with the 'Associationists', but most of these were short-lived and poorly supported. The really significant and spectacular growth of soccer came at about the turn of the century and occurred above all at *junior* level, especially among schoolboys and youths. In 1900, the *Brighouse Echo*, centred in a strong rugby playing area, was giving its first tentative coverage to soccer. Within six years, it could claim that 'there are now in this locality more football clubs that play under association rules than under the rugby code.' By 1907 the *Yorkshire Observer*, claiming that 95 per cent of Bradford's younger generation were now soccer players, argued that rugby, 'cannot under any circumstances regain its former glory until there is a revolution in the taste of juveniles.'[16]

Soccer was making varying degrees of headway at about the same time in other areas including the East Riding of Yorkshire, South Wales, partially 'unconquered' regions of the Lancashire textile belt between Rochdale and Oldham, and parts of the south and east midlands. What was responsible for these changes? To some extent, the points raised in the previous chapter suggesting that soccer was structurally superior as a game played a part here, a new audience enjoying the game as they encountered it for the first time. By comparison, rugby did not always project a positive image. Rugby Union often exuded elitism and conservatism, while the newly established Northern Union was beset by organisational and financial problems in its first decade, resulting in a number of clubs disbanding or, as will be seen, changing codes. Northern Union's attempt to maintain support for the game led to a number of rule changes which some commentators claimed only served further to alienate or confuse fans.

Three factors, however, seem to have been especially important, two of which demonstrate the influence of 'nationalising' forces overriding local specialism. The role of state education was vital in this regard. Team sports had begun to appear as an extra-curricular supplement to drill from about 1880 and, by the mid-1890s, it was clear that soccer was increasingly preferred as the winter game. Its advantages were obvious. The rules were relatively simple; it could be played on hard surfaces in the many schools without access to playing fields; and it was suitable and comparatively safe for the physically underdeveloped and undernourished youngsters that schools so often had to cater for. Bradford Schools Athletic Association in fact moved to soccer in 1895–96 after a boy received a serious leg injury playing rugby. Schools were thus to be vital seedbeds for the game's great expansion in the late nineteenth and early twentieth centuries.[17] A second 'nationalising' force came in the shape of the press. National papers, sporting journals such as the *Athletic News* (1875) and local papers employing soccer enthusiasts did much to advertise soccer. The emergence of professional soccer in Bradford in 1903, for example, owed much to skilful lobbying by the soccer correspondent of the *Yorkshire Sports* Saturday special.[18]

Finally, the politically astute and highly expansionist Football League rarely missed an opportunity of encouraging the game in rugby's heartlands or, indeed, wherever the professional game was weak. This skill was first demonstrated by the admission in 1893 of its first southern member, in the form of a very modest Woolwich Arsenal side. In the 1900s, such examples multiplied. When Manningham Northern Union club abandoned rugby for soccer in 1903 and reformed as Bradford City, the League gave them immediate entry into the Second Division, even though a playing squad had not even been assembled. Leeds City and Hull City were allowed entry in 1905 on the basis of potential rather than actual playing record, Bradford Park Avenue joined in 1908 despite having managed only thirteenth place in the Southern League in their previous debut season, and Huddersfield Town followed in 1910, only two years after their formation. Certainly, the two rugby codes were able to maintain a powerful hold in some areas and some of the newly established soccer sides led a perilous existence for some time. However, by 1914, and perhaps as early as 1906, soccer had clearly established itself as the national winter sport.

Southern League football in the 1900s. Queens Park Rangers (hoops) play Southampton. (*Football Association*)

The increased popularity of the game in the south provides further evidence in this regard. The bitter opposition to professionalism found in many southern county associations was undoubtedly a factor retarding the growth of the game in the south: Arsenal became the first southern professional side as late as 1891, closely followed by Millwall and Southampton.[19] The premier football competitions were then, not surprisingly, dominated by clubs from the north and midlands. In 1914, only six of the 40 Football League clubs (Arsenal, Bristol City, Chelsea, Clapton Orient, Fulham and Tottenham) were situated in the south or west, although Luton had briefly been members from 1897 to 1900. Only Tottenham and Southampton, both as Southern League clubs, threatened midland and northern FA Cup hegemony, Spurs winning the trophy in 1901 and Southampton reaching the final in 1900 and 1902. However, southern and particularly metropolitan soccer culture was actually much stronger than this at first suggests. First, the Southern League offered professional and semi-professional southern clubs a credible alternative to the Football League. Although at all stages of its existence its standard was generally inferior to the Football League, it supplied the stronger clubs with a number of attractive fixtures, while at the same time saving them expensive travel fees. Moreover, some southern and particularly London sides were tremendously well supported. Even before they joined the Football League in 1907 and 1908 respectively, Fulham and Tottenham regularly attracted crowds of over 20,000 for top fixtures, far bigger attendances than those achieved by many First Division sides. Even some of the less well-supported Southern League teams drew larger crowds than their counterparts in the League's Division Two.[20] Yet again, the two best-supported Football League teams in 1913–14 were Chelsea, who averaged 37,105 after finishing eighth in the First Division, and Spurs, who drew an average of 28,020 after finishing only seventeenth. The records, while incomplete, suggest that Chelsea were, in fact, the best-supported League club for five of the eight seasons between 1907–8 and 1914–15, including the 1909–10 season when they were relegated.[21] Such statistics, apart from raising interesting issues about the discriminatory powers of Chelsea supporters, underline that while football's most successful sides in terms of playing record were still to be found in the game's initial heartlands, soccer had established a mass base in the capital, where its massive advantage in terms of population was at last coming into play.

Football's Personnel

i Administrators

The Football Association and the Football League forged a working relationship that, although often effective and productive in the face of a common enemy such as the players' trade union, was often marked by tension and conflict. The League accepted the FA's position as the game's overall governing body, but fiercely defended its autonomy in its own sphere. The FA in turn broadly respected that autonomy, but kept up a constant pressure to minimise the commercial element within League football and the professional game in general. It must be stressed that every issue that divided the FA from the League was parallelled by a similar division *within* those bodies, partly because there was an ever-growing overlap in terms of personnel between the two. Clear differences could be seen, however, in their philosophies and cultures.

The FA was particularly anxious to control the transfer system which many of its members found distasteful, making several efforts to restrict its operation between 1899 and 1904. Having decided merely to monitor the transfer market for evidence of improper practice from that point, the first ever £1,000 transfer fee, taking Alf Common from Sunderland to relegation-threatened Middlesbrough in 1905, re-activated the FA's reforming spirit and it attempted to impose a maximum £350 fee on all future dealings. However, this proved impossible to police and the scheme was abandoned after three months.[22] The FA was also active in attempts to control wage levels and bonuses, imposing the maximum wage and outlawing bonuses in 1900, initially against the will of many League sides. More vigorous disputes arose over these issues in 1908–10. Other FA measures designed to contain commercialisation included restricting the dividend that clubs could pay shareholders to 5 per cent from 1896, the strong discouragement of betting on soccer matches and a determined campaign to remind professionals of their role in a master-servant relationship. The restriction on their administrative role has already been noticed, but their behaviour on and off the pitch was also closely controlled. As late as 1923 Charles Buchan, a professional captaining England in an international against France, was reprimanded for the apparently disrespectful gesture of shaking an amateur team-mate by the hand in a post-goal celebration. Buchan recalled too the refusal of an FA official to pay the players' expenses until they were safely on the boat home, informing Buchan that 'I am determined that they shall go back with their money in their pockets.'[23]

To some extent, tensions between the two governing bodies, and indeed between the FA and other leagues, simply resulted from their separate functions. The FA secretary from 1894 to 1934, Frederick (from 1930, Sir Frederick) Wall, saw the administration of the FA Cup and England's international matches as his central tasks, but he was always intensely aware that he had to 'look after all football and not a part'.[24] However, this sense of duty to the thousands of clubs beyond the professional leagues does at times appear to have been be as much rationalisation of, or excuse for, policies and behaviour that were rooted more in a set of social attitudes than in objective sporting priorities. While the FA–League conflict can never be reduced to a simple matter of southern patricians and professionals against northern and midland 'trade', social differences along these broad lines undoubtedly did structure the relationship. Of the 28 individuals who served on the League Management Committee between 1888 and 1914, only two came from the south, compared with fourteen from the midlands and six from Lancashire. Eleven of the committee were either shopkeepers or small businessmen and only three were drawn from the professions. None appear to have had a public school education.[25] The influx of League club and local county representatives into the FA's governing bodies over the period from the early 1880s obviously altered the social structure of an organisation once dominated by elite, often southern-based, social groups. By 1906, the Leicestershire FA, for example, was represented by the clerk to the National Union of Boot and Shoe Operatives. However, the FA continued to exhibit a rather more elevated social tone than the League. In 1903, 17 members of the 46 strong FA Council were drawn from the professions and, in 1906, at least nine of its, by then, 52 members were public schoolboys.[26] At least to some extent, the philosophical and practical differences between the two bodies were rooted in their different social complexions. The League's willingness to embrace at least some of the values and procedures of the commercial entertainment industry stemmed from the competitive, business-orientated culture of its leading figures. The FA's stress on service to a wider community and the sanctity of wider sporting values in turn reflected the mores of the professional and allied classes.

Interestingly, the FA's attempts to restrain the impact of professionalism and commercialisation were not enough to satisfy a significant minority of the game's adherents, particularly in the south, who had been erecting a *cordon sanitaire* around the professional game ever since the 1885 compromise. The abolition of the residence qualifications for professionals in May 1889 led to the resignation of Old Etonian president, Major Marindin, and five vice-presidents, all from southern clubs. N. L. Jackson of the Corinthians suggested that the FA should effectively divide into amateur and professional sections.[27] In 1893, the FA Amateur Cup was founded, partly as a compensation for professional domination of the FA Cup. Almost immediately, however, that too became dominated by working-class sides, beginning with Middlesbrough's defeat of the Old Carthusians in 1895. Many old boys sides were happy to decamp to the Arthur Dunn Cup, established in 1902–3.

In July 1907 supporters of a strictly amateur game ('amateur' defined as a player who received only legitimate travelling and hotel expenses) finally broke away from the FA to found the Amateur Football Association.[28] The stimulus for this was the conflict that followed the refusal of the Middlesex and Surrey FAs to bow to an FA directive of March 1905, instructing that all county associations must now accommodate professional clubs. Backed by a number of southern sporting journals, especially *Amateur Sport Illustrated* and *Amateur Football*, the AFA speedily recruited some 500 clubs including the Corinthians, most of the old boys sides and Oxford and Cambridge Universities, as well as winning official recognition as football's ruling body from the Rugby Football Union and the Hockey Association. The majority of clubs remained loyal to the FA, however, which was astute enough to impose a ban on its clubs playing AFA affiliates. In particular, amateur sides in the north and midlands showed no inclination to support the break-away, the AFA failing to register a single club to the north of Nottingham in 1913. The social and practical realities of provincial society clearly made the 'pure' amateur ideal a hard one to sustain for those who wanted to maintain their sporting interests.

The AFA's limited success with recruitment, coupled with the FA's maintenance of control over the international side selected for the Olympic Games in 1908 and 1912, led to a partial climb-down, with the rebels returning to the parent body as an affiliated society in February 1914. The whole incident, though, demonstrates the power that an idealised notion of amateurism continued to hold for many, especially in the Home Counties. While it is dangerous to make unsubstantiated links between sporting and political contexts, it is possible that part of amateurism's appeal emanated from the concern felt in some southern elite circles about the increasing challenge posed to their political and social position by the emergence of progressive political forces, in the shape of the Labour Party and new Liberalism. The election of a Liberal government in 1906, one which was to take on an increasingly radical reforming agenda after 1908, can only have added to these concerns. The AFA revolt was very much a rebellion of the old order, its leadership drawn virtually exclusively from a public school elite. It is also perhaps significant that it chose as its first President Old Etonian Lord Chief Justice, Lord Alverstone, Attorney-General in three Unionist administrations. Bold defence of amateurism was, arguably, rooted in something far deeper than just the narrow 'sporting' arena, much of its potency arising from its political value as a symbolic rejection of unattractive elements of mass culture and, thereby, mass democracy.

The secession also places the FA and some of its most prominent figures, especially Frederick Wall, in a slightly more positive light than the one in which it is often portrayed. Wall is best known to us through his autobiography where his patronising observations on the professional game, his snobbery and sexism and his predilection for celebrating an innocent golden age of soccer before the late nineteenth-century 'fall' – his proud claim to have been sufficiently uninterested in results as to have eaten a rump steak just before a key cup tie is noted in number of books – have made him a fairly soft target for late twentieth-century observers. However, while the FA undoubtedly placed barriers in the way of the commercial game and helped maintain clear class distinctions within it, the extent of the reaction against it, especially in 1905–7, demonstrates that far more extreme positions were possible, and that they were successfully countered.

ii. Directors

Football clubs were initially just that, voluntary organisations comprised of voting members and run by committees. The financial exigencies stemming from the growth of gate-taking and eventually professionalism, however, led to the transformation of the leading clubs into limited liability companies. Small Heath, later Birmingham City, was probably the first club to make the change in 1888 and, by 1921, Northampton Town and Nottingham Forest were the only two of the League's 86 clubs not to have followed suit.[29] The pioneering work of Mason, Tischler and Vamplew has revealed that rather more skilled working men and small tradesmen held shares in football clubs than might have been expected.[30] This was especially the case with clubs that were either relatively small or which were at an early stage of their development. At the same time, it is apparent that working-class shareholders often owned only a very small number of shares and held them only as a token of support for the club, rather than as an attempt to exercise power. Vamplew suggests that before 1915, manual workers comprised some 37 per cent of shareholders but held only 18 per cent of shares. The major shareholders and, above all, the great majority who became directors, came from far wealthier backgrounds, with perhaps only 20 per cent of all directors drawn from the combined ranks of manual and clerical workers.[31]

Consideration of the motives which drew middle- and upper-middle-class men onto the boards of football clubs has proved a fertile topic for academic speculation, shedding as it does potentially valuable light on the role and function of local elites and their relationships with subordinate social classes.[32] Many contemporaries liked to believe that the motive was essentially an 'innocent' one, there being 'no desire to obtain any reward beyond the success of the club, and, through that, the success of the sport.'[33] It is undeniably the case that many directors were genuine football enthusiasts, anxious to retain involvement with sports that they had played or watched as young men. Similarly, ensuring the 'success of the club' was often viewed as an opportunity for civic service, a chance to enhance the reputation of the town and settle scores with rival local communities. However, historians would be naive indeed if they did not search for less

Frederick Wall, Secretary of the Football Association 1894–1934. A rigorous disciple of the creed of 'managed professionalism'. (*Football Association*)

selfless motives. To what extent did the desire for financial gain act as an incentive? With dividends fixed at 5 per cent (this was increased to 7.5 per cent after the First World War), opportunities to make significant *direct* profits were obviously limited. Many clubs were able to pay a reasonably regular dividend, but most profit was absorbed in the maintenance of financial reserves, transfer deals, and above all, ground improvements.[34] Possibilities for indirect benefit were probably more substantial. Certainly, there is evidence that individuals in the building, catering and drinks trades used football club directorships to award themselves contracts, with only Newcastle United actually banning individual directors from the tendering process.[35] On occasions, directors clearly acted with their own interests uppermost in mind. In 1903, for example, brewers on Manchester City's board voted against relocation plans lest a move should interfere with match-day drinking activity at their own establishments; the move eventually went ahead.[36] Tischler suggests too that the business acumen of directors allowed them to 'make and conceal extra income'. This claim is hard to substantiate and, ultimately, fairly unconvincing. The corrupt director was a staple of sporting fiction throughout the twentieth century, but supposition is a poor substitute for hard evidence. In regard to this point, and indeed, to the issue of financial motivation in general, it might be justifiable to swap one untested assertion for another and record the directors' oft-made claim that they invariably spent more on their clubs than they took out. It is worth noting here the case, albeit an extreme one, of Preston North End's William Sudell, who was imprisoned for three years in 1895 for embezzling £5,000 over a five-year period from his employees, largely, it would seem, to boost the club's resources.[37] In general, profit-maximisation, either for the benefit of individuals or the club, was not a major consideration for the football club directors of Victorian and Edwardian England.

The possibility that directors used the game as a mechanism for exerting party political influence, and, perhaps more fundamentally, as an instrument of social control, is a second area that needs consideration. There is undoubtedly evidence that individuals did use football directorships for political ends. The most remarkable case concerned Middlesbrough chairman T. Gibson Poole who, as a Unionist candidate in the 1910 General Election, not only recruited members of the team to speak for him at meetings, but tried to bribe Sunderland players in the hope that a Middlesbrough win in a key local derby would enhance his electoral prospects. In fact, he lost the election and received a life ban from football.[38] This was, of course, the desperate measure of a rather sad figure and scholars stressing the game's potential to influence political and social attitudes usually have a slightly more subtle scenario in mind. Tischler, for example, sees the game as part safety valve, allowing spectators to vent potentially subversive energies and passions, and part mechanism for the incorporation of working-class culture by elite groups. Although rather unspecific about the nature of the values 'learnt' through professional soccer, he argues that 'the sport that captivated millions of working people also incorporated and institutionalised the principles of social organisation that were the basis of bourgeois hegemony. The establishment of such relationships seems to have been worth a meagre five per cent return.' Dunning and Sheard have also argued for the rugby and football club to be viewed as 'a vehicle for social control'.[39]

Obviously this is a difficult area; those seeking to use soccer in such a way would hardly be inclined to deposit proof in the record office. It seems perfectly reasonable to put forward such arguments; after all, many late Victorian and Edwardian socialists were highly critical of professional sport precisely because of the opportunities that it provided for the employing classes to deflect the working classes away from their 'true' political and economic interests.[40] It does, however, posit a rather conspiratorial view of the historical process. Apart from implying a working-class passivity that probably underestimates their capacity for critical thought and independent action, it also suggests a ruling class blessed with a purpose and programme of far greater coherence than was actually the case. It would be foolish to deny that directors were aware of the range of political benefits that flowed from involvement with sport, but it is perhaps best to see this as only one of an amalgam of motivating factors, not all of them fully articulated or even understood by the parties involved, that encouraged involvement on the boards of football clubs. Individuals gained a variety of personal benefits and pleasures from their role as directors, and it is perhaps at this level that the root of motivation should be sought. The desire, especially for older men, to be involved not merely with the sport but with the whole culture of youthful masculinity was probably one powerful attraction. Again, the simple exercise of power held its rewards for some, while for others it provided a status and *kudos* denied to them in other areas of public life. Some of these things might in turn have conferred political benefits, but many individuals were simply content to enjoy the pleasures and bask in the sense of importance that a seat on the board seemed (and seems) to induce.

iii. The Professional Footballer

By 1914 the footballers' trade union claimed that there were 4,740 professional players in England located in 158 clubs.[41] Despite the presence of a small and dwindling number of exceptional amateurs such as Vivian Woodward and the Rev. K. R. G. Hart, these declared professionals formed the elite of the English game, the backbone of club and international football.

The Reverend K. R. G. Hunt. An amateur with Leyton and the Corinthians, he gained two full England caps in 1911 and wrote on football tactics. (*Football Association*)

Evidence as to their social origins is scanty, but Mason's patient research suggests that the 'first generation of professional footballers was largely drawn from the ranks of skilled manual workers.'[42] These young men were opting for a career that offered considerable financial, social and emotional reward for the best and the luckiest. However, it was also one which increasingly placed restrictions on individual behaviour and mobility and which could be cruel to those who did not reach the required standard, or who suffered injury in what was, by late twentieth-century standards, a primitive medical culture.

Football League professionals operated under a code of labour regulation designed partly to maintain reasonable levels of equality between clubs, and partly to control labour costs. Central here was the rapid establishment of what became known as the 'retain and transfer system', fully established by 1893.[43] Initially, the Football League intended that a player could only represent one club per season, but this was immediately changed to allow for movement between clubs. Compensation in the form of a transfer fee (technically a fee which purchased the registration document) rapidly became the norm. Players could not join a new club, however, without the permission of their existing one, a restriction compounded by the fact that the League supported the clubs' right to maintain a player's exclusive services if they wished. The League resisted freedom of contract fiercely, arguing that it would allow a few wealthy clubs to recruit the best players; clubs had to be able to hold key players if a balanced and thus economically viable competition was to be maintained.

By the end of the century, wage restrictions were also in place. As is often the case when reconstructing occupational histories, there is no single body of data that provides definitive material on wage rates in the 1880s and 1890s. Indeed, it is not even clear how many players were actually full-time professionals. Scattered evidence suggests that by the early 1890s such players were probably still a clear minority and were receiving about £3 a week during the season, £2 during the close season.[44] A small number of 'star' players, however, were able to command much higher wages. Nick Ross, linchpin of the outstanding Preston side of the 1880s, was reputedly paid £10 a week on his transfer to Goodison Park in 1888. Obviously, there were also inducements to sign for new clubs (£10 was the supposed maximum from 1891) and various bonus systems. A very small number of top players could further enhance their income through their (modest) fees for representative and international matches and for off the field activities including the endorsement of such products as 'Oxo', leading cigarette brands and various liniments, as well as writing or 'ghosting' columns in the football press. In such a culture, the football agent made a first appearance, matching clubs and players for a suitable fee. One observer believed the trade to be only 'in its babyhood' in 1891 and wage restrictions and a hostile FA, for whom the agent's private profit violated the principles of the game, ensured that it never reached maturity in this period.[45]

A number of less affluent clubs became increasingly concerned about rising labour costs in the 1890s and there was much discussion of the benefits of a maximum wage. In 1893, Football League members actually voted in favour of such a device, but the three-quarters majority needed to effect change was not obtained. It was in fact the Football Association, anxious to be seen to exercise influence over the League and concerned that high wages would prove detrimental to good sportsmanship, which introduced the maximum wage of £4 per week in 1900.[46] The same meeting also voted to outlaw match bonuses. A number of wealthier clubs initially tried to resist the move, but it was introduced in time for the 1901–2 season. As partial compensation, players were to be awarded a benefit after five years, in case of accident or if forced to retire due to injury. Some 12–15 per cent of players, almost all in the Football League and Southern League, received the maximum by 1914.

Once again, the introduction of restrictive conditions was soon being justified in terms of the need to maintain a balanced competition and limit the power of wealthy clubs. As for those clubs, the player militancy

Millwall players training at the turn of the century, sit-downs clearly preferred to sit-ups. (*Football Association*)

of the next decade persuaded employers of the value of the maximum wage and their opposition died away. Opposition was also less vociferous because clubs found ways of flouting the system in order to reward key players. The bonus restrictions were certainly ignored, and some clubs paid leading players well above the maximum. Glossop, Manchester City, Middlesbrough and Sunderland all failed to disguise their various schemes and fell victim to Football League punishments between 1904 and 1907. The Manchester City evasion was on such a scale – leading players were receiving £6 10*s*. a week plus win and draw bonuses – that all the directors were forced to resign, the secretary and manager were suspended *sine die* from all football activity and seventeen players were suspended, fined and banned from playing for the club again.[47]

Just how hard players worked to earn their money varied according to the club's regime. Most clubs trained every weekday from the relatively leisurely time of 10 a. m. until lunchtime, with some further afternoon and occasional evening sessions. Training consisted of various combinations of skipping, sprinting, brisk walking, work with clubs and dumb-bells and ball practice. It is interesting to note that from the earliest days of the English game, some commentators complained that players were not encouraged to develop sufficient ball skills. It was a regime that was an easy target for satire, Arnold Bennett noting that before important games, clubs often 'took the teams off to a hydropathic establishment far, far distant from any public house. (This was called "training".)'[48] In terms of the number of games played in a season, regular players could certainly face heavy demands, especially if they were contracted to a side with a penchant for end of season tours and friendlies, presumably undertaken to gain extra revenue. Millwall, Derby and Aston Villa played 65, 58 and 56 matches respectively in 1895–96, while Everton played 17 games in 25 days in the April of the same season.[49] Club policy towards the off the field needs of their players varied dramatically, but many do seem to have adopted fairly paternal strategies with regard to the provision of insurance and financial assistance to injured players.

In comparison with most of the rest of the manual labour force from which they had come, professional footballers generally enjoyed a fairly comfortable lifestyle. They were obviously not immune to the problems that beset the working class in general. 'Industrial' injury, as noted above, was a serious hazard, while the diseases that afflicted the poor had often taken hold of footballers before their improved standard of living and superior fitness could come to the rescue. Nick Ross only briefly enjoyed the fruits of his transfer to Everton, the ex-roof slater dying of consumption in 1891, aged only 31. The advantages, however, were clear. Many footballers earned a great deal more than the £2 a week ceiling that even skilled tradesmen rarely passed above, while successful benefits could provide a valuable hedge against poverty in later life. Footballers also enjoyed the privilege of a flexible work routine, high job satisfaction and considerable standing in the local community. Actual and alleged incidents of match-rigging placed the occasional question mark against the professional footballer's probity, but by 1915 his respectability stood far higher than had been the case in the late nineteenth century.

It is not clear whether these differentials in standard and quality of life were maintained after retirement. Some (perhaps a majority) undoubtedly returned to their previous trade or something broadly akin to it, while others, probably a much smaller group, experienced quite considerable upward or downward social mobility. The annals of most clubs seem to include at least one ex-player similar to Preston's once-renowned goalkeeper James Trainor, effectively destitute towards the end of his life and reduced to soliciting help from teams visiting Deepdale.[50] At the other end of the scale, a significant minority of individuals were able to take pubs or shops and move into the relative safety of the lower-middle class. Few

Bob Crompton, full back with Blackburn Rovers from 1896–1920 and winner of 41 England caps. Originally a plumber, he eventually became manager and a director of the club. (*Football Association*)

ex-players, however, ended their days as wealthy men. Mason, for example, could find only ten ex-players who had gone on to become football club directors, a move which he sees as a clear indicator of upward social mobility among professional footballers.[51] Overall, the picture drawn here suggests that, before 1914, and indeed for a long time thereafter, the professional footballer remained very much a part of the working-class community both during and after his career.

Given the many problems that players faced and the general growth of trade unionism within British society from the late 1880s, it is not surprising that attempts were made to unionise professional footballers.[52] An abortive effort was made in 1893 and the short-lived Association Footballers Union was founded in 1897–98, but it was not until December 1907 that a permanent union emerged in the form of the Association Football Players' Union, led by Manchester United's Charlie Roberts. The passage of the Trades Disputes Act in 1906, which improved unions' legal rights, was a crucial spur here, although it is possible that at least some inspiration was derived from the music hall performers' strike in early 1907. This action, which was directed at restrictive contractual practices broadly recognisable to professional footballers, at least demonstrated that workers in an isolated and individualistic occupation could be mobilised.[53] Seeking reform on the issues of transfers and the maximum wage, as well as fighting for industrial injury compensation under the 1906 Workmen's Compensation Act and a range of other friendly society type benefits, the AFPU initially recruited reasonably well. It was certainly strong enough to trigger a confrontation with the game's authorities in 1909. The FA,

Charlie Roberts. Manchester United centre half from 1904 to 1913, many believed that his pioneering activity within football trade unionism limited his England career to just three games. (*Football Association*)

backed by the League, was particularly hostile to the Union's desire to affiliate to the General Federation of Trade Unions, and at one stage demanded that players leave the Union or have their registrations cancelled. A players' strike seemed a possibility, but an agreement was eventually reached in August, whereby the Union agreed to work under FA rules on wages and conditions, provided that the FA acknowledged the Union's recourse to the law on contractual issues. Even then, the FA refused to grant recognition unless the Union agreed not to affiliate to the GFTU. A subsequent ballot saw a vote of 470–172 against affiliation.

The Union continued to operate up to 1915, although its finances were seriously weakened by its failure in the 1912 Kingaby case, a test case brought against Aston Villa in order to challenge the retain and transfer system.[54] Membership slid from a height of 1300 in 1908 to perhaps 400 by 1915. A Union minute from April 1915 noting that 'expressions of regret were made at the lack of interest shown by the majority of players in their own welfare', captures the mood well.[55] Over the period from

1907, the Union clearly had some success in fighting cases for individuals and, although it almost disappeared during the war, the AFPU established a permanent structure for football trade unionism.[56] Ironically, however, a major outcome of its efforts may have been the unification of the football establishment against both unionisation and reform of the retain and transfer system and maximum wage, thus creating an even more problematic industrial relations climate within the game. Overall, the events of 1907–15 showed the imbalance in power relationships between 'labour and capital' in soccer. They also underlined the sheer scale of the problem faced by those who sought to unionise a group of workers who were geographically diverse, reasonably well-paid, certainly in terms of the range of job satisfactions that Vamplew refers to as 'psychic income', and who were often desperate not to spoil their chance of success in a notoriously short and unpredictable career.[57]

Patterns of success and failure

This chapter ends with a brief consideration of the relative share of playing success enjoyed by the 59 clubs that competed in the League at some stage between 1888 and 1915. Such a study further illuminates a number of areas already debated as well as providing material useful for later comparative purposes. The League's concern with quality control, as exemplified by the maximum wage and the transfer system, was also evident in areas relating to promotion and relegation. When the Second Division was created in 1892, relegation and promotion were initially settled by a series of 'test matches', played on a knock-out basis and contested by the bottom three clubs in the First Division and the top three in the Second. These matches were re-organised on a mini-league basis in 1896, although this too was abandoned after a notorious game involving Stoke and Burnley in 1898. With both sides needing just one point for a First Division place, they concocted a goalless draw so dire that a Stoke paper could claim that 'the teams could have done without goalkeepers, so anxious were the teams not to score.' The spectators became so bored that they took to playing with the ball every time it came among them.[58] Finally, in 1898, automatic relegation and promotion, reflecting form across the whole season, was introduced. A rigorous re-election procedure was also established, with the bottom four clubs expected to apply for re-election every year. The system was well used, with 15 clubs being voted out between Stoke's dismissal in 1890 and Glossop North

End's in 1915.[59] The League's recent origins coupled with the availability of a strong pool of sides seeking admission clearly prevented the re-election process from being coated with the weight of historical tradition and sentiment that so reduced its effectiveness for much of the twentieth century.

How successful were all these strategies in producing a balanced league? John Harding has talked of a 'super-eight' (Aston Villa, Everton, Liverpool, Manchester City, Manchester United, Newcastle, Sheffield Wednesday and Sunderland) that dominated the game by the early Edwardian period, and there is no doubt that a small number of sides took a significant share of the major honours. Four clubs, Villa, Everton, Sunderland and Newcastle, took 50 of the 108 possible First Division top four places between 1889 and 1915 and 15 of the 54 possible Cup final places in the same period.[60] Overall, however, a reasonably competitive situation did exist. Ten different clubs won the championship over the 27 years, while 18 won the FA Cup, progress in which was, of course, rather more prone to the influence of good fortune. Only Aston Villa and Sunderland ever came close to dominating English football for lengthy periods. Villa won the championship five times between 1894 and 1900 and took the Cup twice in the same period, achieving the 'double' in 1897. Sunderland in their turn managed five championships spread relatively equally across the period from 1892–1913.[61] In general, though, even the best teams tended to find that their success came in relatively concentrated periods often followed by spells of greater or lesser decline. Preston North End, so dominant between 1888 and 1893, found themselves relegated three times between 1901 and 1914; Liverpool were relegated in 1904, only three seasons after winning the championship; Sheffield United entered a very thin phase following a championship and two FA Cup successes between 1898 and 1902. Things were a little less competitive in the Second Division, where Darwen could only muster nine points in 1899 and Loughborough and Doncaster an even worse eight in 1900 and 1905 respectively. Even here, though, the position had improved considerably by 1915. The League had some reason to be pleased with its efforts.

There were, though, some factors that just could not be legislated for. Even at this stage of the game's development, and despite all the control mechanisms in place, it does seem that the simple fact of population size had an impact on playing success. No town with a population of below 100,000 was able to support a championship-winning side, with Preston (117,000) at the beginning of the period and Blackburn (133,000) at the end, the smallest towns to manage this.[62] The Cup, less dependent on sustained achievement, provided a better avenue for the small town club, as was demonstrated by Bury (1900 and 1902), Barnsley (1912) and Burnley (1914). At the same time, the endless struggles of clubs like Glossop North End and Gainsborough Trinity showed that League football was not really sustainable in communities with populations of under 30,000. Obviously, success ultimately depended on an often intangible blend of managerial skill, the quality of the scouting network and the chemistry of the team. Nevertheless, while a large population base and the concomitant increased support it generated did not guarantee success, it most certainly helped.

3

Football and its Fans, 1885–1915

Crowd size and social structure

THE NUMBER OF PEOPLE attending football matches rose almost continuously from the 1880s. Allowing for the fact that most observations must be based on estimated figures, it would appear that there were especially significant rises in the late 1890s and again after about 1906. In 1905–6, only Newcastle and Aston Villa had average attendances of over 20,000, whereas by 1913–14, 15 clubs had reached this figure.[1] Although real wage rates were generally higher between 1900 and 1913 than in the 1890s, the overall trend for the Edwardian period was towards stagnation and decline. While personal finances remained an important factor in structuring leisure habits, the increase in attendances after 1906 does suggest that watching soccer had become a habit which people were ever more willing to take up and ever less willing to give up, even if that meant going without other pleasures or even necessities.

Richard Holt has argued that loyalty to team overrode most extra-economic considerations, claiming that 'calculations of climate or league standing came second to just turning up, just being there to support your team and to identify yourself with thousands of others who felt the same.'[2] Certainly, Chelsea, Everton and Liverpool all seem to have experienced rising attendances in the immediate pre-war period despite declining playing records, suggesting that team success was not necessarily a major factor in attracting fans. Holt is on less certain ground when discussing climate. Excessively cold or wet weather was often offered as the explanation for smaller attendances by local journalists and it seems likely that people were sufficiently worried about discomfort and, more importantly, the possible medical effects of a good soaking on often almost entirely uncovered terraces, to exercise some caution.

Most fans saw their teams largely at home matches. Economic considerations limited away visits beyond attendance at 'local derbies'. Sets of supporters would, however, arrange visits to important cup ties, most notably the FA Cup final, and there would normally be an annual club trip where large numbers of fans would travel to a game at some distance from home. Arrangements for such events were often in the hands of the nascent supporters' clubs, which appear to date back to the Scottish 'brake' clubs, or travel saving clubs, of the 1880s.[3]

Evidence relating to the social composition of football crowds before 1914 is fragmentary, but a fairly clear picture can be constructed. In terms of social class, crowds at Football League matches were predominantly drawn from the skilled working and lower-middle classes, although Mason suggests the possibility of increased semi-skilled working-class attendance after 1900.[4] Social groups below that level were largely excluded by the admission price. In 1890 the Football League, quite possibly in a deliberate attempt to limit the access of poorer (and thus supposedly 'rowdier') supporters, raised the minimum adult male admission price to *6d.* This was relatively expensive in comparison with the costs of many other public forms of popular leisure: minimum admission to the music hall, for example, was often set as low as *3d.* or *4d.* while the cinema was cheaper still.[5] Boys and women were usually admitted for *3d.* Initially, women were often given free admission, a practice which continued in Scotland, but English clubs were clearly deterred by the loss of revenue that resulted from over-zealous use of the privilege. Preston North End, for example, changed its practice after some 2,000 women turned up for a game in April 1885.[6]

Given such a pricing regime, many supporters could only follow their teams from a distance or find ways of glimpsing them whenever possible. The young Charles Buchan was reduced to watching the last ten minutes of Arsenal's home games when the exit gates were opened, a rather ironic situation given that he was son of a blacksmith at the Woolwich Arsenal. He claimed to have sold a schoolbook to raise the money to see an Arsenal-Sunderland cup replay.[7] A middle-class element formed a significant minority at most grounds, usually situated inside the grandstands that had begun to emerge in the early 1880s. Mason's phrase describing such supporters as representing 'a bourgeois island in a sea of working-class faces' seems particularly apt, for football stadia were certainly designed with the 'popular' element uppermost in mind.[8] In 1905, Chelsea's Stamford Bridge ground housed 61,000 of its 70,000 capacity on the terraces, while in the same year Fulham's revamped Craven Cottage placed 40,000 on the terraces and only 5,000 in a new stand which they proudly boasted was 'absolutely safe in the most boisterous weather.'[9]

Regular attenders tended to be aged between about 18 and 40. Younger fans were presumably often excluded for financial reasons, while for older ones, the cost was likely to be married to poor health as deterrent factors. Those propagandists who call for the 'return' of the 'traditional family' game, when fathers and sons attended together in large numbers, clearly know little about the history of the game before the 1950s. The clear majority of spectators were undoubtedly male. Women certainly did attend matches, but it is probable that women's attendance rates fell from the 1890s as free admission was removed and as grounds became fuller and less comfortable. It is possible that young working-class girls and women were more likely to have been present in significant numbers at FA Cup ties, particularly as supporters of visiting teams. Observers certainly noted this to be the case at ties in Birmingham in 1902 and Bradford in 1911.[10] Arguably, the 'special' nature of these matches rendered them surrogate feastdays or holidays, which thereby legitimated female attendance. It is certainly significant that most observers noted the youthfulness of working-class women supporters. The 'leisure' of most married working-class women was generally far too hedged around with practical and ideological restrictions – lack of free time, the notion that formal leisure was the breadwinner's reward, concerns about 'respectable behaviour' and 'good mothering' – to allow for attendance at a football ground.[11] Many women, of course, had absolutely no wish to attend, grateful of the space that their menfolks' absence created for necessary domestic tasks or a brief period of 'time off'.

Crowd culture

Research into soccer crowd culture both in the period before 1914 and later has been dominated by the issue of crowd disturbance and hooliganism. This is undoubtedly an important area of study and will receive attention shortly, but more 'normal' patterns of behaviour must be considered in some detail. In this regard, the most obvious but perhaps the most crucial point is that, even on the popular terraces, there was no single style of spectator or spectating. Football crowds were an amalgam of various, essentially male sub-cultures. As will be seen shortly, some groups showed a propensity for violence, some gambled, some swore. The *Preston Herald* was not alone in criticising the language of football fans, nor claiming that their behaviour had a detrimental impact on the players' behaviour.

I have no wonder at rough games being played at Burnley when the

> players are urged to excesses by frank, rabid and I was going to say thick-headed partisans, who did not scruple to call out from the stand to the players to 'go' for a North Ender: "Punch his – ribs in, punch his – legs off," and much more filthy.

A reporter at a Nottingham Forest–Bradford City match in 1911, on the other hand, found a group of visiting supporters 'singing a hymn tune to the strain of concertinas' before the game started.[12] The latter pattern of behaviour was obviously less frequent, but the key point is that so-called 'rough' and 'respectable' cultures mingled in the football ground. Indeed, it is perfectly possible that individuals criss-crossed between them over the course of the ninety minutes, according to the state of their temper. It is important to acknowledge these differences; blanket generalisations about *the* football fan have blighted debate about the game since the late nineteenth century and historians should be careful not to endorse unhelpful stereotypes.

This is not to deny the existence of a definite atmosphere and specific modes of behaviour and custom. On the terraces at least the outcome was a rich mixture of colour, noise and humour, rooted in an intriguing blend of both long-established and rather more modern popular cultural forms and expressions. While the team colours, ribbons and rosettes, the crow-scarer rattles and the occasional drums and other instruments would not have looked out of place at a pre-industrial fair, or at a Georgian election, many of the songs and slogans were drawn from the contemporary music hall canon. A reporter at the 1911 Bradford City-Burnley cup tie, for example, noted that a rendition of Harry Lauder's 'I love a lassie' placed 'a serious strain on the permanence of the stands.' The same reporter was mystified by the provenance of the 'Stick it Jerry' favours worn by numerous Burnley fans in celebration of their goalkeeper Jeremiah Dawson. A music hall regular could have informed him that this was the catchphrase of a leading Edwardian music hall performer.[13] It would be interesting to know more about the timing and emergence of spectating styles and habits. Liverpool's club historian has claimed, for example, that the wearing of colours, rosettes and scarves only became common at Anfield from about 1907.[14] Evidence in this area is likely to be extremely fragmentary, but it might cast potentially interesting light on shifts in the generational and class basis of the football crowd.

Individual crowds exhibited distinctive flavours and characteristics. At the most basic level, this involved particular sets of supporters becoming associated with specific songs and chants. In the 1890s, for example,

Sheffield United supporters adopted the music hall drinking song, the 'Rowdy Dowdy Boys', while Southampton followers developed what the local paper termed their 'distinctive Yi! Yi! Yi! chant.'[15] Similarly, local customs and trades were celebrated by highly decorated mascots, and teams seem to have been happy to adopt nicknames which emphasised local connections and idiosyncracies. There may have been deeper manifestations of distinctive club cultures of the type noted by observers of the modern game.[16] Students of the game at local level should be alert to scattered hints relating to levels of noise, verbal abuse, praise, 'sporting' behaviour, commitment, preferred style of play and so forth.

The rewards for the football supporter were numerous. The game itself provided (usually) excitement, spectacle, colour and noise. It was a focal point of the week, a pleasurable end to the working week for the many who went, almost literally, from work to play as Saturday shifts finished, a fixed item in a not always certain world. Football also provided endless material for conversation, each game ripe for comment and dissection, first in anticipation, then in reflection. For those with a reasonable level of disposable income, football lay at the centre-piece of a weekend cultural practice which extended well beyond the duration of the match. The game might be preceded or succeeded by a visit to the pub, while supporters from outlying villages would often combine attendance at the match with a visit to the variety theatre or cinema. A whole panoply of forms of gambling surrounded the game, while a whole culture of collecting football memorabilia had begun to take shape by 1900. Most teams produced matchcards, and by 1914 a number of top sides produced programmes on quite a lavish scale. The very first football cigarette cards were probably those produced in the Ogden 'Golden Guinea' series in the later 1890s, while soccer postcards were common almost from the moment that the standard-size postcard emerged in 1899.[17]

At another level, a number of commentators have also pointed out that supporters could (and can) enjoy a certain sense of control, or at least a very realistic hope of swift reward through their involvement with a team. While political, economic and theological systems were not always to be trusted and often dangled the promised land beyond arm's reach, soccer offered the follower of even the poorest side a reasonable hope of immediate gratification in terms of victory, exciting incident and skilful play. Ironically, to shout and swear, even to cry, was in this context a rational form of behaviour. Many contemporaries and many historians term this rich cluster of pleasures 'escapism' or an antidote to 'the monotony of everyday life'. Clearly there is something in this, but it is unhelpful to stop at this initial level of analysis. Apart from the fact that such reasoning makes many assumptions about the everyday life of individuals of whom, for the most part, we have no knowledge, it also underestimates the centrality of sport in the lives of many people. As I have argued elsewhere, until all scholars appreciate that people's leisure activities were not just some fringe activity or ornamentation, but often a vital and defining part of their existence, then the function of popular recreation and culture will simply not be understood.[18]

It is hardly surprising that in the often febrile atmosphere this culture generated, football supporters sometimes indulged in outbreaks of what contemporaries variously described as 'riot', 'disturbance' or, after the word was coined following Bank Holiday incidents in 1898, 'hooliganism'.[19] While much hysterical journalism of the 1960s and 1970s, and some stimulating but ahistorical sociology of the same period, claimed football fan violence to be a new phenomenon, no serious scholar of football history now denies the existence of such events in the period before the 1960s. It is clear that a raft of activities including pitch invasions, attacks on players and match officials, the destruction of parts of grounds and fighting between rival groups of fans both inside and outside the ground punctuated soccer history in the period to 1914 and beyond. Tales of referees running from grounds and of sober citizens scattered by running gangs can make a rich source of almost pleasurable anecdote from the safe distance of 80–100 years, but the worst incidents were frightening to those caught up in them. Preston North End players and officials were attacked by a crowd of '2,000 roughs' following their 5–1 victory at Aston Villa in 1885. The Villa fans, apparently antagonised by a running feud betwen two opposing players and by a comment made to them by a North End player, mobbed the visitors in their changing tent, forcing them to escape 'Indian style' into a wagonette which backed up into the tent. They were pursued for some time by a crowd throwing 'sticks, stones, mud and every available missile'. A member of the Preston party reported themselves 'covered [with] showers of spittle'. The most spectacular footballing disorder of the period occurred at Ibrox Park, Glasgow in 1909. The crowd's anger at the failure to play expected extra time following a draw in a replayed Scottish Cup final resulted in a pitch invasion, the destruction of the nets and goals, the burning of pay boxes ignited with whisky, and pitched battles between fans and the police. Well over 100 people were injured.[20]

What academics do disagree upon is the frequency, scale and social significance of such events. Were they an infrequent aberration stemming from problems related to the game, or were they common events that manifested deeper social forces and tensions in English society? On the latter point, most commentators agree that local rivalry, part reinforced and part generated by soccer conflict, did provide the fuel for some outbreaks of disorder. Bad blood clearly existed in the 1890s between supporters of Darwen and Blackburn, for example, and between those of Preston and Burnley. Beyond this point, however, there has been much debate.

Perhaps the most restrained views on this issue are those expressed by Tony Mason. He is struck both by the peaceableness of the typical crowd, kept comfortably in order by what the *Athletic News* termed 'half a dozen flat-footed Robertos', and by the lack of 'any significance outside the context of the particular footballing occasion' possessed by those isolated events which did occur.[21] Wray Vamplew in an important early article was slightly more impressed by the scale of the problem and more persuaded of the possibility that such disturbances might reflect wider social tensions. Nevertheless, in general, he still appears to see disturbances as untypical and most frequently related to specific 'footballing' incidents such as unexpected postponements of matches and poor refereeing decisions.[22] A far more radical position has emerged from the work of researchers at Leicester University who have concluded that, while in no way the norm, 'there can be little doubt spectator disorderliness was a problem of considerable proportions at Association football matches in this period and that none of the historians who have studied it so far has come even close to capturing the scale on which it occurred.'[23] Extrapolating from local research based mainly on Leicester newspapers, combined with use of FA records, they claim that there may have been over 4,000 incidents of hooliganism at all types of football between 1894 and 1914, with particular peaks of activity between 1894 and 1900 and 1908–14.[24] They also show a far greater willingness than most other commentators to connect hooliganism with wider social currents, suggesting, for example, that there may have been a link between outbreaks of football violence and the presence in the crowd of members of youth gangs, the so-called 'scuttlers' or 'peaky blinders' which existed in a number of urban areas.[25]

The twin problems facing all students in this field concern the related issues of historical record and of definition. If we rely on 'official' FA records then certain key incidents, especially those that took place away from the ground, are likely to be missed, leading to a serious underestimate of the problem. If, on the other hand, the 'Leicester' approach is adopted, and a detailed trawl of local newspapers carried out with the aim of recording all incidents of crowd disturbance, there is a danger that large-scale and relatively trivial events will be conflated and the overall scale of the phenomenon exaggerated. Central here, of course, is the issue of definition. 'Hooliganism' was, and still is, a hugely subjective category: it is this very slipperiness that gives it its power in the hands of law and order lobbies. A few lads shouting in the street might well fit the term for a frightened resident near a football ground, but be of little moment for a policeman who has witnessed a full-scale riot and who is used to policing the city centre at night. Whether the contemporary press recorded such an incident as 'hooliganism' or 'horseplay', or simply ignored it altogether, depended very much on the inclinations of the journalist and the paper. At the time of a 'moral panic' over youth culture it might receive attention; at other times it might be ignored. The issue is further complicated by the fact that late Victorians and Edwardians (or at least their police forces), for all their concern about law and order, probably had a higher tolerance of a certain degree of disorder in and around sporting events than has been the case in the last thirty years.

A series of reports in the *Bradford Daily Telegraph* and the *Yorkshire Observer* from 1911, relating to Bradford City's trip to Nottingham and to the visit of Burnley supporters to Bradford the next Saturday, are helpful here. (These reports carry rather a lot of weight in this chapter, but they do provide an unusually detailed level of description and comment.)[26] These reports record behaviour which would almost certainly have courted police attention post-1965, but which does not appear to have led to anything beyond some anger among middle-class observers and mild press criticism at the time. Such behaviour included the pouring of beer into a rival fan's coat pocket, running on the field to give friends 'a laugh', pelting the visiting mascot 'with volleys of orange peel, banana skins and clods of earth', rowdiness in restaurants and the jostling of passers-by on the pavement. As far as can be ascertained, the only arrests stemmed from an incident in a Nottingham pub where some 'youths' (actually aged in their mid-twenties) were arrested for stealing glasses. On neither occasion does it appear that a report of any trouble was made to the FA. The language of the press is especially interesting. The *Daily Telegraph* was certainly more critical – especially of Burnley's *women* supporters – in its

Monday edition than it had been on Saturday afternoon, following incidents on the Saturday night and the *Observer* noted the mayor of Nottingham's claim that the events of Saturday night were 'a disgrace to all football followers, whether from Bradford or anywhere'. However, for much of their coverage, both papers adopted an almost avuncular, even at times jovial tone, the *Daily Telegraph* seeing 'something irresistibly infantile' about the Burnley contingent. How does the historian working through the local press record these events: football hooliganism by many people's standards in the late twentieth century, but clearly a less clear-cut issue for contemporaries?

Overall, for all these reasons, definitive measurement of the problem is impossible. Perhaps the best conclusion might be that hooliganism *defined as the outbreak of actual violence* was not normal, but it was far more frequent than has usually been assumed. Furthermore, a sometimes very boisterous undercurrent accompanied most games, and an edge of violence or aggression was often not far below the surface at games where fans with strong traditions of rivalry came into close proximity. It is perfectly possible that the hooligan problem would have been a lot greater if economic circumstances had allowed fans greater travel opportunities. Most incidents were probably sparked off by events on the pitch or were related to the organisation of games, but the presence of significant numbers of young men alert to the possibility of 'laughs' or adventure made disturbances more likely. We certainly should not dismiss the possibility of something resembling a 'hooligan sub-culture' existing at this time. Such a group appears to have attached itself to the Leeds Parish Church Rugby Club. Following an incident in 1890 when a referee had to escape from the home crowd by means of 'scaling a fence and taking a boat across the river' before taking refuge in a house, Yorkshire Rugby Union officials admitted that five other referees had turned down the fixture, and acknowledged that the club had to deal with particularly difficult fans.[27] It is perfectly possible that local research might generate similar evidence in regard to soccer clubs.

Interpreting the fan

Gender

Supporting a football team clearly involved the construction and expression of identities and beliefs which had resonance well beyond the sporting arena. One indisputable function of soccer was its capacity to build and articulate certain notions of male identity. Much of Richard Holt's pithy summation of sport's general role in this regard can undoubtedly be applied to football specifically.

> Sport has always been a male preserve with its own language, its initiation rites, and models of true masculinity, its clubbable, jokey cosiness. Building male friendships and sustaining large and small communities of men have been the prime purpose of sport. Women have been banished to the sidelines both literally and metaphorically, except for a minority of public schoolgirls.[28]

Soccer provided a locale into which men could escape from domestic and family obligation, an escape which indeed, because of the economic imperatives which underpinned it, helped define their status as head of household. It gave them a language, an argot which could be used wittingly or otherwise to exclude women, or indeed those men who withstood the game's attractions. It also provided a topic of conversation which could bind male relationships which otherwise would have little foundation, and which offered a useful distraction from other more troublesome emotional, social or political issues. Martin Amis's delineation of one of sport's central emotional functions rings as true for the period before 1914 as it does for its late twentieth-century fictional setting.

> Out on the street they couldn't talk about Nicola Six because that's what they were going back to Guy's place to talk about. As they turned into a quieter avenue their own silence grew louder. Guy chose a subject which had often helped him out in the past.
>
> 'Are you going to the match?'[29]

Place

A second important contribution to the management of social identity stemmed from the game's central role in the shaping of affiliations to locality and region, a topic only recently beginning to receive its due attention from historians.[30] Soccer confirmed the sense of 'being from Bolton or Blackburn, Bury or Sheffield'.[31] Holt's stress on football's capacity to confer 'symbolic citizenship', a sense of belonging to a community that was no longer easily knowable and manageable, is especially useful here. 'In a world where industrial production and urban life had cut loose the more intimate and human scale of the past . . . supporting a football club offered a reassuring feeling of being a part of something even if the crowd itself were for the great part strangers to one another.'[32] All this is leading us into the intriguing territory of the 'imagined community', where idealised notions of community produced empowering myths through which people expressed their hopes and aspirations. In a seminal essay focusing on the north of England, Jeffrey Hill has skilfully stressed the latter element, showing that celebration of sporting achievement, especially as structured by the local press, contained a very powerful element of wish-fulfilment. This was evident, for example, when newspapers described the crowd welcoming home cup-winning sides as though it represented one essentially united community.

> There is no doubt that people of all sorts did turn out to welcome their teams home, but perhaps the wish to amplify this occasional event into a more generalised image of the authentic nature of community reveals an all-too-keen awareness of the actual disharmonies present in the everyday life of northern towns. The image of the seamless community existed, perhaps, more readily in the imagination than in reality.[33]

To acknowledge Hill's point is not to argue that the forms of territorial consciousness discussed below were mere inventions. The myths that sustained them were rooted in lived historical experience. However, the symbolic as much or even more than the 'actual' must be considered here. Much of what follows is at an essentially descriptive level. Future historians must seek to explore these ideas further and, in particular, to examine the ways in which different groups manipulated these languages for social and political benefit.

The sense of local, civic pride was never more intensely and graphically expressed than at celebrations which followed the League and Cup successes, ironically, so often delivered by players with no local connections. The pattern of civic footballing celebration was well established by the end of the 1880s and remained in place at least until the 1960s. The central ingredients, almost clichés of the civic repertory, involved the triumphal greeting of the team at the station, often with a band or bands in attendance to play Handel's 'See the conquering hero comes', a procession through the town, and finally, a public dinner at which civic dignitaries thanked the team for bringing such honour to the community. Huge numbers representing a true cross-section of the local population could be mobilised on these occasions.

The level of playing success necessary to activate such celebration eluded many sides, of course, and it was the local press that carried much of the daily burden of boosting sporting civic patriotism. This could be done in many ways apart from merely trumpeting local success. Achievements in rival towns could be denigrated. The *Accrington Times*, for example, although deigning to give a detailed match report of neighbouring Blackburn Olympic's historic victory over the Old Etonians in the 1883 FA Cup final, gave almost equal space to games involving local clubs Accrington, Church and Enfield, and was less than enthusiastic about events at the Crystal Palace in its sports editorial. 'The Olympians also won the English Cup . . . One has seen and heard so much of this victory that it is a relief to leave this subject.'[34] Again, while never slow to offer constructive criticism, local papers were always anxious to defend the honour of the local representatives. In 1895, the *Preston Herald* strongly disputed reports that Preston's 9–1 away defeat in a friendly at Millwall was the result of drunkenness, explaining that North End's poor form in fact stemmed from tiredness caused by the journey, Millwall's rough play and the poor refereeing which had presented Millwall with at least four goals.[35]

Much of the above discussion is especially relevant to the smaller towns in which one club emerged as the dominant footballing force by the 1880s and thus became the town's external representative. The issues were potentially rather more complicated in larger cities. By 1914, London, most obviously, but also Birmingham, Bradford, Bristol, Liverpool, Manchester, Nottingham, Sheffield and the Potteries were all communities potentially divided as much as united by soccer. In general, it would appear that geographical and organisational factors, rather than social, political or cultural ones, structured patterns of club allegiance in cities and large towns. Bradford Park Avenue to a degree served the working-class communities of Horton in the west of the city, while Bradford City drew its support rather more from the Manningham district, a mile or so to the east. Similarly, Bristol City was essentially a south Bristol side while (then non-league) Rovers was rooted in the Eastville region in the north-east of the city. Rivalry between Liverpool and Everton stemmed from a conflict over the management style of Everton chairman John Houlding, which led to a break-away group decamping to nearby Goodison Park, forcing Houlding to found Liverpool in 1892 in order to find a use for the Anfield Road ground.[36] There is really no evidence to support the often made claim that sectarian rivalry underpinned the clubs' rivalry in this period. Neither club recruited players exclusively from one religion or another, and they supported local religious charities even-handedly. Mason's comment that even within the city itself, he had 'detected a little uncertainty as to which club was associated with which religion', is especially revealing.[37] The eventual decision as to which Liverpool side to support was rooted in a plethora of individual preferences rather than any clear social element. Even in towns and cities where loyalties were passionately divided, however, a strong civic sense could still emerge. In 1906, Liverpool's League championship and Everton's FA Cup success were celebrated by a cartoon in the *Liverpool Daily Post and Echo* showing the rival captains arm-in-arm astride a ball, with vanquished foes lying behind them.[38] Whatever the rivalry (and, indeed, perhaps *because* of it) Liverpudlians could unite as proud members of England's premier soccer city. In this cartoon and other cultural expressions lay the basis of many powerful and sustaining myths about Liverpool which were to play a major role in both the city's self-perception and outsiders' views of it. They will be returned to later in this book.

Obviously, an individual's loyalty to a particular club was not pre-ordained by accident of birth. Since the 1960s, support for the local team has clearly become far less important a factor in deciding fan allegiance, but it is possible that from much earlier in the century some individuals may have opted to ignore the ties of locality. One possible example of this, admittedly from a slightly later period, concerns the 1,000 Bradfordians who went to Wembley in 1928 for the Huddersfield–Blackburn cup final, with 'the majority of them' sporting Huddersfield colours.[39] This may have been a gesture of Yorkshire solidarity, or they may have been drawn largely from the marginal areas and villages around southern Bradford which were to an extent in Huddersfield's sphere of influence. However, simple preference for the successful neighbour over the modest local sides may well have played a role. The opportunity to support a 'big' team as against or alongside the local one was greatest in London. Here Chelsea, perhaps Tottenham and, at the end of the period, Arsenal, were prototypes for the 'glamour' sides of the post-sixties era. Arsenal's move from Plumstead to Islington in 1913 was made not merely to connect the club with the far larger base of support offered by the working-class communities of north London, but also because of its proximity to the main line stations at Kings Cross and Euston, which opened the club up to a much wider base of support. Chelsea was effectively an 'invented' club, joining the League before a team had been assembled. Its great advantage lay in the huge Stamford Bridge ground which, although situated in the territory already served by Fulham, had a main entrance almost next to a railway station and thus, like Arsenal, could draw support from well beyond the immediate area. The huge level of support for the club noted in the previous chapter is presumably partly explained by this.

Local patriotism could, of course, act as a building block for wider loyalties and affiliations.[40] Although identification with an immediate locality exerted the strongest influence, local rivalries were often suspended or ignored for long enough to allow various types of regional identity to emerge. At present, most of our knowledge here relates to the so-called 'north–south' divide. The dominance of northern teams in the FA Cup led to the almost annual invasion of London by northern fans, allowing full journalistic reign to the discussion of the supposed differences between the often hazily defined north and south. These 'differences' were long-established in popular cultural representations. Northern writers focused on southern condescension, snobbery and its stark contrast of wealth and poverty and compared this with the decency, plainness, inquisitiveness and simple good sense of the northerner. Southern protagonists tended to place a different gloss on these latter characteristics, viewing them instead as naivety and lack of sophistication. The most famous slur on the character and habits of the northern supporter was that delivered by the *Pall Mall Gazette* in 1884, in the course of its observations on the supporters of Blackburn Rovers. They were described as 'an incursion of Northern barbarians . . . hot-blooded Lancastrians, sharp of tongue, rough and ready, of uncouth garb and speech. A tribe of Sudanese Arabs let loose in the Strand would not excite more amusement and curiosity.'[41]

In fact, it is probable that this piece was written by the son of one of Blackburn's most esteemed residents, Dr Edward Morley, a leading Rovers committee man and member of the FA Council.[42] Whether the young Morley was merely being playful, guying the prejudices of the London press, or taking fearful vengeance on his home town, is unclear. However, while historians should beware of quoting this uncritically as evidence of southern hostility, the quote does stand as a useful exaggeration of a common view of the provincial in particular and northerner in general, whether soccer fan or otherwise.

Northern fans countered with their own myths. One concerned the supposed 'hardness' of northern teams, an extension of the belief commonly expressed in northern popular culture of the innate superiority of areas where wealth was created by 'real' (that is physical) work rather than by whatever largely invisible enterprise it was that kept the south so wealthy. The pleasure that the Barnsley crowd took in seeing Swindon's amateur forward and ex-theological student Harold Fleming, a young man who in Holt's memorable phrase 'compounded the crime of coming from the south by being middle class', being kicked out of a cup tie in 1912 would seem to be an extreme example of this.[43] There was, too, the belief among northern and especially *north-eastern* fans that they were both more passionate and more knowledgeable than their southern counterparts. This self-image, still a potent one at the end of the twentieth century, sometimes received reinforcement from informed outsiders. Charles Buchan, for example, a Londoner who started in the Southern League and then played for Sunderland from 1911 to 1925 before returning south to Arsenal, was a definite supporter of this view. Such notions are, of course, almost impossible to test in any concrete way. In the cricket world a similar belief in local expertise was propounded by the citizens of Sheffield and there, too, supposedly expert testimony could be called upon. The problem is whether such testimony is in any sense objective, or merely an unwitting absorption of the myth.[44] Whatever the reality, such myths should engage the historian, providing as they do important examples of the way in which provincial England expressed its opposition to the south, and to the capital in particular, through recourse to the symbolic terrain of sport and culture.

The study of regional identity is still in its relative infancy and it is important to recognise that a set of attitudes, rather than one set attitude, could be expressed. Throughout Southampton's cup runs of 1900 and 1902 the town's *Football Echo and Sports Gazette* constantly emphasised that the team was carrying the reputation of the south against a north and midlands who had for too long assumed superiority. 'In spite of the long start the North and Midlands have had, consequent on the snobbiness and the craving after the genteel among our sleepy and behind-the-times local associations, we are catching up, and apparently at a very decent rate too.'[45] Interestingly, the 'southern' identity projected here contained a strong anti-amateur, perhaps even anti-upper-middle-class element, that chimed in remarkably well with many northern representations of the southern elite. Clearly, narrow regional and wider class identities co-existed in many interesting ways

Class

While historians have been in broad agreement as to football's capacity to build a cluster of identities relating to gender and geography, there has been far less common ground when examining the game's role in the reflection and construction of class consciousness. The main focus has been on the nature of *working-class* self-expression and self-identity, a central issue for social historians in the last the three decades. At the risk of simplifying the debate, at one extreme writers argue that football was essentially in the hands of a knowing and manipulative ruling class which controlled the game in its own interests, thus denying the working class authority in both sporting and wider social contexts. The most dramatic examples of such arguments are to be found in the writings of European Marxists such as Bruno Rigauer and Jean-Marie Brohm. Brohm, for example, who amalgamates insights derived from Althusser and Foucault as well as the Frankfurt Marxists, has argued that sport has invariably served as a stabilising factor.

> The spectacle of sport magnetises enormous crowds – up to a million 'live' and up to a billion via television. As the biggest mass spectacle, sport operates as a sort of catharsis machine, an apparatus for transforming aggressive drives. Instead of expressing themselves in the class struggle, these drives are absorbed, diverted and neutralised in the sporting struggle.[46]

Brohm and others have been concerned largely with later twentieth-century sport but some historians of football's early development have shown a sympathy for such ideas. Tischler, for example, closely echoes Brohm's words when he contends that, 'commercial-professional football, like other entertainments controlled and financed by the bourgeosie, arguably created a safety valve through which pressure generated by industrial capitalism could pass safely, without endangering the basic relationships of society.' He moves on to suggest that, 'It may indeed be appropriate to reconsider the value of designating football as a "working-man's game" in anything other than a superficial sense.'[47]

Alternatively, others, often working within less prescriptive Marxist traditions, have claimed that working-class supporters have, to an extent, appropriated the game and imposed their own world-view on it. In this way, they deflected the thrust of ruling-class ambition and perhaps even sharpened their sense of class identity and class interests. The late Stephen Jones stressed the working class's capacity for independent thought and action, arguing that in the sphere of popular leisure working people were 'not sacrificial lambs to capitalist enterprise and domination . . . the Proletariat, in brief, discovered in modern sports *possibilities* for the culmination and advancement of their own interests.'[48] Similarly, sociologist John Hargreaves, although ultimately seeing football as dominated by the bourgeosie has emphasised the way in which working-class supporters invested games 'with their own character and transformed them in some ways into a means of expression for values opposed to the bourgeois athleticist tradition.' In particular, he stresses their 'vociferous partisanship, a premium on victory, a suspicion of and often a disdain for, constituted authority, a lack of veneration for official rules, mutual solidarity as the basis of team-work, a preference for tangible monetary rewards for effort, and a hedonistic "vulgar" festive element'.[49] Although one might quibble with the extent to which some of these features represented distinctly working-class characteristics, there is clearly much in this argument. The new culture of mass spectatorship rejected much of the largely middle-class ideology that drove the sporting revolution of the mid-nineteenth century. The working class undeniably took over what had been intended as a school of moral instruction and turned it into a popular theatre.

While such action, conscious or otherwise, can be seen to have to some degree blunted elite ideological ambitions, it is not at all clear whether this represents quite the scale of popular victory that is implied in some accounts. The move to interpret popular culture as a key site of working-class 'resistance' to the ideological control of dominant groups has been an exciting and important tendency within social history from the 1970s. However, there is always a danger that such an interpretation will be strained too far, and that, in the words of one critic, we will 'over-invest the actions of members of popular culture with either too much power or knowledge.'[50]

Focusing for the moment purely on power-relationships specifically within football, while the working classes might have imposed themselves on the game, they exercised little real control over it. They could admittedly exert influence, as when in 1909 the Leicester Fosse directors were forced to call a general meeting when fans threatened to rebel over the imposition of an admission surcharge for the Christmas Day game. In general, though, fans were rarely consulted, and there is not much evidence that they actually wanted to be. In the Leicester case at least, they also appear to have been remarkably pliant once their views had been aired, the meeting voting not only to allow the surcharge, but to volunteer one for the Boxing Day game as well. While writers like Tischler certainly underestimate the popular capacity for independent thought and action, they are surely right to see the location of sporting power in a small number of mainly bourgeois hands.

Extending the debate from football to the wider social arena, it is obviously extraordinarily hard to draw direct links between sport and political culture. We can speculate – and should do – but hard evidence is virtually impossible to find. It is difficult to disagree with Mason's comment that football helped assist individuals to locate themselves within social groups, and that, by 1914, playing and watching the game 'had become one of those things which working men did'.[51] In that way, the game perhaps helped to shape a sense of class but one which did not necessarily translate into any political programme or show any notable hostility to other groups. Football, then, perhaps generated a consciousness of class rather than class consciousness. Beyond that it is hard to go. As is so often the case in this type of debate the same material can often be used to support antithetical cases. The boisterousness of the terrace might, for example, be viewed as evidence of the popular seizure of the game, of working-class autonomy and resistance, but it might equally be viewed as providing an escape valve which allowed for the dissipation of energies which might otherwise have fuelled political and industrial radicalism. Indeed, it might be argued that it performed both these functions at the same time. Ultimately, interpretation will depend largely on the political standpoint of the individual historian.

Football and its place in society

This final section attempts to assess the place of professional football in English national life by 1914. How 'respectable' had the game become, and how secure was its place within national culture? Football, and indeed popular culture in general, was in many senses a soft target, attacks on which prevented the deeper analysis of contemporary ills that was often required. As popular support for the game grew it could in Fishwick's phrase 'be blamed for the failure of whatever cause one happened to espouse.'[52] Churches, struggling to hold congregations in what was an increasingly troubled time for organised religion, and political parties and organisations, especially socialist and radical ones, were a notable source of such comments. Simple competition for numbers was not the nub of the issue, of course. As already noted, many in left-of-centre groupings believed that sport was a de-radicalising element, deflecting supporters from political paths, while religious spokesmen found much that challenged Christian purpose and priorities. In 1900 a Bournemouth Congregationalist minister expressed such views with considerable ferocity, stating that 'to him the professional footballer was a monstrosity. God did not design a life to be spent in kicking a leather ball about. It was a perversion of God's meaning of life.'[53]

Further criticism came from within the ranks of those concerned with the fitness of the imperial race, a central topic of national debate in the late nineteenth and early twentieth century. In such discourses, 'spectatorism' was the target. The typical sentiment was that expressed in an article in the *Westminster Review* in 1903 when the rather aptly named Robert Sturdee demanded that the nation's males 'did not substitute a passive interest for an active participation in the game. It is not thus that football will redeem our national physique.'[54] Hostile references to hunched-shouldered, cigarette-smoking football crowds were not unknown in the literature of the Scouting movement, founded in 1908, one of the most powerful forces for national discipline and regeneration in an age that saw many such movements. Such attacks on 'passive' consumption found further reinforcement in writings from right across the political spectrum which were critical of the whole range of what we now call 'mass culture'. The music hall, the early cinema, and popular literature were all criticised in the same way, and often in the same breath, as football.

The problem for the historian, however, is to determine just how typical these effusions were. It is interesting in this regard that, when wishing to cite evidence of hostility to the game, historians tend to draw from a very restricted body of sources: many of the quotations and references given above will be familiar to those with a grounding in the existing literature. Future writers might attempt a detailed content analysis of a cross-section of contemporary journals to test the scale of the anti-football tendency. It might also be worth subjecting some of the most cited sources to rather closer scrutiny than has often been the case. Almost every book on the social history of football notes Charles Edwardes's piece 'The new football mania', published in the *Nineteenth Century* in October 1892, as prime evidence of middle-class hostility to the game. There is no doubt that Edwardes had some harsh things to say about football and especially its fans, foul in smell and language as they 'flock to the field in their workaday dirt, and with their workaday adjectives on their tongue.'[55] He expresses, too, concern that the game has taken on an exaggerated importance in the lives of the industrial working class. At the same time, however, there are *positive* comments in his article. Professional footballers are praised for their behaviour and a decline in serious injury is posited as evidence of the improving quality of play. Much of the article, written not by a first-time observer but by an individual 'present at considerably more than a hundred league matches', takes a relatively benign tone and is far less censorious than many pieces of late Victorian social comment.[56]

In the final analysis, certainly by the Edwardian period the level of support for the game across the whole social spectrum is more striking than the level of hostility. Ironically, detailed written evidence for this is harder to find than the evidence of hostility. As ever, silent majorities are harder to hear than vocal minorities. In general, supporters of the game from the 'respectable classes' offered sustenance through deed rather than word, and the written records of most value are not articles directly debating the game's merits but press reports of cup tie celebration, obituaries of civic 'worthies' and the general anecdotes of town life. Therein lies the obvious but vital point, that football quite simply could not have reached the level of public attention that it commanded without very substantial support from various sections of the middle and upper classes. As already noted, local and national politicians were ever more anxious to associate themselves with footballing success. Employers actively assisted the game by granting permission to the game's many part-timers to leave work early in order to train or play. On occasions, factories were closed to allow attendance at crucial games, usually cup ties replayed on weekdays. Such actions may have been a pre-emptive and reluctant acknowledgement of the threat of mass absenteeism encapsulated in the fan's supposed motto, 'if your work interferes with football, give it up', but a shared sense of the importance of the game may well have played a part.[57]

Further evidence for the hold of the game is provided by the fact that, perhaps for the first time, northern manufacturers and businessmen at least could be celebrated for their sporting contribution as much as their business or political careers. By 1914, Bradford textile manufacturer A. H. Briggs, 'in whose bank book' the prosperity of Bradford Park Avenue had been 'largely written', could be acknowledged as by no means the only magnate whose 'notability . . . is based upon a hobby.'[58] Perhaps the game's ultimate accolade came in 1914 when King George V attended the FA Cup final, the first time the event had been dignified by an official royal visit. No particular fan of the game, the king and his advisers were nevertheless astute enough to realise that the monarchical embrace of popular culture, no matter how light, had much to recommend it as the crown sought to build its repertoire of 'democratic' practice. His visit would have been impossible unless football's place in society was secure.

His witnessing of Burnley's defeat of Liverpool came only months before the game faced its most serious test, the outbreak of the First World War in September 1914. The Rugby Football Union suspended the new season almost immediately. The cricket season was virtually finished, but the game could still provide a good source of patriotic example, as when the Yorkshire captain, A. W. White, left the dressing room during a game with Lancashire to join his Territorial regiment.[59] The Football League and FA Cup programmes (and that of the Northern Union), however, continued, laying the game open to accusations of unpatriotic behaviour at a moment of national crisis. There were certainly those only too anxious to make those claims, one writer arguing that soccer should remain 'the exercise of the munitions workers who suffer so much from varicose veins, weak knees, cod-eyed toes, foul's liver and a general dislike for a man's duty.' In such an atmosphere, the publicity that followed match-rigging by at least four players in a Liverpool-Manchester United game in April 1915 could not have come at a worse time.[60]

Powerful as the anti-football campaign was, it does seem to have been confined essentially to the south. Yet again, the north–south, amateur–professional narratives seem to rise to the surface. Those northern commentators who saw the campaign as largely another chapter in the conflict over the game's soul that had erupted in 1884 and 1907 were probably correct. The game's denigrators also studiously ignored the many services that the game made to the war effort. Footballers acted as recruiting sergeants, both by example and exhortation, and grounds were used as recruiting centres on match-days. At the end of the 1915 season, patriotic virtue, coupled with the serious fall in gates occasioned by the war, led to the suspension of the League programme, a hastily arranged regional competition supplying England with its only regular senior football until 1919. The campaign against the professional game had some successes, a number of grammar schools turning to Rugby Union during and after the war in recognition of its ruling body's patriotic stand in 1914. However, soccer survived its test. It was too deeply entrenched to be weakened fundamentally by its vocal, powerful, but ultimately rather isolated enemies.

4

Football, Economy and Society, 1919–1939

THE IDENTIFICATION of clearly definable historical periods is no less a problem for the historian of football than for the historian of any topic. Although the revival of League football in 1919 and its suspension once again in September 1939 provide convenient boundaries within which to frame these next two chapters, the 'inter-war' period is a far from neat category when discussing the game's development. A number of changes which took place from the early 1930s, especially those relating to the media coverage of the game, almost seem to lead into a new era. The period was also extremely complex in terms of the wider social and economic context.

This chapter is concerned mainly with changes in the way in which the game was played and managed and its relationship with wider patterns of social and economic change. It is essential to begin with the briefest survey of the economic structure and climate. The dole queue has cast a long shadow over the nation's collective memory and many people still associate the period most strongly with the spectre of unemployment. There is, of course, much justification for this. The immediate post-war years evidenced a boom in trade which rapidly turned to a slump in 1920, resulting in the first manifestation of the high unemployment that was to be such a marked feature of the next two decades. Between 1921 and 1939 the unemployment rate amongst the insured workforce averaged 14 per cent, peaking at 22 per cent in 1932. Unemployment rarely fell below 1 million in the 1920s and was never to do so in the 1930s. Such figures, however, capture only part of the picture. Although almost all parts of the country experienced difficulties at the height of the depression in the early 1930s, the overall economic experience was typified by remarkable levels of regional and occupational variation. Certain industries, such as motor car and electrical goods manufacture, for example, prospered, while the older export-led heavy industries such as coal and cotton struggled. Many parts of England prospered in the inter-war period and even in more vulnerable regions some towns, such as Consett in Co. Durham and Halifax in the West Riding, largely escaped serious unemployment because of peculiar features of the local economy. The result was rising prosperity for many. Real wage rates grew by perhaps as much as a third over the period from 1913 to 1939, with the rise almost continual from 1929. At the same time, the opportunity to enjoy this increase in disposable income was much increased by a fall in the hours of work from an average of 54 hours before 1914 to 48 hours by 1939, and by improvements in transport. The estimated number of passenger miles travelled on coaches and buses increased sixfold between 1919 and 1939.[1]

This emphasis on material improvement should not blind us to the real problems and tragedies of the period. The overall climate, however, was a propitious one for the continued growth of the leisure and consumer goods industries, and football, along with the many other areas of social life, such as the popular press, cinema and broadcasting, with which it grew in a mutually stimulating symbiosis, was a major beneficiary. In the immediate post-war prosperity, the Football League felt confident enough to commence an ambitious programme of expansion. In 1919, both divisions were increased from 20 to 22 clubs. Then in 1920, a Third Division was added, comprising 22 clubs drawn from the Southern League. There was initially some concern as to whether northern football was economically strong enough to be embraced in this process, but, in 1921, a twenty-strong Third Division North was founded.[2] Over the period as a whole, average attendance at First Division matches increased from 23,115 in 1913–14 to 30,659 in 1938–39. The number of clubs affiliated to the FA rose from 12,000 in 1910 to 37,000 by 1937. A. J. P. Taylor described the inter-war cinema as 'the essential social habit of the day'. For many young men at least, football had an equal claim to this honour.[3]

'Lucky Arsenal': *the rise of southern football?*

While many individuals expressed concern that the expansion of the Football League weakened its quality, its officials were at least now able to claim that it was a truly national body. By 1921, most towns of any significant size had a Football League club and only a very few, mainly rural, counties did not have a representative. Indeed, the League was now more than just an English body, with six Welsh sides joining between 1920 and 1921.[4] In terms of its long-running rivalry with rugby, and especially Northern Union, its 'colonising' days were effectively over.

West Bromwich Albion, League Champions in 1919–20. The League title was not to return to the midlands again until 1954. (*Football Association*)

There were a few marked successes at the beginning of the period, most notably that experienced by Huddersfield Town. Unable to establish a strong foothold in a Northern Union area, the club almost went out of existence in 1919 when two leading directors, seeking to fill a potentially lucrative gap following the FA's disbanding of the Leeds City club for allegedly making illegal payments, considered relocating it in Leeds. A determined fight back by supporters coupled with an unexpected turn-around in their playing fortunes were the key steps in a revival which saw Huddersfield become the country's premier League side in the 1920s. In general, however, patterns of sporting preference were effectively established by 1920. In some areas, notably the Yorkshire heavy woollen district, south-west Lancashire, Cumberland and Cornwall, soccer had to be content to remain the junior partner.

One of the most common claims concerning soccer's 'social geography' between 1919 and 1939 is that the expansion of the League and, above all, the varied regional patterns of economic experience, led to the rise of southern and midland teams at the expense of those in the 'traditional' northern heartlands. The most authoritative commentators on the period, such as Nicholas Fishwick, are anxious to emphasise that the story is a complex one. However, the thrust of their argument is clear. Fishwick, for example, argues variously that 'London and clubs from the better off parts of the Midlands dominated football for much of the thirties', that 'the grip of the traditional areas was weakened noticeably', and finally that in this period 'southern clubs dominated professional football for the first time.'[5]

In fact the issue is rather less clear. The following table demonstrates that in terms of simple geographical location, there were at best, only modest changes in the overall geographical balance of power across the inter-war period.

Table 1. *Geographical location of First Division teams, 1915–39*

	1914–15	*1928–29*	*1939–40*
'Textile' Lancashire	5	4	4
Lincolnshire	—	—	1
London	2	2	4
Manchester	2	2	1
Merseyside	2	2	2
Midlands	3	4	4
North-east *	3	2	2
Southern	—	1	1
Wales	—	1	—
Yorkshire	3	4	3

* Includes Middlesbrough, technically in the North Riding of Yorkshire.

Obviously, analysis of different seasons would give a slightly different picture, but the general picture would not alter. As regards the issue of levels of playing success, it is perhaps easiest to begin with the midlands. As the selection of quotations from Fishwick's work shows, it is quite common for writers to bracket the region with a 'rising' south in some statements, but exclude them from others. This implied uncertainty as to the actual level of achievement is understandable. At one level, some midlands sides, especially those from towns with lower than average unemployment, enjoyed much improved playing records in this period. Leicester finished as League runners-up in 1929, Derby finished in the top six on six occasions between 1929–30 and 1938–39, finishing as runners-up in 1930 and 1936, and Wolves finished second in the two immediate pre-war seasons. In the lower reaches, Coventry were Third Division South champions in 1936 and soon became a force in the Second. However, only West Bromwich (1920) won a championship and only Aston Villa (1920) and West Bromwich (1931) won the FA Cup. Of the seven midlands sides which competed in the First Division in the 1930s, only Derby and Wolves enjoyed any measure of success, most of the others spending much of their time in the lower half of the table.[6] In terms of attendances, another useful indicator of sporting health, Villa were consistently one of the best-supported clubs in the country and most sides enjoyed good crowds during their spells of relative success. However, some midlands sides attracted far smaller crowds than their playing record or their town's economic strength might have led people to expect. Derby, for example, consistently drew crowds well below the divisional average, despite both their relative success and the fact of the town often enjoying one of the lowest unemployment rates in the country. Overall, there was clearly no fundamental shift in the midlands' soccer fortunes in this period.

There *is* more evidence of the 'rise' of southern football, both in terms of escalating attendances and success on the field. Arsenal's record in the 1930s was (one has reluctantly to admit) quite remarkable. Tottenham's FA Cup victory in 1901 represented southern football's sole success in major tournaments until 1930. Indeed, the record was so slim that the occasional writer has appropriated Cardiff's 1927 Cup success for the 'south'. This changed dramatically as Arsenal took the championship five times between 1931 and 1938, including a hat-trick of titles in 1933–35, and the FA Cup in 1930 and 1936. Arsenal players also made a huge contribution to the home international sides. The team was the best-supported in the league for nine consecutive seasons from 1929–30 to 1937–38; in 1934–35 their 46,252 average gate was 11,500 higher than that of their next biggest rivals. Moreover, the skilful eye for publicity held by both Herbert Chapman and his successor George Allison placed the club in the public gaze to an extent that was truly novel. No club had ever dominated English soccer on and off the field to this extent. A number of other southern sides also came to prominence. Two London clubs, Brentford and Charlton, new entrants via the Third Division South in 1920 and 1921 respectively, arrived in the First Division in the mid-thirties and achieved immediate success. Charlton were runners-up in 1936–37 and then fourth and third in subsequent seasons, while Brentford (sited in an extremely prosperous area) managed a top six position in three of their four seasons in the top division. Portsmouth, in their turn, won the FA Cup in 1939.

However, in at least two important ways, emphasis on southern success, and the concomitant northern 'decline' which will be addressed shortly, has led to the construction of a misleading history. First, stress on the

'North and South'. Arsenal's George Hunt takes on the Manchester City defence at Highbury in 1937. (*Popperfoto*)

south's post-1919 record does tend to underplay its strength in the Edwardian period. As already noted in Chapter 2, despite its limited playing achievements, the southern game was in a fairly healthy state. Chelsea and Tottenham were among the best-supported Football League teams, while the Southern League contained a number of sides of very respectable quality, often drawing on a strong basis of support. The Southern League should be seen as part of the overall structure of the professional game in Edwardian England rather than, as can be the case, being excluded on what are, to some extent, rather artificial administrative grounds. The key point, however, is that the pre-war/inter-war contrast is less dramatic than often suggested: the inter-war rise was part of a longer-term trajectory of growth.

Alongside this it is hard not to conclude that the 'rise of southern football', at least in regard to playing success, is in fact a rather sweeping term for what was actually the 'rise of Arsenal'. The record of southern achievement listed above is thin indeed when Arsenal's record is subtracted. Moreover, some southern sides passed through difficult periods at this time, sometimes because of the problems of form, quality of players, injuries, morale and poor management that can beset any side, but also because they sometimes shared the economic problems of northern towns. Spurs were relegated from the First Division in 1927–28 and again in 1934–35, and West Ham in 1931–32, not to return until 1958. Chelsea averaged only thirteenth place during the 15 seasons they spent in the top division. At the lower end, only three of the 15 sides promoted from the Third Division South between 1921 and 1938 went on to reach the First Division, while newly formed Thames United resigned from the League in 1932 after just two disastrous seasons.

The corollary of all this, of course, is that the 'traditional' areas were actually extremely resilient. Even in the economically troubled 1930s, northern sides managed six Cup victories while Everton (twice), Sunderland and Manchester City all succeeded in interfering with Arsenal's run of championship successes. Again, it terms of attendances, the older established sides held their own. As late as 1938–39, only seven of the 20 best-supported League sides came from the south. It was not, in fact, until well after the Second World War that any major shift in the game's geographical balance of power really took place, and even that may have been less dramatic than is sometimes thought.

The relationship between local economic health and sporting success has been touched upon several times in the above discussion, and it is time to address this issue in more detail. At the height of the depression in the early 1930s, the majority of clubs experienced a drop in gates and, thereby, varying degrees of financial difficulty. The First Division average fell from just under 26,000 in 1927–28 to just over 22,000 in 1932–33. Problems were especially acute in those towns with a reliance on single industries badly affected by unemployment. Between January and May 1932, Blackburn saw home gate receipts plummet by £250 per match and were forced to sell four players to relieve the situation. In the next season, they recorded nine gates of under 10,000; four-figure gates were almost unknown in the more prosperous 1920s. Overall in 1932–33, Blackburn Rovers saw a 32 per cent fall in attendances in comparison with the 1926–27 season, against the background of a local adult unemployment rate of 34 per cent. Over the same period, Middlesbrough, suffering from 44 per cent unemployment, experienced a 46 per cent fall.[7] Fishwick has drawn attention to Swindon's similar financial struggles as the Great Western Railway shed labour. Large crowds could still be attracted to key matches, 36,000 watching Blackburn's 1932 Christmas fixture with

Everton, while interestingly some clubs seem to have had greater success than others in holding supporters. In October 1932, the Sunderland *Football Echo* wondered how Sunderland managed to maintain their support 'at a fairly high level [in] the hardest hit area in England' at a far better rate than Sheffield Wednesday. In this instance, local pride does appear to be supported by the evidence. In 1932–33, Sunderland's unemployment rate ran at 48 per cent, Sheffield's at 34 per cent. Yet in 1931–32, Sunderland, finishing only fifteenth in the First Division, enjoyed average gates of 23,000, only 2,000 less than in the prosperous 1928–29 season when they had finished fourth. Wednesday, however, despite finishing third, recorded an average of only 17,000, a fall of 10,000 from 1928–29, when admittedly, they were champions.[8] Perhaps non-quantifiable variables, such as the north-east's supposed extra passion for the game, came into play in such situations.

Bill McCracken, Newcastle United defender and expert user of the 'off-side' tactic. (*Football Association*)

How did all this relate to patterns of individual team success? Loss of revenue due to unemployment was undoubtedly a major factor in Aberdare (1927), Durham (1928), Ashington (1929), Merthyr (1930), Nelson (1931) and Wigan (1932) losing Football League status. Admittedly, it must be said that many of these towns had such small populations that they were in any case desperately vulnerable to financial crisis. Larger teams could also be troubled, however. West Ham's relegation from the First Division in 1932, Newcastle's and Sheffield United's in 1933 and Blackburn's in 1935, all owed something to reduced economic capacity due to falling gate revenue over a lengthy period. Yet among both large and small clubs, the 'fit' was never a neat one. Everton won the championship in 1931 and 1939, and the Cup in 1933, against a background of an unemployment rate well above the national average. Similarly, Sunderland's

Frank Barson, in Aston Villa colours. Barson enjoyed a fearsome reputation as a tackler. (*Football Association*)

1935 championship and 1937 FA Cup success were both achieved with local unemployment running at two-and-a-half times the national rate. The 1938–39 season almost produced an inverse relationship between economic situation and sporting success. All four divisional champions, Everton, Black- burn, Barnsley and Newport, were situated in towns experiencing unemployment of between 20 and 30 per cent, at a time when the national average was just under 12 per cent. However, Leicester and Birmingham, both experiencing below average unemployment, saw their teams relegated from the First Division, and three southern sides finished in the bottom six.

As Arsenal's record showed, prosperity was a great advantage. It certainly did not guarantee success, however, and a lack of it did not necessarily preclude success. The maximum wage, for all its evils, and despite all the ways it could be breached, provided some protection to clubs in troubled areas, as did sheer fan loyalty. A club's achievements were more often the result of being able to draw on a substantial population base, good management of scarce resources and good management of the requisite 'players for the job', than the workings of specific social and economic forces.

The *game*

Comfortably the most important rule change of the period was the alteration of the offside law in 1925. As the regulation had been established, when an attacking player received the ball in the opposition half, he had to have three opponents between him and the goal in order to remain onside. Gradually, the 'offside trap' had emerged, a strategy which usually involved a defending full back moving forward as the ball was played towards their goal, in order to render at least one attacker offside. Most football literature attributes this tactic to the post-war Newcastle defence marshalled by Bill MacCracken. However, it would seem fairest to see MacCracken and his team-mates as the perfecters of a ploy that had been maturing for some time. Charles Buchan and several other informed insiders regarded the immediate pre-war Notts County full backs, Morley and Montgomery, as its first major exponents.[9] Whatever its origins, it led to a decrease in the number of goals scored and there was concern that this, coupled with the endless stoppages that resulted, was undermining the game as a spectacle. In 1925, the Football Association agreed to alter the law by reducing to two the number of players that were needed between an attacker and the goal. The short-term effect was immediate, the first season under the new rule seeing 6,373 League goals scored as opposed to only 4,700 in the previous one.

Compensatory changes in tactics soon followed to counter this shift in favour of the forwards. Increasingly, teams began to deploy the centre half, previously used quite extensively as an attacking player, in a more overtly defensive position, with the label 'stopper' applied to the new role. This was usually combined with the use of a midfield 'linkman' (or men) whose job it was to take the ball from the stopper and supply the forward line. The new line-up was labelled the 'M/W' formation, defence and attack lining up as if on the points of these letters. As ever, there was probably no single 'inventor' of these ploys, but the new pattern of play was most strongly associated with Arsenal, who perfected it in the early 1930s. Defender Herbie Roberts and midfielder Alex James occupied the key roles.[10] The change in the offside rule and the tactics used to counter it were widely believed to have sped the game up by encouraging a long passing game at the expense of the slower, more methodical approach of the earlier period; the quick long ball into the opponent's half clearly gave the maximum advantage to the attackers under the new rules. Interestingly, defences gradually re-asserted some authority as the 'stopper' became the norm and as new variants of the 'offside trap' took root. By 1937–38, the number of goals scored per game had fallen back to under three for the first time since 1924–25.[11]

Other minor but interesting tactical and rule changes emerged in the period. Arthur Grimsdell of Tottenham Hotspur was one of a number of players reputed to have developed the art of the long throw-in during the early 1920s.[12] In 1924, it was agreed to allow goals to be scored direct from a corner kick, thus effectively rendering the corner a direct free kick. In January 1925, Everton's Sam Chedgzoy infuriated Spurs fans, and amused everybody else, by exploiting a previously undetected loophole in the drafting of the legislation and dribbling the ball straight from the corner spot into the goal. The authorities hastily let it be known that the player taking the kick was not supposed to touch the ball twice in succession, and speedily clarified the law in time for the 1925–26 season.[13] From 1929 it became (theoretically) obligatory for goalkeepers to stay still when facing a penalty, while from 1939 the numbering of shirts became compulsory.

The game was probably not as physical as it had been in the 1880s and 1890s. Writing in 1924 of David Russell, the Preston centre half of the 1880s and 1890s, the veteran journalist J. A. H. Catton claimed that the modern referee would have had 'something to say about dangerous play and the honest vigour of his charges', particularly his habit of bringing 'high balls down to the grass with a foot in the vicinity of the opponent's ear.'[14] There is enough corroborating evidence to suggest that this statement represents more than the mere straining after comic effect. Nevertheless, most sides had at least one hard man, or 'killer', in contemporary parlance, and none more famous than Aston Villa's Frank Barson, who actually managed to be sent off in his own testimonial

Huddersfield Town, 1921–22. Three consecutive Football League Championships awaited. Manager Herbert Chapman, arguably the most influential manager in the history of the English game, sits on the far left. (*Huddersfield Examiner*)

match.[15] On some occasions physical intimidation was adopted more or less as a team tactic in order to quell superior opposition. 'Perseus', the *Lancashire Daily Post's* football correspondent, was regularly angered by the tactics adopted to neutralise the skills of Alex James during the player's spell with Preston in the 1920s. 'It is a long time since I watched a game in which the elbow and the foot were used to stop a man so often', he complained after a visit to Chelsea in 1926. Portsmouth were accused of the 'persistent playing of the man, not by the shoulder but by the arm and the foot, cutting him off by the knee and the ankle, with the ball left severely alone'.[16] Cliff Bastin's attempt at diplomacy during his account of the tactics used by Third Division Walsall in their famous FA Cup defeat of Arsenal in 1933 fails to disguise his real view as to the level of foul play they adopted. Interestingly, however, it also suggests an acceptance of the legitimacy of a highly physical approach in games of this sort.

> Walsall could not have complained had five men of their men, at least, been sent off the field in the first quarter of an hour . . . Do not misinterpret me. I don't want to level an indictment at the Walsall players. They played a little too vigorously, perhaps, the game which was right in the circumstances.[17]

At certain times particular sides gained a reputation for a markedly robust style of play. In 1936–37, for example, Wolves headed the 'cautions' table, 15 players amassing a total of 17 bookings, mainly for foul play. When the club wrote to the FA to dispute a caution given to Stan Cullis, the club was sent a curt reply and effectively accused of condoning their players' poor record. Conversely, Gateshead, Gillingham and Hartlepools had no players cautioned, an interesting reflection of the fact that clubs in the lower divisions had far better disciplinary records than those in the First and Second.[18]

The level of concern over the issue of excessive foul play was coloured by the wider social context. In March 1920, the FA held a commission of enquiry into a game between Chelsea and Bradford City which reported that: 'We are of the opinion that the match was played with a vigour and recklessness which is calculated to bring the game into disrepute.' The players of both sides were 'severely censured', but at the same time, the report noted that: 'The referee and the linesmen are deserving of censure for not exercising greater control.' In the next season Bradford City were involved in another rough game, this time with Barnsley. One Bradford paper deemed the game 'the roughest ever seen in Bradford, and the referee

(Mr Botterill of Manchester) should have exercised a firmer control of the players than he did . . . The men repeatedly squared up to each other, and there was more than one bout of fisticuffs.'[19] While it might have been the case that these *were* excessively violent games, it is interesting that both took place in a period when industrial militancy was at a high level, and when there was much public debate about a perceived loss of discipline among the working class. Footballers might have found their behaviour under particular scrutiny at times like these. It is also significant that the match officials were targets for criticism in these and other reports; they were clearly believed to have a wider function as upholders of public standards in troubled times.

Managing the game

The 'secretary-manager' had become established in the game by 1900, as the professional game generated ever more burdens for the clubs. A few, such as ex-schoolmaster Tom Watson who built highly successful sides at Sunderland and Liverpool in the 1890s, appear to have been heavily involved in signing, selecting and training players, but many others were ultimately administrators or clerks. Almost all were decidedly subservient to their boards of directors. The inter-war period, and the 1930s in particular, saw the beginnings of what were to be fundamental changes in this relationship. At the same time, managers came to play a far greater role in the public's perception of the game, as the press, part reflecting reality, part constructing it, increasingly talked of club actions in terms of managerial activity.

The two individuals most commonly associated with these changes were Herbert Chapman and Major Frank Buckley, to some extent the prototypes of the 'technocrat' professional manager so common from the late 1950s. Chapman, one of only three men to have taken two different clubs to Football League titles, saw Huddersfield Town to the first two of their hat-trick of championships between 1924 and 1926, before guiding Arsenal to the Cup in 1930 and the League in 1931 and 1933. The club were half-way to another championship when Chapman died of pneumonia in January 1934. Buckley, manager of Wolverhampton Wanderers from 1927, was unable to lead his side to Cup or League success, but he certainly made the Wolves side of the late 1930s a highly successful and much talked-about club.[20] Nicholas Fishwick has made the perceptive point that managers obtained the greatest power in clubs where directors had a

While directors, and, less frequently, managers, shaped policy and tactics, others organised crucial day-to-day activity. Here, trainer Will Scott takes Preston players through a typical 1930s' training routine. (*Lancashire Evening Post*)

limited tradition of close involvement, or where a club was in the midst of a crisis from which the board was happy to be led. The latter situation certainly fits Chapman's experience at both Huddersfield and Arsenal. Huddersfield had come close to extinction only weeks before he joined them, while the life ban imposed in 1928 upon Arsenal's high-profile chairman Sir Henry Norris for financial irregularities made the Arsenal board less likely to interfere with the work of a man who had already demonstrated great ability at another club.[21]

Chapman and Buckley were very different temperamentally. Chapman built a close, almost fatherly, relationship with his players, who clearly had enormous affection for him. Cliff Bastin recalled that he 'broke down completely' after Chapman's funeral.[22] Buckley was very much the martinet, although equally respected. However, a number of shared features marked them out from most of their predecessors and contemporaries. Absolutely crucial was the autonomy they achieved in regard to issues of team selection and tactics. Chapman actually refused dressing room access to anyone other than players and team officials in the half hour before a match. Their training methods, especially Chapman's, placed much more emphasis on the development of ball skills than had been normal. Both showed an enhanced concern for players' welfare, with Buckley constructing a paternalistic structure which included a hostel for younger players and the provision of further education facilities. Both men had a tremendous flair for publicity which raised their own and their clubs' profiles. Chapman, for example, wrote a series of articles for the *Sunday Express* in which he explained the tactics of modern football and enthusiastically championed such causes as floodlit football, even suggesting the need for heated grandstands if this was to become a commercial reality.[23] Buckley's most famous coup was his claim in 1935 that his players had been fed monkey secretions to enhance their performance.[24]

Obviously, all this represented the beginning of a trend rather than a full-blown change. Many successful (and unsuccessful) clubs continued to be run by often dictatorial directors rather than by managers. The successful Preston North End side of the late 1930s was very much dominated by director James Taylor who had control over all significant matters regarding team selection and club policy. It was Taylor who turned the young Tom Finney from an inside left to a right winger in the late 1930s. The Newcastle United board still chose the team until well into the 1950s. Interestingly, even Arsenal to some extent moved away from the Chapman model on his death by appointing director George Allison as manager. Allison was probably a better manager than some accounts give him credit for. He had some playing experience at a reasonable junior standard in Durham, and he had proved a knowledgeable commentator for the BBC from the late 1920s.[25] However, he was hardly a great tactician and was not close to the players, as their obvious disapproval at his appointment demonstrated. The one gift he shared with Chapman – in fact he probably surpassed him in this area – was that for earning publicity. It was perhaps this, combined with the knowledge that the coaching staff was sufficiently strong to carry him, that led to his appointment.

Stephen Wagg sums up all these rather contradictory elements well, when concluding that while Chapman and Buckley were exceptions, they provided a pointer to the future; the manager 'can be said to have commenced the transition from sacrificial clerk to tactician-horsetrader'.[26] It was in the interest of all parties that this should continue. Managers desired the *kudos*, the rewards and, above all, the freedom of manoeuvre; players wanted to work most closely with those who knew the game well, while the press sought both a source of information and a human 'hook' upon which to hang stories. Even directors came to see the benefits that a skilled manager could bring on the pitch and his value as a scapegoat when things went wrong.

Administering the game

A number of issues relating to the style and structure of the game's administration are dealt with elsewhere in this and the following chapter, and this section is therefore relatively brief. The social complexion of both the Football League and the Football Association changed little over the period. They remained, particularly the League, highly conservative bodies throughout the inter-war years. The FA might best be described as 'Reithian' in spirit. Just as John Reith saw the BBC as a force for public good in the face of commercial pressures, too important a medium to be prostituted by easy association with gimmickry and novelty, so football's ruling body fought hard to insulate the game's essential values from what it felt were the vulgarities of the marketplace. This approach led to a whole variety of protective policies including strong opposition to the pools, club lotteries and the use of football grounds for dog-racing, as well as to women's football, the men's game on Sundays and participation in floodlit matches. The FA also showed no great desire to be at the heart of developments in world soccer. Disputes over the organisation of fixtures with the defeated powers and an English objection to the allowance of broken time payments for players in the Olympic Games led to the FA leaving the Federation of International Football Associations in 1920 and again in 1928. This second disaffiliation led to England not contesting the World Cup in 1930 and 1938, a decision which, at the very least, prevented a realistic assessment of the true strength of the English game. However, just as Reith's BBC showed flexibility as it evolved, so the FA showed some signs of a modernising tendency in the later 1930s. This was largely due to the appointment of Stanley Rous, a leading referee and games master at Watford Grammar School, as secretary on Wall's retirement in 1934.[27] Rous's attempt to foster good relationships with the BBC was just one of the features of an approach which showed greater awareness of the social context in which the game was being played.

The amateur–professional conflict that had so bedevilled the FA from 1880 to 1914 was no longer quite such a central issue after 1918. Rugby Union and hockey absorbed many past and potential malcontents, and the new generation of players in the old boys sides seemed to work rather more happily with the grain than some of their predecessors had done.

The Corinthians abandoned their policy of not playing in tournaments in which prizes were given and entered the FA Cup for the first time in 1923. They were clearly a popular attraction, 80,000 seeing them at Newcastle in 1928. They also still saw themselves as the standard-bearers of good sportsmanship. It is claimed that in one game in the 1930s at which the referee failed to appear, the Corinthians captain played *and* refereed, actually awarding a free kick against himself at one stage.[28]

Nevertheless, as disputes in the international arena showed, the issue of amateurism was still a live one. There were periodic concerns over payments and inducements to 'amateurs' in non-league football, none more dramatic than the campaign of 1927–28 which saw the FA suspend 341 players and over 1,000 officials from clubs in the Northern League.[29] There were also interesting cultural manifestations that suggested the FA was not alone in seeking to bolster the amateur ideal. *The Times* continued to give extensive coverage to amateur games, while many national year-books such as *Whitaker's Almanac* still listed amateur tournaments ahead of professional ones in their summaries of the season's results.[30] Again, as will be seen in the next chapter, even the popular culture of the age still often celebrated the amateur at the expense of the professional. Society still had its reservations.

Playing the game: soccer stars, soccer slaves

The professional footballer plied his trade under a much brighter media spotlight in the inter-war period and this clearly had considerable impact upon his social and economic position. The 1930s in particular saw the game's leading performers adorned with the trappings of stardom that, while restrained when compared with developments in the late twentieth century, were certainly on a different scale from what had gone before. Regular exposure in a booming popular press, colour photos on football magazine covers, appearances in newsreels and even cameos in the occasional feature film made a small number of individuals into 'household names'. Financial rewards from the outside interests that inevitably flowed from this attention could be considerable. Bill 'Dixie' Dean, Everton's legendary centre forward, was supposedly able to earn up to £50 a session for advertising or endorsing products. During their campaign to lure Alex James from a reluctant Preston North End in 1929, the ever-resourceful Arsenal found him extra income by installing him as a sporting equipment demonstrator in a London department store.[31] Even players from the lower divisions, while obviously not in receipt of the same rewards as their First Division counterparts, were to some extent invested with a new degree of prestige in this new atmosphere.

Looking the part. Preston's Harry Holdsworth and Bill Tremelling endorse 1937 fashions. (*Lancashire Evening Post*)

Against this must be set the very real constraints that professional footballers worked under. The maximum wage was set at £9 per week in 1920, only to be lowered to £8 in 1922, with the possibility of additional 'talent money' of £2 for a win, £1 for a draw. Probably only about 20–25 per cent of players were on the maximum at any one time and, as ever, many professionals found themselves in a trade from which they could swiftly be removed by injury, loss of form, or their club's response to financial vicissitude.[32] The retain and transfer system continued to cause problems. Most players were on one-year contracts, renewable in May. Clubs, especially those in financial difficulty, were not averse to discharging a player at that point only to reappoint him the next September, in order to avoid paying summer wages. Players could still be held against their will if clubs refused to release them when another club made an offer, while in yet another manifestation of this essentially feudal set of labour-capital relations, clubs could insert clauses into contracts which restricted a player's off the field activities. Harold Gough, a long-serving Sheffield United player, was sacked and transfer listed in 1924 for taking a public house in preparation for his retirement, in contradistinction of a contractual obligation on the club's players by the temperance-oriented club. He was even asked to refund all wages paid to him since he had obtained the licence. The club set his transfer fee at an artificially high £2,000 and Gough consequently never played professionally again.[33]

Faced with such a system, players were sometimes reduced to indulging in what was effectively unprofessional conduct, and simply stopped giving of their best. Even when footballers continued to behave honourably, a poor game while transfer rumours circulated could easily lead to insinuation. The final months of Alex James's career at Preston were dogged by debate over his level of commitment. Obviously, collective protest and bargaining presented another possible avenue. The Players Union continued to try and improve players' conditions, but the period as a whole was not a fertile one for the Union. The reduction of the maximum wage in 1922 resulted in a serious decline in membership as individuals, especially the less-established players who were more open to boardroom pressure, accepted personally negotiated deals rather than risk resistance. For much of the period, the Union was, in Fishwick's memorable phrase, 'a Red Cross rather than a Red Army', fighting compensation cases for players forced to retire through injury, or forcibly retired by clubs on the pretext of injury as part of a cost-saving exercise.[34] Membership levels gradually recovered from 398 in 1924 to reach 1,314 in 1935 and almost 2,000 by 1939. This was testimony both to the work of Jimmy Fay, appointed secretary in 1929, and to the real body of grievance that continued to simmer over the maximum wage and the contract system. The late 1930s saw a rise in militancy, and talk of a strike threat in early 1939 led to protracted but ultimately unproductive talks between the League and the AFPTU.

For all these problems, however, it is still tempting to see this period as a positive one, at least for those players who held regular first team places for a reasonable length of time. The financial rewards gained from the game itself were still modest, although just how modest depends on the occupational group chosen for comparison. While even obscure film actors and variety performers often earned more than the best-paid players, and a few exceptional boxers and golfers earned far more, the professional footballer's position was still far preferable to that of the manual working class he had (usually) left behind. In 1938, skilled engineering workers received a wage of some £3 10*s*. for a 47-hour week, while an engineering labourer received £2 10*s*.[35] There were, too, the psychological and emotional rewards that the game brought, even if it was only the status that accrued to those who had once been on 'City's' books. One undoubted benefit to players and to the game in general in this period flowed from the generally highly respectable image that the popular media gave to the professional footballer. Written, and more especially pictorial, representations showed him as respectable, amiable, fun-loving in a fairly innocent way, and hard-working. Players were usually pictured at work on the pitch or in training, but off-duty shots usually revealed smartly dressed groups of young men playing golf, indulging in a moment of posed horseplay, or in a happy family group. This image probably genuinely reflected the lifestyles and attitudes of most professionals but, captured by an ever more powerful media, it played its role in cementing the game ever deeper into the national culture.

Women's football

One of the most striking aspects of the inter-war and the immediate post-war game was the emergence of women's football.[36] There had been a very small amount of women's football before 1914, mainly associated with public school girls, but the war and immediate post-war period opened up opportunities for working-class women to play the game. Many women players seemed to have gained their initial enthusiasm while serving

Manningham Mills Ladies Football Team, Bradford, one of the many women's teams that flourished before the FA deemed the game 'quite unsuitible for females' in December 1921. (*Bradford Heritage Recording Unit*)

as munitions workers. This was certainly the case with the most famous of all women's teams of this period, the Preston-based Dick, Kerr Ladies, the club growing from an informal side raised to play male workers at the Preston munitions works in 1917.[37] The return to peacetime working conditions did not end the desire to play and, by 1920–21, there appears to have been the possibility of a genuine blossoming of the women's game. There were at least 150 teams in England by the end of 1921, playing mainly friendly matches for charitable purposes. The leading clubs, particularly Dick, Kerr, and Hey's Ladies, a Bradford Brewery team, commanded impressive attendances for their matches. 53,000 paid £3,115 to see Dick, Kerr play St Helens in a charity match at Goodison Park on Boxing Day 1920.[38]

Obviously, the charitable function helps explain these very high figures and some probably attended merely to pour scorn, rather than to admire the athletic spectacle. Standards were also probably not very high in many cases, as would be expected in any game at this stage of its development. However, these factors should not be allowed to obscure the genuine commitment and ability of many women players. They took the game extremely seriously and trained hard, sometimes, as with Huddersfield Atalanta, with help from male professionals.[39] At the same time, there are signs that the women's game was sinking roots in football's wider popular culture. The *Football Special* newspaper started a weekly 'Football Girl' column, while women players featured, albeit briefly, in the football adventure literature that was establishing itself at this time. In 1922, Amalgamated Press's 'Football and Press Library' produced two popular novels centred on the women's game, Steve Nelson's *Nell o' Newcastle* and Dan Gray's *Bess of Blacktown: A Mill-lass Footer Yarn.* Both books, true to the spirit of this type of literature, covered much else beside football. The adventures of Nell's factory side brought the reader tales of murder, blackmail, fortunes recovered from swindling relatives as well as true love, but it also addressed some of the key events and issues of the time, and, particularly, the hostility that could be engendered. For example, the words of a carter, when asked to watch their game, provided a pithy encapsulation of one version of the case for the opposition to the women's game.

> What! Waste my afternoon off watching a lot of girls try to play a game they know naught about! Haw, haw, haw! Not so likely lass . . . Twould be better if you lasses left the football to men as can play it, an' get on wi' courtin' an' gettin' married as girls were meant to.

Perhaps the most interesting feature of this book was its ending, indicative of a sense of the possibilities for the women's game at this time. Nell inevitably marries, in this case, a local entrepreneur who had sponsored a women's league, and thanks football for bringing to her to this state of grace.

> 'How I shall always love football, Phil – apart from the excitement and thrills of the game.'
> 'Because –' he prompted.
> 'Because it brought me you', she said softly, her eyes like stars.

However, she *does not* give up the game on marriage, an outcome which might have been the expected closure of a book with such a potentially 'disruptive' theme.

By the time Nell's adventures became available to the public, however, the factual situation was far bleaker than the fictional one. It is not clear whether women players saw their activities as in any way a conscious challenge to male hegemony, either in sport or in society in general. Nevertheless, even the more obvious motive of simply desiring to extend their recreational life produced vigorous opposition. The most effective attack came from the Football Association whose criticism gained in volume over the course of 1921. On 5 December 1921 the FA finally announced that women's teams could no longer use the grounds of any of its affiliated clubs. This move was disastrous for the women's game, robbing it of both essential facilities and the credibility that use of such facilities conferred. FA opposition was buttressed by claims that women were being paid to play (if this was true, it is indicative of how serious the game was becoming), and that receipts from charity games were being siphoned off by the organisers, for 'other than charitable objects'.[40] In the final analysis, though, such arguments were essentially a rationalisation of deeper prejudices. Frederick Wall had long been opposed to the women's game, his experiences of a match in 1895 leading him to the – unexplained – conclusion that 'the game was not suitable for them.'[41] The FA's statement which accompanied the ban in December 1921 demonstrated similar sentiment, its council feeling 'impelled to express their strong opinion that the game of football is quite unsuitable for females and should not be encouraged.'[42] Women's football was, of course, also the victim of a much wider historical process whereby many of the social and economic gains made by women in the First World War were speedily and deliberately reversed.[43]

Women's football was far from universally condemned. The size of attendances, the interest expressed in popular literature and, perhaps most significantly, the help given by professionals suggests some considerable interest and sympathy. It would also be misleading to assume that all opposition came from male quarters. A number of women doctors recycled old warnings about the dangers that excessive exercise posed to women, while at a more mundane but probably more troublesome level, a number of players were not supported by female family members and friends.[44] Whatever the source of opposition, the FA's decision fundamentally weakened the nascent women's game. A number of sides managed to continue, using stadiums that were not under FA jurisdiction; revealingly, rugby grounds were often made available. Dick, Kerr Ladies managed a much publicised and successful tour of the USA in 1922, and a Ladies Football Association was founded in December 1921 to try and overcome the reverse in fortunes. However, while the women's game did not disappear, it lost the purchase that it had so swiftly gained. It was not until the late 1960s that it resurfaced to any significant extent.

Watching the game

The inter-war football crowd drew on a rather broader social constituency than had previously been the case. Mason suggests that it was in this period that the game began to be watched 'by representatives of all sections of the working man more or less in proportion.' It is also probable that middle-class support grew over this period. For the working-class fan, however, regular attendance was still not a guaranteed feature of social life; the most marginal changes in financial situation could alter leisure habits dramatically. The minimum admission price rose, first to *9d.* in October 1917, a measure necessitated by the introduction of the Entertainment Tax that was to be levied on clubs for another fifty years, and again to 1*s.* immediately after the war. Andrew Davies has noted how even skilled workers in regular employment in 1930s Manchester could experience difficulty in finding the necessary money. This was a particular problem for those who moved to the satellite towns and council estates around the city, where the resulting higher rents and transport costs had a detrimental effect on their budgets.[45]

The unemployed fan, for all the resilience noted above, had especially serious problems. During the initial onset of unemployment after 1920, some clubs appear to have offered reduced entrance rates for the unemployed, despite Football League hostility.[46] Throughout the early 1930s there was constant pressure from clubs in areas badly affected by unemployment to persuade the Football League to allow such a policy. However, successive Annual General Meetings between 1932–34 could not be persuaded to provide the necessary two-thirds majority. A strong element of financial self-interest was only thinly disguised by the often rehearsed argument that such a scheme was both unfair to poor fans in regular employment and open to abuse.[47] Reduced admission to reserve games (which, by raising attendances, was probably in the financial interests of clubs) was the only consolation offered. Unemployed people's loss was graphically demonstrated by the enthusiasm with which they flooded back to the game when the opportunity arose. Merthyr Town's gates, for example, rose from 500 to 4,000 in 1932, when the club left the Football League for the Southern League which allowed a 2*d*. minimum admission. The Pilgrim Trust's observation of Liverpool's unemployed lining the streets on match-days to watch other spectators going to the game is a well-known but still potent reminder of the social and emotional costs of unemployment.[48]

Several commentators have claimed that women's attendance increased in the inter-war period.[49] There is little hard evidence for this, although it is obvious that women did attend and that individuals could sometimes take on a central role in spectator culture. Blackburn Rovers's main mascot at the 1928 Cup final, for example, was the seventy-year-old Mrs Catterall, who attended the game armed with a blue and white plumed canary in a blue and white cage.[50] Women clearly played a prominent part in the civic celebration of footballing success. They were well represented in the huge crowds that turned out to greet Blackburn Rovers in 1928 (and 'fainted by the score' according to one report) and 'women predominated' in the 50,000 crowd that gathered in the late afternoon to greet Preston's victorious side in 1938.[51]

Fan culture was very much as it had been before 1914. It was at its most colourful, but probably least spontaneous, on the away trips organised by supporters' clubs. These events became an ever more frequent feature of this period and seem to have institutionalised some of the carnival element. In 1921, for example, 2,500 Bradford City fans set off to Burnley in train compartments festooned with posters declaring the occupants to be 'The Swankers', 'The Toffs', 'Jock's Pals', and, more prosaically, 'the Laisterdyke Cricket and Athletic Club'. The presence of alcohol – a 'dray load of beer' accompanying each of the trains – left the way open for rather more spontaneity later in the day. Again, in 1928,

Wembley-bound Huddersfield Town supporters covered the carriages, guard's van and engine of a football special with balloons, streamers and slogans announcing the arrival of 'Now Town, the Wonder Team'.[52] Fans still appear to have sung on the terraces, the *Football Favourite* magazine offering the words to dozens of songs for a period in 1927, including such unlikely bedfellows as 'The Wearin' of the Green', 'The Minstrel Boy' and 'My Old Kentucky Home', as well as footballing versions of popular tunes. This led to 'Kick, Kick, Kick, Kick it', to the tune of 'Chick, Chick, Chick, Chick, Chicken', and 'Keep the Forwards Scoring', sung to Ivor Novello's, 'Keep the Home Fires Burning'. The historical record has not yet revealed whether these pieces attained any popularity![53]

A rather more aggressive side was still present. Journalists and managers consistently criticised the barracking of home players, which could extend from ironic cheering in remembrance of some recent sin, as when Swindon supporters thus acknowledged every action of a goalkeeper blamed for a cup defeat the previous week, to real displays of hostility.[54] T. E. Maley, attempting to rescue Bradford Park Avenue's woeful 1920–21 campaign, was only one of many managers who appealed to the supporters' sense of English decency in an attempt to stop such demonstrations.

> Players are very human and resent being made the butt of vulgar abuse by ill-mannered spectators . . . so much has been heard of the Australian 'barracker' during the present tour of the MCC team that one dreads the thought of it spreading to this country. Surely the sport-loving Englishman is too fair-minded to indulge in the same practice.[55]

Football has never been entirely free of crowd disorder, and the inter-war period was no exception. Queens Park Rangers (1930), Millwall (1934) and Carlisle (1935) all had their grounds closed for periods following disturbances. Sections of the Millwall support, indeed, enjoyed something of a reputation for disorder in the 1930s.[56] There were innumerable other incidents and punishments, as when the Football League banned boys from attending Bradford City matches for a spell in 1921 after a referee was reputedly pelted with stones and orange peel. The numbers of police on hand for big matches – Sheffield Wednesday would have over one hundred on call in such cases – shows at the very least a belief in the potential for trouble.[57] However, most commentators see the period between 1919 and 1939 as a relatively peaceful one in this regard. As has been stressed in one detailed study, the frequency with which such a relatively innocuous habit as barracking was reported by the press suggests that minor indiscretions now stood out.[58] It is also significant that the two major episodes of public concern over crowd behaviour, in 1919–22 and the later 1930s, were both shaped by wider contextual factors which may have led to the exaggeration of the scale of the problem. The earlier period coincided with great concern over a supposed decline in public discipline following the wave of industrial militancy after the First World War, the second with a determined campaign by Stanley Rous to raise the status and image of the game. For the most part the crowd was typified by a pattern of behaviour in which 'enthusiasm was not incompatible with restraint.'[59]

At the opposite end of the scale, supporters' clubs appear to have become an ever more frequent element of the football landscape between the wars. The National Federation of Football Supporters' Clubs, founded in 1926–27, had some 150,000 affiliated individual members by 1934.[60] Drawing their leadership mainly from the lower-middle and middle classes, these bodies saw themselves essentially almost as servants of the clubs rather than as pressure groups acting on behalf of fans. The National Federation's motto 'To help and not to hinder' is indicative in this regard. Two major functions of the supporters' clubs were to raise money and to provide a source of free labour for ground improvement schemes. For some clubs these efforts probably meant the difference between survival and extinction. Certainly many ground improvements could not have taken place without them. Luton Town Supporters' Club raised £20,000 (at least £1.5 million in current terms) towards such improvements in the 1930s, and this figure does not include the labour provided.[61] A further function was to police the rest of the crowd and generally educate fans in good sporting habits. This would certainly account for Bradford City Supporters' Club organising lectures on 'Referees' and 'The Laws of the Game' in 1922.[62]

All this effort was expended in return for remarkably little actual control over the affairs of either specific football clubs or the game in general. Supporters were only given seats on the board in exceptional circumstances, while the Football Association appears to have given remarkably little recognition to these acts of self-sacrifice. Stanley Rous was a vice-president of the NFFSC from 1935 but did not actually attend a national conference until 1980.[63] Most striking of all was the fact that, for the most part, these most active supporters showed little interest in challenging the status quo, or in taking a major role in influencing the direction that the game was to take. This may have resulted partly from the 'policing' element noted above. It has been suggested that the supporters' club could become something akin to 'a conspiracy to reform the behaviour of the working class', and this mentality may sometimes have overridden the possibility of developing other agendas.[64] In the long run, however, the desire to help not hinder reflects the deep hold that football clubs exerted on their community. Football, for its devotees, was not like any other form of commercial entertainment. People joined a supporters' club and contributed to its efforts much as people did when embracing church or chapel, Labour Party or working men's club. It was a cause, and, for many, helping it was reward enough, especially if it raised the possibility of at least some personal contact with directors, managers and players.

5

Football and English Culture, 1919–1939

THIS CHAPTER explores three overlapping aspects of football's relationship with the wider cultural, social and political currents of the inter-war period. It begins with a consideration of the interaction between professional football and various elements of the media and popular culture, which seeks both to demonstrate the central role that the media played in the game's growth in this period and to consider some of the potential impact that its coverage had on both the game and wider social attitudes. This is followed by an examination of soccer's role in the construction and realisation of various social and political identities, and finally, an assessment of the changing status of the game within English society between 1915 and 1939.

Football and the media

Football's increasingly prominent place within English society was both reflected and reinforced, especially in the 1930s, by the much enhanced attention it received in many elements of the national media. Nicholas Fishwick is surely correct in seeing media attention as crucial in helping bring about 'the transformation of football into a national game of importance to more people of different social classes.'[1] The press had already played an important part in this process before 1914, but the sheer growth of the so-called popular press in this period, and its overt use of sporting coverage as a weapon in circulation wars, made its role even more significant. In 1920, the *Daily Mail* was the only daily with a circulation in excess of one million: by 1940 while its own sales had grown to 1.45 million, it had been overtaken by the *Express* (2.6 million), *Herald* (1.75 million) and the *Mirror* (1.65 million). The rise of the Sunday paper was equally dramatic, the circulation of the *News of the World* and the *People* rising from 3 million to 7.5 and 4.6 million respectively, in the period from 1925 to 1947.[2] By the late 1930s, both papers devoted some 10 per cent of their space to football, having at least doubled their coverage since 1920.

The 1930s saw something of a stylistic revolution in football reporting, pioneered by the *People* but rapidly, if sometimes reluctantly, followed by many other papers. Influenced to an extent by American models, it featured shorter sentences and paragraphs; more gossip, often with a somewhat 'anti-establishment' slant; a rather aggressive, combative tone; and action photography of a much improved quality, which helped both to glamourise the game and to undermine the credibility of referees. The *People* also initiated use of the back page for football and sporting coverage, thus reinforcing 'the separation of sports news and real life at the other end of the paper.'[3] Some sections of the press were little touched by these developments, *The Times*, for example, still tending to give at least as much coverage to amateur as to professional sport and to utilise the factual narrative as the dominant mode of reportage. Such an approach made perfect commercial sense for a paper whose readership was generally but little exposed to new cultural currents, but for the more popularly based papers failure to change could be fatal. One victim was the *Athletic News*, once the 'footballer's bible' but, despite attempts at modernisation by its last editor Ivan Sharpe, reduced to being merely the back page of the *Sporting Chronicle* from 1931.[4]

The local press continued to make a central contribution to football's robust health. The football special, usually priced at a penny or twopence, was a ubiquitous feature of Saturday-night urban life, while local titles gave regular coverage on other days of the week. Local papers retained the old mix of loyalty to the club coupled with a spirit of constructive criticism, couched in a language often not very far removed from that of the late nineteenth century. In 1930, Preston's Bobby Crawford, for example, was given the following tutorial by the *Preston Herald*.

> Crawford is a grand little player, but he has two cardinal faults. At times, he wanders too much into the middle and too often leaves the opposing outside right with a perfectly open passage . . . In the second place Crawford is rather too slavish in his attentions to Harrison. He might with advantage distribute more of his favours in the direction of McClelland and some of his other colleagues.[5]

Over the period as a whole, local papers increased and diversified their coverage of the game and its personalities. This was partly the result of stylistic shifts particularly noticeable in the 1930s. Although most local papers did not take on quite the sensationalist tone of some of their national counterparts, they certainly attempted to move away from the previous minute-book-like coverage and presentation of events. Editors seeking more 'human interest' found the footballer a promising topic. Interestingly, by the late 1930s players' wives and families also began to come under the spotlight, as when the *Lancashire Daily Post* ran a feature on the 'Preston North End wives' in the build up to the 1937 FA Cup final.[6] This perhaps reflected women's increased interest in the game, but it certainly reflected the press's increased interest in women readers.

One of the central sporting functions of all newspapers and journals, local or national, was to provide information on the football pools which had been introduced in the early 1920s. Indeed, the supposed quality of pools information was a vital selling point in the circulation war. Although obviously not a form of 'media' as such, it seems useful to deal with them at this point. Gambling on football was as old as the game itself, but the skill with which the pools were marketed elevated them above mere 'gambling', and they thus served both promoters and the game well. The pools were a form of the long-established fixed-odds coupon betting, designed to circumvent the Ready Money Football Betting Act of 1920. Passed at the behest of the Football Association, this act banned all betting save that involving credit, a provision clearly aimed at working-class gamblers who rarely had access to such facilities.[7] The pools were legal because stake money was collected *after* the fixtures were fulfilled, thus rendering the wager a credit transaction. Efficiently run, offering both the self-appointed expert and the dabbler the chance of success and skilfully marketed with adverts, magazines and celebrity cheque presenters, the pools rapidly became a national institution. By the mid-1930s, some 5–7 million people were 'doing the pools', at a cost of £30 million per year and generating work for some 30,000, mainly female, employees.[8] The pools habit bit rather more deeply into the social life of both the unskilled working-class and women than the game itself had succeeded in doing, thus helping, in a modest way, to secure an enhanced place for football in contemporary society.

The football authorities remained fiercely opposed to the game's association with any form of mass gambling: concern about 'respectability', fear of possible match-fixing and the belief that gambling denuded already scant working-class budgets fused in a powerful mixture. Their campaign reached its height in February 1936 in the famed 'pools war', when the Football League resorted to sabotage by refusing to announce the fixture list until two days before games were due to be played.[9] The pools companies, supported by large sections of a decidedly partial press, launched a powerful counter-attack which seems to have had considerable popular support. On 9 March, much to the delight of the beleaguered companies, barely surviving on hastily arranged schemes which asked punters to predict home team results against unknown opposition, the League backed down and chose once again to adopt a legislative route. It was not until the late 1950s that the League accepted the benefit of receiving payment from the pools companies in return for guarantied use of the fixture list, a suggestion first made by the Pools Promoters Association in 1934. In the wider context, this defeat, and the rise of the pools in general, represented a small but significant defeat for the custodians of Victorian values at the hands of a partnership between business calculation and popular aspiration, a theme manifested in many other areas of popular culture in the inter-war period as a mass consumer culture took ever clearer shape.

No other area of the media gave the game quite such a constant and varied coverage as the press, but other forms could play a significant part. In 1922, when the then British Broadcasting Company was in its infancy, only 1 per cent of UK households held a wireless licence. By 1930, the figure had risen to 30 per cent and by 1939, 71 per cent, by which time some 8,900,000 licensed sets were in use.[10] At first the BBC, dedicated as it was under Sir John Reith's stewardship to the raising of public taste, concerned itself relatively infrequently with professional sport. However, driven by the challenge of developing new technical skills and by the first glimmerings of a willingness to explore new areas of national life, the Corporation soon discovered professional soccer. Its first commentary on a professional match took place on 22 January 1927, Arsenal and Sheffield United the two sides thus making history. Games were usually carried on the London station and relayed to other parts via the Daventry transmitter, although local stations, at that stage still an important part of the BBC network, often carried alternatives of greater interest to their audiences.[11] On 12 March 1927, no fewer than four different matches were broadcast, in full or in part. Later in the year, the Cup final was relayed for the first time, the presentation giving due attention to the presence of royalty and the massed singing of 'Abide with me'.[12]

The BBC's leading commentator in the early period was the journalist and Arsenal director, and later manager, George Allison. He possessed a rather less detached style than that more normally associated with the BBC, his commentaries sprinkled with cries of 'By Jove' and exhortations such as 'Shoot, man shoot'. He even claimed to have invented action during a tedious game between Hull City and Port Vale.[13] In his modest way, he thus added to the slightly more popular flavour that gradually suffused the BBC in the 1930s. An interesting solution to the problem of listeners visualising the action was devised in the form of a chart in the *Radio Times* with the pitch divided into numbered squares. As the ball moved around, a background voice (initially that of Derek MacCullough, 'Uncle Mac' of 'Children's Hour') called out the number of the square where the ball was located, allowing the audience to follow the game.[14]

In the period to 1931, over a hundred games were broadcast. However, opposition from the Football League was mounting and in June 1931, it banned all broadcasts of its fixtures. The most fervent critics of soccer broadcasting were the smaller clubs and especially those of the Third Division North. Already badly affected by the onset of unemployment, they argued that the broadcasting of leading matches reduced their attendances still further. Although the Empire Service, founded in 1932, was allowed to take some games, this ban stayed in force until after the Second World War. The Football Association, particularly after Stanley Rous took the helm in 1934, was rather more sympathetic and although the 1929 FA Cup final was not broadcast owing to a dispute over fees, subsequent finals, many internationals and even some other cup matches were broadcast during the 1930s. The end of the decade witnessed the first attempts to transmit television coverage and the few thousand potential viewers within range of the Alexandra Palace aerial saw pictures (almost inevitably) of Arsenal playing Arsenal Reserves in September 1937. The FA Cup final was first shown in its entirety in the following year.[15]

Overall, the BBC's adoption of the game and of the Cup final in particular was extremely important. One of the BBC's most important cultural roles was to provide, via the transmission of a set of national rituals, a tangible, binding sense of nationhood.[16] Once added to this ritual calendar, which by the early 1930s included the Boat Race, Empire Day and the King's Christmas broadcast, events gained a *kudos* and a rank that was quite distinctive. The BBC thereby coated the 'people's game' with an aura of respectability that few other mechanisms could have provided. At the same time, of course, football coverage helped give the BBC a marginally more democratic flavour.

Cinema was to play a far smaller role in the game's development. Newsreel footage of games had been shown before 1914 and this continued into the 1920s and 1930s. The Football League had no objection, deeming the subsequent publicity an inducement to attendance at matches. At least two feature films were made using football as a focal point. *The Lucky Number* (1933) was a Gainsborough comedy which included guest appearances from Cliff Bastin, Eddie Hapgood and other Arsenal players, while the same club received even greater attention in *The Arsenal Stadium Mystery* (1939). This comedy thriller, starring Leslie Banks, was based on a book written in the previous year by crime-writer Leonard Gribble.[17] Obviously, these two films are insignificant within the overall context of film production at this time, but it is an interesting commentary on the 'Arsenal syndrome' that an aspiring novelist and two film companies were alert to the potential offered by the club, and that it in turn recognised the publicity value of the media. *The Arsenal Stadium Mystery* was an especially good public relations vehicle for the club in general, for the players involved, who received £50 a week for their efforts, and for George Allison, who clearly relished his screen opportunities. *The Lucky Number* was set firmly in a working-class milieu and its main character was a professional footballer. *The Arsenal Stadium Mystery*'s central characters, however, were not the cheerful, bantering professionals, but the amateurs of the Dark Trojans, a Corinthians style public school old boys side, whose star player was murdered during a cup tie with Arsenal. There are hints here, therefore, that professional football was not always seen as quite respectable (or interesting) enough to be at the heart of a cultural product designed for a cross-class audience.

Gribble's opportunist novel was unusual in placing football at the heart of its plot, for novelists, both 'serious' and 'popular' to use a useful but simplistic distinction, generally paid the game little heed. Arnold Bennett and J. B. Priestley both touched on it quite effectively, but the game was never invested with the rich cultural significance attached to cricket.[18] This is not to say that soccer had no popular literature, for it spawned an enormous body of work. However, it was produced largely by specialist writers working for the numerous journals, comics and magazines aimed at young men and boys which were so much a feature of this period. Such literature was not a new product. The *Boy's Own Paper* had included sporting stories from its inception in 1879, as had the many others that followed in its wake.[19] The inter-war period, however, saw a substantial increase in the space devoted to sport in general and soccer in particular by both existing publications and the many new ones that entered the market.

This rich area of popular culture will be glimpsed here through

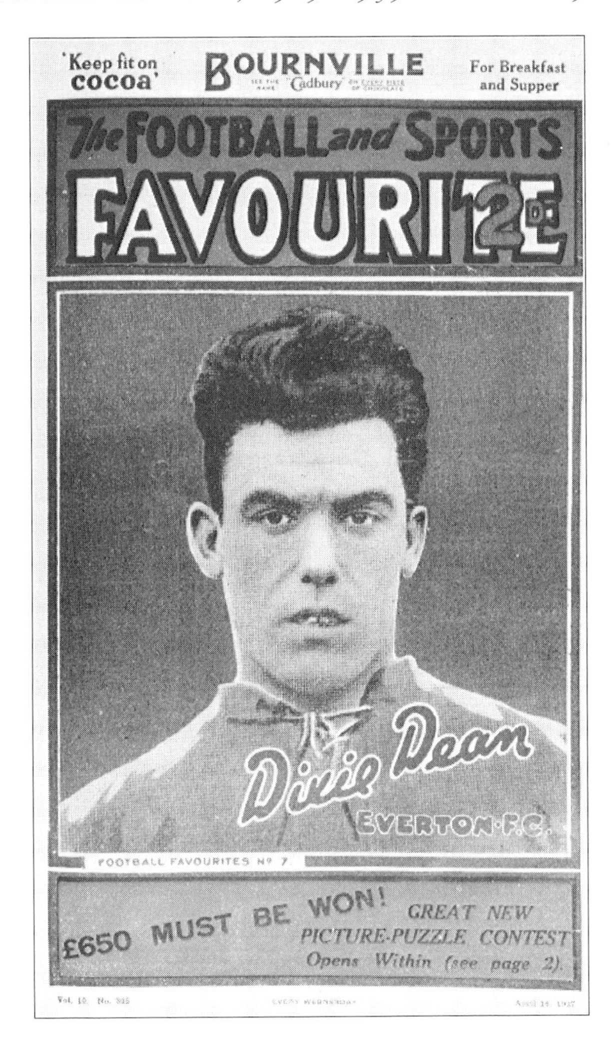

Dean was an especially favoured pin-up. (*British Library*)

consideration of just one title, the Amalgamated Press's *Football and Sports Favourite*, launched in 1920, and the closely associated series of full-length popular novels which appeared in the same company's 'Football and Sports Library'.[20] Although no circulation figures are available, both the paper and the novels survived for a long enough period for them to be taken as reasonably significant elements of contemporary sporting literature. The *Favourite* was a 2*d*. weekly which combined photographs, cartoons, sporting gossip and features on teams and individual players, with adventure serials carrying a strong sporting flavour. The 'Library' produced two sixty-four-page novels per month, at 4*d*. each. Although football was not the sole focus of either publication, it certainly gained the largest amount of attention. Little is known about the complexion of the readership, although the presence in the *Favourite* of guess-the-result competitions carrying £300 prizes and the strong love story element in many stories would suggest that adolescents and young adult males made up a substantial proportion of the intended audience. However, the fact that it took on the title *Boy's Football Favourite* in 1929, without any substantial change in content and approach, suggests that this group co-existed with a significantly younger readership.

The *Favourite* gave its readers a strong sense of identification with the game's stars, a process enhanced by the pull-out photos that became a feature of this and most other similar papers in the 1930s. However, it is the fictional star that is of interest in this context. The substance of the soccer sporting adventure was quite brilliantly captured by E. S. Turner in a passage which, while affectionately satirical, only fractionally overplays the extravagant and exotic plot lines that typified the genre.

> No one is likely to forget the long and unflagging sequence of stories about football matches in which the lemons were poisoned at half-time, in which rascally backs hacked the home forwards with boots containing poisoned nails, and bogus referees blew poison darts at players . . . [of players] who spent the week shaking off kidnappers and trying to clear his own or his father's name. It was all he could do every Saturday afternoon to break through the crook's blockade and reach the ground in time to score the winning goal.[21]

C. Malcolm Hincks, Arthur S. Hardy, Alfred Edgar, Walter Edwards and the other authors who laboured so productively in this field, were all able to match (and mix) these plots with ones of equal devilishness.

Certain key themes ran throughout these stories. Rather unexpectedly, almost all of them involved a serious, and always requited, love between hero and heroine. Winning goals, heavyweight boxing titles and crucial sixes were invariably followed by the hand of the trainer/manager/director's daughter. In the Sports Library's anonymous *What's the Matter With Millport* (1922), Barry Boyland's beloved, Constance, even managed to collapse into his arms on the pitch, her headlong flight from kidnappers coinciding with his vital cup goal. As already stated, these titles were not aimed exclusively at boys. However, the prevalence of such romantic episodes should lead to some reconsideration of the assumption that boys' literature traditionally served to keep the opposite sex at a very safe distance.

Less surprising themes and stock devices of popular fiction encountered in these stories include the crooked director, virtue rewarded by the

Constance faints into Barry Boyland's arms, one of the many incidents and adventures enjoyed by the free-scoring player-director of Millport Athletic. (*British Library*)

discovery of true (usually aristocratic or upper-middle class) social origins, the importance of 'fair play' and sporting behaviour and, relatedly, the centrality of the amateur tradition. As comments on *The Arsenal Stadium Mystery* have already suggested, amateurs invariably enjoyed a privileged status in sporting popular fiction. Its star footballers were invariably amateurs, unless lost fortune (or lost memory) dictated otherwise, in which case amateur status was reverted to as soon as wrongs had been righted. Such amateurs bore no trace of snobbery, the need for the game to be kept free of social division forming a strong and recurrent theme. Thus Jack Grant, amateur centre forward with Birningham Rangers in Charles Pickford's *The Team With the Bad Name* (1922), refuses to play for a local, purely amateur side on the grounds that they were 'a set of prigs and snobs' who would exclude a good player if he happened to be poor. 'If you're going to bring class distinction into football, you're going to kill the game right away', he tells his family *en route* to guiding his side

Bellingham City's flying forward is cruelly thwarted in the *Football Favourite*'s 1927 serial, 'You Ought to See The Old Club Now', by leading sports fiction exponent, Arthur S. Hardy. (*British Library*)

to an honourable defeat in the FA Cup final.[22] Inevitably, however, the constant emphasis on the value of the leadership that could be provided by financially uninterested amateurs actually put class distinction at the very heart of sporting discourse. Once again, suppressed concerns about the professional game surface in the 'safe' territory of fiction. Professional footballers, and by extension the working class, were not quite to be trusted.

Broader social themes were also touched on in this literature, with class, regional and, above all, national and racial stereotypes drawn and reinforced with striking clarity. The *Favourite* regularly featured the adventures of Jock McJulius, a member of an 'anything tried' agency often involved in matters sporting. A huge, kilted African-American, Jock spoke in sub-plantation dialect and was once memorably referred to in the casual racism of late empire as 'the Big Nig'.[23] Nell Harmer's football team, noted in the previous chapter, included the black goalkeeper Topsy

Johnson, famed for her 'happy grin that showed all her perfect white teeth' and whose injury, when she struck her 'woolly head an ugly blow on the goalpost', so nearly cost Hood's XI victory in a crucial game.[24]

Quite what impact these stories of Pulton North End, Millport Athletic, Beauchampton United and Everpool had upon their readers is unclear. At the very least, they fulfilled some of the major traditional functions of popular fiction by providing both a rich source of inspiration for personal fantasy and a comforting imaginary landscape in which justice and goodness always prevailed. Most readers were certainly able to work out that the real world was not populated exclusively by long-armed goalkeepers and free-scoring centre forwards with chronic amnesia and silver mine concessions in South America, but their capacity to interpret the social agenda is less certain. With the exception of the coverage given to the women's game, the world-view offered to them was most definitely a highly conservative one. People knew their place and married in accordance with it; gentlemanly leadership brought benefit; foreigners were different and often funny. In recent years, of course, scholars have become adroit at teasing out alternative, even radical readings of such apparently conservative forms of popular culture.[25] It cannot be denied that the messages inscribed in popular culture are there to be absorbed, ignored, debated or deflected, according to the reader's individual views and circumstances. Nevertheless, it is hard to come away from this material without concluding that sporting fiction offered remarkably little in the way of a challenge to dominant social and political attitudes.

Football, politics and identity

Rather less has been written about the relationship between soccer and the construction of modes of political and social consciousness in the years between 1914 and 1939 than has been the case for the preceding period, but as the discussion of popular literature has shown, there is plentiful scope for debate. The arguments aired in Chapter 3 concerning the relationship between soccer and political mentalities can certainly be returned to here. The premier historian of inter-war football has quite rightly stressed the speculative nature of such an enterprise, arguing that, 'It is difficult to show . . . that the working class might have been more radical but for football or some other equally attractive substitute . . . it is easier to show that football reflected political crises and social mores than that it had much effect on them.'[26] It is obviously impossible to show any correlation between soccer and specific patterns of political or trade union activity. The political and industrial landscape changed considerably while football remained a constant, with matches attended by working men in militant or more peaceful times, in both Labour and trade union strongholds and in less radical areas. The various inflections of political and industrial culture were ultimately rooted in the political and economic sphere, not in the sporting one, and much of the explanation for the nature of inter-war working-class culture and consciousness must be sought in these areas.

Speculation, though, should still take place. It is inconceivable that something which drew the time, energy and money of so many people did not have ideological repercussions for at least some of them. There is material available to give succour both to those who see the game embodying a working-class radicalism, however attenuated, and those stressing its conservative role. In the period after 1919 the balance of speculation probably lies with the latter group. The soccer ground admittedly remained an arena in which large numbers of working men could come together in a boisterous mass and feel, if not a sense of class unity, then at least a shared ownership of the game. Such an argument, however, is too thin to carry much interpretative weight. 'Real' power remained firmly in the hands of the propertied classes and supporters exercised remarkably little influence. As the professional game became ever more secure within the national culture, terrace behaviour offered far less of an implicit challenge than it had in the late Victorian and Edwardian political and social climate. Furthermore, those arguing for football's capacity to serve as an escape mechanism can seize on many new developments in this period. Growing media coverage and the emergence of the pools certainly added to the attraction of what Orwell memorably termed 'life on a fish-and-chip standard'.[27] Above all, football was a fixed feature, a source of guaranteed enjoyment and debate and, as such, arguably helped maintain social stability. Many on the left certainly argued that sport was a de-radicalising force and although they, like their nineteenth-century predecessors, were often guilty of seeking easy explanations for complex issues, it would be wrong to dismiss their arguments out of hand. A mass soccer culture had much potential as a social balm, although one not necessarily consciously manipulated by social elites.

The game's capacity to reflect and define local and regional identities remained strong after 1918. In one sense, the Cup final became less of a colourful battle between two localities in this period. In an attempt to avoid a repeat of the potentially disastrous overcrowding that occurred at the first Wembley final in 1923, subsequent finals were made all-ticket events, with large numbers of tickets distributed across the whole country through the local football associations. The FA's rationale for the change emphasised the need to acknowledge that the FA Cup was a national competition to which dozens of clubs, including a large non-League contingent, had made a contribution. This affirmation of a residual Victorian 'the-game's-the-thing' attitude also had the effect of reducing the number of fans from the two competing clubs, subtly altering the social composition of the crowd and somewhat diminishing the carnival spirit. One paper claimed that the ticket system 'is killing the Cup Final as a festival of enthusiasm and high spirits.'[28]

A Cup final visit, however, still offered considerable opportunity to impose local identity upon the capital and not only at the match. It was an excuse for a sightseeing excursion to London, for northern supporters at least still a very distant place in an age before motorways and high-speed trains. Indeed, it is obvious that many took advantage of cheap rail and coach excursions without ever intending to visit the match. Even those attending the game took maximum advantage of the day. In 1922 the *Yorkshire Observer* noted long queues at Madame Tussauds where the captains of Preston and Huddersfield had been 'done in wax', and at Trafalgar Square and the Tower.[29] A serious and moving element was introduced with the construction of the Cenotaph in 1920. Visiting fans brought wreaths in club colours in honour of their town's war victims, often singing hymns before leaving.[30] All sections of the press reported these events through the language of the 'provincial invasion', deploying the now obligatory narrative of provincial gullibility/cunning versus metropolitan sophistication/over-confidence, depending on the writer's allegiance.

One recent historian has warned that we should beware of exaggerating the sense of local separatism and northern 'difference' when examining this cultural spectacle.[31] Jeffrey Hill has argued that while northern fans were to some extent indulging in a display of local patriotism, they were ultimately simply taking the chance to bask in the national spotlight for the day. Indeed, Hill argues that the Cup final became ever more a *national* event from the early 1920s, a process stimulated by the game's move to Wembley, the presence of the monarchy and the increasing influence of the BBC. Hill's stimulating essay is surely correct in pointing to the fact that local identity has often served as the central building block of national identity. 'Englishness' or 'Britishness' was often predicated upon an awareness of the supposedly special characteristics that a locality gave to the a national confection: the 'best' English man or woman was from phlegmatic Yorkshire, homely Lancashire or wherever. It is also probably the case that memories of the 1914–18 conflict and the increasingly national complexion of the media allowed greater possibilities for the expression of national attachment than might have been the case in earlier periods. Nevertheless, particularly in the 1930s when many in the north of England felt that they were bearing an unfair burden of economic hardship, the 'taking' of London can be interpreted as, to some extent, a symbolic attempt to settle scores.

Comparison with the biennial invasion of London by Scottish supporters is instructive here in that while it shows the clear limits to displays of English local and regional identity it also locates such displays within a tradition of sub-political sporting 'nationalism'.[32] The presence of national costumes, banners with such slogans as 'Forget Flodden and Remember Stirling Bridge and Bannockburn' and what one historian has called the 'war-like metaphors of the media' demonstrates that, for the Scots anyway, the England-Scotland fixture had a edge and a significance beyond most northern excursions to London. 'The trip to Wembley had become part of a sturdy sub-culture of symbols, slogans, heroes and myths which sustain an apolitical, invented, but palpable sub-nationalism which combines a strong identity of being Scottish with a very weak national project.'[33] The English regional political project was even weaker, of course, as were its sub-political sporting manifestations. However, this description of Moorhouse's will not sound utterly unfamiliar to those who have examined notions of local, provincial and regional pride within England at this time.

The point becomes stronger if the focus moves specifically to the operation of what might be termed 'northern-ness'. A general dislike of southern and more accurately metropolitan dominance was perhaps even stronger after 1918 than before. In the sporting arena it often surfaced in the local press, as when Sunderland's *Football Echo* claimed during a criticism of the value of floodlit football that 'the Metropolis generally takes the lead for the rest of the country to follow like sheep through a gate.'[34] Its most frequent manifestation, however, came in the form of the often intense dislike that many northern supporters had for Arsenal. This sentiment was well known and often acknowledged by journalists in a gently humorous way. When seven Arsenal players were chosen for the

England side in 1934, the *Daily Mail* mused that it would 'be a pretty sight at the game to see northern onlookers as patriotic Englishmen, sinking their feelings and shouting "come on Arsenal"'.[35] A hard edge underlay the humour, however. To an extent the club's unpopularity was rooted in nothing more complex than resentment at its success. Moreover, the Arsenal had a reputation for plucking victory from unpromising situations, a knack which led to them earning the 'lucky Arsenal' label which dogged the side until it was replaced by 'boring Arsenal' in 1970. Arsenal personnel, with some justification, argued that 'luck' actually described the ability to absorb pressure and then counter with break-away goals.[36] Hostility could also flow from the team's approach to a particular game, as was the case in the championship decider at Preston in April 1938. Here, in an immensely physical game that saw the home side lose 3–1, 'the booing of the Arsenal was almost continous'.[37]

At the heart of much of this bad feeling, however, was the symbolic role that was ascribed to the club. Arsenal quite simply represented southern domination, their sporting success held to mirror a (much simplified) wider social and economic picture. Writing in 1956, George Scott recalled how, in his native Middlesbrough, Arsenal were disliked for coming from 'the soft south, from London, from the city of government, where, it was imagined, all social evil was plotted and directed against places like Teesside.'[38] Here was a club, so it appeared, that had purchased success, bringing the best players from all over Britain, denuding the provinces, and to a lesser degree Scotland and Wales, of skilled footballers. This replicated the process which saw industrial change and unemployment force workers to move south in search of new opportunities. It must be acknowledged that the club also had enemies closer to home. Many West Ham supporters were persuaded that the supposed 'West Ham way', a strategy born of financial necessity involving the avoidance of expenditure on transfers and the use of local talent, gave the club a moral superiority over its north London rivals.[39] The notion of the embattled East End community invoked here served a very similar symbolic purpose for local people to that offered by ideas of an oppressed 'north'. Being close to the privileged could be as painful as being supposedly out of their sight and mind.

These issues re-connect with the discussion of soccer's role in the creation and expression of class identity and political culture that began this section. Did the territorial allegiances formed and/or expressed by the game divide the working class within itself and unite local communities across class lines?[40] It is tempting to believe that the major shaping influences were rooted in the economic and political sphere, but the game had the power to generate negative images about other usually more distant parts of the country. The discourse of 'northern-ness', for example, perhaps implicated the southern working class in the perceived conspiracy against the industrial provinces, in such a way as to create intra-working-class fractures. Speculation is, of course, once again the order of the day. At the very least though, football's fiercely local and regional roots probably did few favours for the leaders of the organised labour movement.

Football and the national culture

At all times between 1918 and 1939, professional football had its enemies; socialists viewing it as the opiate of the people, religious leaders concerned about its impact upon congregations, individuals caught up in boisterous crowds. However, what was so important about the period after 1919 was that the number of opponents, and the frequency and volume of their opposition, seems to have diminished. Some of them had quit the field of battle, sniping at the game only occasionally from within the ranks of the amateur sporting establishment. More significantly, the level of support and recognition for the game from within various sections of middle and upper-middle-class England, appears to have risen. The evidence for this is often scattered and anecdotal, but it is significant. In 1927, Charles Clegg was knighted for his services to the game, the first individual to be thus honoured. President of both Sheffield Wednesday and United, and president of the Football Association, Clegg, a solicitor by profession, had been a sometimes reluctant but key architect of 'managed professionalism', while also fighting a stern battle against the influence of drink and gambling within the sport. By the 1930s, the popular press could portray him as part of a reactionary old guard. His knighthood rewarded a safe unchallenging view of the game, but it was an important recognition nevertheless.[41] There were other less formal but important examples of the game's changed position. On 8 March 1922 St Luke's Boys School, Preston, 'closed early to allow boys to attend a cup tie. This is a special favour granted because of loyal way boys have kept their word not to miss school to attend match.' Neighbouring St Mark's selected ten boys to attend the same game.[42] These may not have been the first recorded instances of such an imaginative form of discipline, but they suggest a more positive attitude than was sometimes expressed in the late nineteenth century.

In February 1933 the *Yorkshire Observer* had great fun with the antics of Leeds city councillors, who found themselves faced with a conflict of interests over a council meeting and a replayed cup tie. Even though the Bradford-based paper's report was firmly set within the long-established tradition of gentle satire at the expense of an overblown neighbour, the incident is suggestive.

> It took exactly 40 minutes to transact business which normally occupies anything from three to six hours. It was a record in post-war brevity. Not the whole of the council had remained for even that expeditious business. The minutes of four committees were moved by someone other than the chairman, for there are several aldermen who sit on the board of directors of Leeds United. And before the brief 40 minutes were up, the ranks of the city fathers had become sadly depleted. Their presence, it was whispered, was required in (or overlooking) another arena. When the Lord Mayor announced, 'that concludes the business', the hurried exit of most of those left was as nearly dignified as the urgency of the situation would permit – but it was not many seconds before aldermen and councillors were packed in the 'bus and motor cars which waited outside the City Hall.[43]

The presence of a 25,000 crowd for this mid-week game suggests that the councillors were not alone in placing pleasure before duty. A rather more serious example of football's enhanced place and status is provided by the remarkable campaign fought by the people of Stoke in 1938 to keep local hero Stanley Matthews at Stoke City.[44] A footballing genius and Stoke's first England player for thirty years, Matthews had requested a transfer after being offered what he saw as an inadequate benefit. In a lengthy editorial, the local paper asked him to reconsider his decision and seven prominent Stoke manufacturers called a public meeting, attended by 3,000 people, designed to force the club to retain the player. One of the manufacturers claimed that, 'Some of our workpeople are so upset at losing him that they cannot do their work.' Strategic hyperbole perhaps, but this set of events really does suggest a level of recognition from civic and commercial leaders on a scale not encountered before 1914.[45]

Some of the factors responsible for the game's elevated status have been touched on already. The role of the mass media was absolutely central here as was, to a lesser extent, the 'Arsenal phenomenon'. The skilfully publicised appearance at Highbury of leading figures in the film world, such as Anna Neagle and Herbert Wilcox, gave the club and the game greater *kudos*. Yet again, the fact that from 1921 the Football League was much more genuinely a national tournament had a part to play. Changes in the political and social climate, though, exerted arguably the greatest influence. To a degree, some of the diminution in levels of criticism and perhaps even some of the increased support for the game was rooted in fairly cynical motives. The 1918 franchise extension increased the electorate from 7 to 20 million, and in this age of mass democracy there were those who saw the game as a necessary escape valve, absorbing the energies that might otherwise have been absorbed by what the *Sheffield Telegraph* listed as 'fanaticism, Communism and discontent.'[46] It is also the case that the new scale of mass democracy demanded an acceleration in the process whereby elite groups adopted ever more circumspect language when discussing popular culture and pastimes. This undoubtedly gave a certain protection to the game.

Rather more positive factors, however, can be divined. Before 1914 football, like many other aspects of popular culture, was often seen by social commentators as a threat, a major site of the behaviour, emotions and characteristics – gambling, partisan support, the holding of false priorities, passive 'spectatorism' – believed to threaten the nation's political, imperial and industrial base. Such views had failed to prevent the game gathering ever more of a hold, but they still had influence. From 1919, however, football increasingly came to be seen not as something antagonistic to the national project, but rather at its very heart. The football crowd had a major role to play here. The decline in 'hooliganism' and the favourable view of spectators that subsequently emerged in newspapers and on newsreel footage gave fans an improved image. Their restraint could be favourably compared with what was deemed the excessive passion to be found in some other parts of the world. Yet at the same time there was still humour and liveliness among English crowds. The football crowd could thus be represented as encapsulating the humour, restraint and balance which were key elements of the English self-image.[47]

The FA Cup final, or at least the manner it which was portrayed by the media, was central to this process. The first Wembley final, in 1923, had an especially privileged role. At least 200,000 people gained access to a stadium which had a capacity of only 127,000. Thousands entered without paying, rushing the turnstiles shortly before the kick off. The start was delayed as a small group of mounted police slowly pushed the crowd back to the touchlines: it is indeed remarkable that the game was ever played, let alone completed. Initially, there was great concern at these events, as ticket-holders complained of losing seats to gatecrashers and observers claimed that a riot had only narrowly been averted. In a Commons debate, the local MP, Oswald Mosley, then an independent, spoke of the future need to protect the stadium and his constituents from 'the hooliganism of an imported crowd and the ineptitude of the . . . authorities', a richly ironic comment in the light of his subsequent career.[48] However, attention increasingly focused on the positive aspects of the afternoon's events. For all the complaints, the fact that only a handful of people were seriously hurt, that such a small contingent of police could clear the pitch, and that the game actually took place were all seen as evidence of the ultimate good sense, humour and discipline of the English people. Above all, it was widely believed that it was the arrival of the king that had averted disaster. Supposedly, thousands turned to the Royal Box and then filed out of the ground, one aspect of their curiosity satisfied. Here was a powerful version of the 'nation as family' image later used so effectively by National Government Prime Minister Stanley Baldwin, a people united under a benevolent popular monarchy.[49] As time elapsed, a momentarily dangerous and potentially disastrous situation passed into folk memory as 'The White Horse Cup Final', in honour of thirteen-year-old 'Billy', which had caught the national imagination. The king and a horse had saved the day.

The notion of the football crowd as an embodiment of the stable, disciplined and ordered nature of English (and, indeed, British) society was further boosted by the addition of the singing of 'Abide with me' to the Cup final ritual in 1927.[50] In 1928 the *Yorkshire Observer*, proud of the contribution made by the thousands of Huddersfield Town supporters present, argued in a revealing editorial that 'The spectacle of that typical sport-loving, merry English crowd lifting their hats as one man, transformed by a single thought into one huge congregation, is a lasting tribute to the depth of religion in the national character.' Moreover, the paper could report that a special court established to deal with spectator trouble at this final had almost nothing to do. Blackburn Rovers supporters 'gleefully clipped the Huddersfield enthusiasts who were never at a loss for good-humoured retorts', but the English working class remained happily and safely at play.[51]

At first sight, it might seem that celebration of the structured, ordered crowd was most likely to be a sensibility of the political right. However, it was also voiced by commentators who stood to varying degrees to the left of the political spectrum. J. B. Priestley's description of the 'Bruddersford' football crowd in his 1929 novel *The Good Companions* is extremely well known, having been quoted in numerous anthologies of football writing.

> It turned you into a member of the community, all brothers together for an hour and a half, for not only had you escaped from the clanking machinery of the lesser life, from work, wages, rent, doles, sick pay, insurance cards, nagging wives, ailing children, bad bosses, idle workmen, but you had escaped with most of your mates, and your neighbours, with half the town, and there you were, cheering together, thumping one another on the shoulders, swapping judgments like lords of the earth, having punched your way through the turnstile into another and better way of life.

Priestley's words are frequently quoted, partly because few other serious writers dealt with the game at this time, but also because he does succeed in communicating a major part of the game's attraction. However, for all its value as an 'objective' source, Priestley's description is best seen here as a discursive device. He was using the idealised football crowd as emblematic of a wider and often equally idealised working-class community, which he and many other leftward-inclined writers, artists and broadcasters turned to as repositories of an essential 'Englishness', to be set against the supposedly mindless, inauthentic products of American popular culture. Football, along with the seaside holiday, the pub, the brass band movement and much else was called to the rescue of an endangered culture.[52]

Towards the end of the inter-war period, football's status received a further boost from the increasing realisation among both the game's and the country's leadership of the sport's value in the political arena. As Richard Holt has argued, 'English football was too self-absorbed to give itself whole-heartedly to the national cause', but there were hints of a change in the late 1930s.[53] This was a process largely denied within the game. Frederick Wall argued that English soccer was unburdened by political values.

> Abroad, international sport has a political aspect. Football in England is not carried on for the purposes of playing a foreign country and gaining a victory. Football in dear old England is merely a sporting entertainment . . . England regards international matches as a game, but continental countries look upon these matches as a test of strength, spirit and skill. Victory increases national prestige, and defeat is a sign of decadence. To them, success is vital.[54]

Once again, football was being coated with a highly positive notion of 'Englishness'.

Wall's comment was actually a highly political statement, stressing the superiority of idealised liberal democratic values. It was also misleading. In fairness to Wall, neither the government, the FA, nor, indeed, the English people gave the game's international dimension the level of importance attached to it by their counterparts in Germany, Italy, the Soviet Union and some South American countries. Furthermore, these early manifestations of both the politicisation of sport and the growth of sporting nationalism in England were modest in comparison with what was to occur in the post-war period. Nevertheless they were present. The British government had blocked the visit of a Soviet side invited by the Communist-led British Workers Sports Federation in 1930, but had proved oblivious to protests over the visit of the German national side in 1935.[55] Most famously, the dictates of appeasement led to insistence by the British ambassador, Neville Henderson, that the English team give the Nazi salute before a game against Germany in Berlin in May 1938.[56] In the immediate aftermath of Munich, the FA wrote to Chamberlain to thank him for averting war and congratulate him on the success of his policy.[57] Internationals against the Axis powers were clearly seen by press and public to have rather more than mere sporting significance. The *Daily Mail*'s statement after England had defeated Germany 6–3 in May 1938 that, 'once again, England had been proclaimed the leading football nation in the world', had obvious political connotations in the context of the period.[58] 'Dear old England' was clearly learning some new habits.

6

Football in Austerity and Affluence, 1939–1961

THE OUTBREAK of the Second World War and the abolition of the maximum wage in 1961 present convenient boundaries for the content of this chapter which deals with an important transitional period in English football. The earlier years saw the highpoint of the footballing culture that had taken shape in the inter-war years. In the late 1940s, huge crowds watched a style of football that was highly familiar in terms of the way it was played, organised and managed. At the same time, the game had never held a more secure place in the national culture. Over the course of the 1950s, however, a set of crucial changes were set in train which were to usher in the 'modern' game in the 1960s.

Football at war

The fact that soccer was played virtually throughout the Second World War without attracting any significant criticism is testimony both to the game's rise in status since 1914 and a new awareness of the importance of leisure provision among the governing classes.[1] Anxious to avoid the opprobrium of 1914–15, the League suspended the 1939–40 season immediately war was announced on 3 September. Within weeks, however, a regional competition was in place, and a Football League Cup competition soon followed. War Office regulations initially demanded that the crowd size was limited to 8,000; entry was by ticket only and sides were to travel no more than fifty miles for matches. Players were given the right to play for any club in Britain and, from 1941, allowed to turn out with more than one club in the same cup competition. However, wages were cut, bonuses outlawed and existing contracts suspended, leaving some players without income. Many players, of course, were soon on military service, a number of them qualifying as PT instructors. Seventy-five professional footballers were eventually to lose their lives in the six years of conflict.

The difficulties of playing in war-time are well recorded in soccer history and folk memory. Games had to be halted for air raid warnings. Key players did not appear, leading, on several memorable occasions, to the call for volunteers from the crowd. Some of these 'substitutes' were hilariously incompetent, others, such as Sergeant-Major Bryson, who scored the winning goal for Blackburn against Burnley in 1941, surprisingly good.[2] Travel arrangements could become a nightmare and kit was often hard to find as clothing coupons came into short supply. There were administrative fallouts as well, with a number of London clubs setting up a London League in opposition to the Football League's plans in 1941–42. There were, however, unexpected pleasures, as internationals suddenly appeared in the most unlikely places as a result of military postings. Standards were obviously extremely variable and new competitions were no compensation for the traditions and rivalries of League and Cup. Nevertheless, soccer's presence contributed to the sense of 'normality', while various war charities benefited greatly from specially arranged games and collections at other matches. The football world was justifiably proud of its distinctive contribution to the war effort.

The game: patterns of success and patterns of play

The Football League underwent a modest expansion after the war, adding another four clubs at the beginning of the 1950–51 season. This allowed for the return of League football to Gillingham, the club having lost its League position in 1938, and its introduction to Colchester, Scunthorpe and Shrewsbury. New Brighton's failure to win re-election in 1951 led to Workington's elevation to League status, thus allowing professional soccer further penetration into what was still very much a Rugby League stronghold. In 1958, the regional Third Division structure was abolished and new national Third and Fourth Divisions created. The four-up, four-down promotion and relegation system that accompanied this began a long overdue process of increasing mobility between the divisions.

The first nine seasons from 1946 were highly open and competitive in terms of the share of club success at the highest level. With the flow of money from hugely increased gates helping to equalise opportunities, seven clubs won the League title, four of them (Portsmouth, Tottenham, Wolves and Chelsea) for the first time. Over the longer period to the mid-sixties, the level of competitiveness was not dramatically different from that of the inter-war years, although no club was quite able to dominate as Arsenal had done in the 1930s. Wolves, who took three championships in the 1950s, came closest to this; the Munich air crash of 1958 may well have prevented Manchester United from emulating Arsenal's achievements. The comparison with the period from the mid-sixties, though, *is* dramatic. While eight clubs won the title in the 15 seasons between 1947 and 1961, only eleven clubs were successful in the 34 seasons from 1961 to 1995, with just five of them, Liverpool (13), Manchester United and Everton (4), Arsenal and Leeds (3), sharing 27 of those titles.[3] Even allowing for the imbalance caused by Liverpool's abnormal level of success, here is stark evidence of the revolution in English football that the changes of the early 1960s were to set in motion.

The geography of football success remained fairly constant before the early 1960s. As the table below shows, the spatial structure of the First Division was typified by variations on a traditional theme, rather than any major changes.

Table 2. *Geographical location of First Division clubs, 1939–61*

	1939–40	1960–1
Textile Lancashire *	4	5
Lincolnshire	1	—
London	4	5
Manchester	1	2
Merseyside	2	1
Midlands	4	6
North-east †	2	1
Southern	1	—
Wales	—	1
Yorkshire	3	1

* Includes Blackpool † Includes Middlesbrough

In terms of success rates, at least in the late 1940s and early 1950s, the 'rise of the south' certainly became rather more than just the rise of Islington. The championship went south six times in the first nine post-war seasons, twice to Arsenal, but also twice in succession to Portsmouth (1949 and 1950) and to Spurs (1951) and Chelsea (1955). Although Tottenham were to record the twentieth century's first 'double' in 1960–61, this record was not sustained. Indeed, in the next 34 seasons, only Arsenal and Ipswich were to bring the championship south of Birmingham.

In terms of the management, coaching and playing of the game, the years after 1945 saw the acceleration and deepening of many of the more 'technocratic' themes which had begun to emerge in the 1930s. Although directors hung on to control in many clubs, managers, especially those first appointed after 1945, increasingly sought greater autonomy in terms of recruitment, selection and tactics. While this owed much to the gradual realisation of the benefits the new managerial style could bring, it is at least worth suggesting that the more egalitarian social and political climate of the war and immediate post-war years may have helped speed the process of change. The football world, like the country at large, was perhaps a slightly less deferential place.

For some, notably Matt Busby, Manchester United's manager from 1945, and Stan Cullis, his Wolves counterpart from 1947, this involved hitherto unknown levels of daily contact with the players and with their training. Busby has, indeed, often been called the first 'tracksuit' manager.[4] For many managers, coaching took on a new importance in this context. A seminal figure here was Walter Winterbottom, an ex-Manchester United half back turned PE lecturer, who was appointed England's first ever team manager in 1946. As well as managing the national side, Winterbottom worked hard to reform the whole basis of the English game via a rapidly expanding network of FA coaching schemes. The FA had first developed such schemes in 1934 in attempt to combat the spread of rugby in schools.[5] After 1946, teachers were gradually joined on such courses by those involved in the professional game.

Initial reactions were mixed, some enthused by Winterbottom's belief that players could be taught new tactics and skills, by judicious use of a blackboard if necessary, others, especially in the popular press, suspicious of this 'intellectual' approach. The reformers were given significant help from lessons learnt at the hands of Eastern Europe. The visit of the Moscow Dynamo side in 1945 and, much more painfully and effectively, the 6–3 and 7–1 defeats suffered by England at the hands of the Hungarian national side in 1953 and 1954 respectively, did much to banish complacency about the English game. The first of these defeats, England's first ever on home soil by a side from outside the British Isles, came as a greater shock to the footballing public than it should have done. As reigning Olympic champions, the Hungarians were an extremely talented side, rather disregarded by a press too anxious to emphasise England's previous home record. This record, while good, had in fact been earned against often limited opposition. Although the press was to remain ambivalent about the coaching revolution for a long time, in the short-term its reaction to 'Magyar magic' was to demand that English players should, like their

The England youth team in 1949–50. Youth policy was seen as essential to the future of the game, although results were more striking at club than international level. (*Football Association*)

conquerors, receive exactly the type of modern coaching and training that many of them had so recently been deriding. Overall, in the climate of the Cold War, England's humbling by communist opposition added an edge to the situation, and the growing (although often denied) belief in the need to maintain both national pride and faith in democracy through sporting achievement became a further spur to footballing change.

Perspiration as much as European inspiration, however, was to play an important part in the spread of the coaching gospel. The Football Association's role was vital here, with its network of coaching schemes and its encouragement of youth and schoolboy football. The establishment of the FA Youth Cup in 1953–54 was one mechanism adopted. Significantly, it was won in its first two seasons by Manchester United's hugely talented youth side, already attracting the epithet 'the Busby Babes'. Boys' literature was also enlisted in the battle for enlightenment, with the *FA Book for Boys*, which appeared annually from 1948 until 1973, especially important. Here was juvenile sporting literature as textbook, a serious work that had no space for stories of last-minute goals unless they were real ones that had been scored by deep-lying Uruguayan centre forwards. The 1954–55

Chelsea's Len Goulden coaches the club's junior players in 1949, a typical illustration from the *FA Yearbook For Boys*. (*Football Association*)

edition, for example, contained articles on the training regimes adopted in different schools, the role of 'backroom boys' such as physiotherapists and, crucially, numerous pieces on various aspects of coaching and tactics by leading players and managers, including Stanley Matthews, Walter Winterbottom and Ferenc Puskas, Hungary's brilliant inside forward and a major architect of England's humiliation. Puskas's elegantly written piece – 'for an effective performance it is not sufficient merely to be fond of playing' – was a remarkable achievement for a man who in 1953 spoke not one word of English.[6] Either his linguistic skills were as great as his footballing ones or the FA had realised the value of putting their words into the mouth of the great symbol of progressive football. The book was liberally sprinkled with tactical diagrams and charts; even the article on the Royal Marines Band's Wembley performance was enriched by sketches of their major marching routines.

This was baptism by total immersion. The book has a period charm now and it is hard to avoid a little levity when writing about it. However, it stands as an important symbol of a determined attempt to change mentalities from the grass roots. The annual *FA Yearbook* also contained regular features on coaching and tactics, often involving an international perspective. Such articles, often accompanied by discussions of the pools, Sunday football and the value of European competition and other controversial issues, suggest that soccer's ruling body was trying hard to meet contemporary challenges and to slough off at least some of its conservative traditions. In this it is hard to avoid comparison with the far more insular agenda of the Football League. This surfaced most noticeably in regard to the European Cup, first contested in 1955–56. The Football League, already worried by the number of friendlies being played against foreign sides, and seeing the tournament as yet another distraction from the domestic game, dissuaded current champions Chelsea from entering. It was not until the following season that Matt Busby, strongly backed by Rous and the FA, took Manchester United into the competition and established a English presence in Europe.[7]

By the late 1950s, most clubs had been penetrated to some degree by the new thinking. At some clubs, it appears to have been the players rather than the management who were the most innovative. The most famous example here is provided by the so-called 'West Ham Academy', a group of players who met and discussed tactics in a local restaurant and who sometimes imposed their ideas on the (usually sympathetic) manager, Ted Fenton. A number of the Academy's members, including Malcolm Allison, John Bond and Dave Sexton, were later to become highly influential coaches and managers in their own right. Although critics of coaching railed against the dangers of stereotyped and rigid patterns of play, what actually emerged was a mixture of plans, formulae and tactics. Arthur Rowe's Tottenham Hotspur side that took the Second and First Division titles in consecutive seasons in 1950 and 1951, played an essentially short passing game, soon labelled 'push and run', based on the attacking players 'running off the ball' into space. Wolves, however, under Cullis, adopted a long passing game, designed to get the ball into the opposition penalty area as rapidly as possible. Many sides experimented with changed formations, ranging from the relatively modest gambit of using a 'roving' centre forward to pull defences out of position, to the 4–2–4 formation sometimes adopted by more tactically literate sides by the early 1960s. It must also, of course, be acknowledged that many spectators continued to witness some highly physical games, comprising tactics which were not to be found in any modern coaching manual.

While it is obviously the case that these various developments had a major impact on the style and quality of the English game, albeit one which was not to mature fully until the 1960s, it is impossible to gauge just how important all these changes were in influencing individual club success. As Stephen Wagg has pointed out, the link between Hungarian success and coaching was more assumed then proved and it is perfectly possible that this was true also in the English context. Sides were sometimes successful because of the peculiar blend of talent that happened to coalesce at a particular time. Similarly, some of the tracksuit managers, including Matt Busby, were not believers in particular systems or set tactics.[8] Whatever the impact that these changes had on the field, in terms of their wider significance, they undoubtedly helped breed a specialist, 'technocratic' culture within football. Expert 'insiders' increasingly saw themselves as ranged against an ill-informed set of 'outsiders', comprising the press, directors, fans, or whichever group threatened or criticised at the time. 'Do you mind, I'm working', are the words Alf Ramsey reputedly used when the Ipswich chairman congratulated him on the club's championship success, while Ramsey watched a reserve game.[9] While such a culture probably raised the autonomy and status of many managers and players at the expense of those who had previously exerted power, especially directors and administrators, it was, arguably, eventually to be one of the factors that was to distance the game from the ordinary fan. Football was ever more prone to be represented by its professional elite as a science that was beyond the comprehension of many and thus above 'lay' criticism. This may eventually have contributed to the attendance problems that many clubs began to face from the 1950s.

Spectators

The most obvious feature of the football crowd in the immediate post-war period was its sheer size as football experienced a massive burst of popularity in a country desperate for entertainment after war-time disruption and austerity. Football League attendances were to reach their all-time peak in the 1948–49 season when 41,271,424 people passed through the turnstiles. It is surely the case that good luck rather than good management was responsible for there being no repetition of the major crowd disaster of this period, at Burnden Park, Bolton in 1946, when 33 died and 400 were injured after barriers gave way behind a goal.[10] The game's appeal was equally marked outside the professional sphere, the Amateur Cup

The Football Special had few of the negative connotations it was to earn from the late 1960s. (*Science Museum*)

final attracting 95,000 on its Wembley debut in 1949. From 1949, however, attendances began to fall, fairly gradually at first, but with the rate of decline gathering speed from the early 1950s. Although the 1956–57 and 1957–58 seasons saw a slight recovery, the 1960s began with the biggest percentage drop in attendances that the League has ever seen, the 1960–61 season witnessing a 12 per cent decline in crowd size. By the end of the 1961–62 season the League aggregate total had fallen to 27,979,000, a decline of some 11.25 million since the 1948–49 peak. The saga of the search for the 'missing millions', a key theme of soccer's post-war history, was well established.

Obviously, considerable care has to be taken here. First, despite its problems, throughout this period soccer was drawing larger attendances than it had before 1939. The 1937–38 season saw an aggregate attendance of 28.1 million and post-war aggregates remained at, or above this level (albeit boosted by the four additional clubs) until the early 1970s.[11] Again, football managed to sustain a far greater level of patronage than many of the other areas of mass entertainment that had boomed in the 1940s, most notably the cinema. There were also a number of counter-trends and variations which are disguised by the macro-figures. First Division clubs lost support at lower rates than clubs in the lower divisions, suggesting a certain level of discrimination operating among fans, while many clubs enjoyed surges of support reflecting periods of success or the availability of especially attractive teams. Indeed, 45 sides with pre-1939 League status experienced their highest seasonal aggregate attendance in the period *after* 1950.[12] Admittedly, almost half of these were recorded in the early 1950s, close to the peak years of attendance nationally. Similarly, some of the records in later years reflect moments of unexampled success by small town or suburban clubs, as when Northampton (1965–66) and Carlisle (1974–75) enjoyed their single seasons of First Division football. However, several clubs that were no strangers to major honours recorded their best aggregate well after the boom years had passed, including Blackburn (1958–59), Everton (1962–63), Leeds (1970–71), Liverpool (1972–73) and Manchester United (1967–68). United's record average of 57,552 was almost 20,000 higher than that of 1960–61, and 12,000 higher than in their title-winning season of 1956–57.

There can, however, be no denying the overall downward trend. It has to be said that much discussion on attendance patterns to date, and indeed much of what follows here, is based to some degree on supposition. Little serious research was conducted into the problem in this period by the football authorities and there has been little in the way of detailed academic analysis. Students of recent leisure history surely have a worthy topic here, one that would benefit from the much needed oral history research that will shed light on the network of innumerable individual decisions that led to the overall decline.

Every commentator in the 1950s had their pet theories. A poem in the 1956–57 *FA Yearbook*, blamed teams not using local players, the lack of skill in the modern game, the rise of gamesmanship and the rise of defensive football.[13] Such offerings, however, were often little more than a rag-bag of ahistorical prejudices. On the point of defensive football, for example, the number of goals scored was actually at its lowest level since 1925 during the boom years of the 1940s and then rose during the 1950s, as attendances dropped.[14] Critics only needed to look at other sports to realise that the game itself had only, at best, very limited correlation with attendances at this time. Rugby League attendances, for example, fell from a record aggregate of 4,950,000 in 1949–50, to just under 2 million by 1963–64.[15] Clearly, wider forces were in operation.

At a very obvious explanatory level, the immediate post-war attendances could not be sustained at such magnitude and a small amount of the decline simply reflects a novelty wearing off. Explanations of the more significant levels of decline that took place from the early fifties are usually centred on the rise of the 'affluent society' that marked the 1950s and 1960s. Such explanations make much sense, but there were many who never had it 'particularly good' and it is possible that, for some poorer fans, the game did actually become too expensive. Minimum admission prices were lowered from their war-time rate of 1*s.* 6*d.* to 1*s.* 3*d.* in 1946, but then rose back to 1*s.* 6*d.* in 1951, 1*s.* 9*d.* in 1952 and 2*s.* 6*d.* in 1960. It is not perhaps surprising that the 1960–61 season saw the loss of some 3.9 million fans from League football. While many of the lost supporters of that season were probably demonstrating discrimination, backed by the money to pursue other activities, others, especially those with low incomes and faced with travelling costs from out-of-town council estates, might simply have found it all too expensive.

Rising living standards and the benefits and distractions that they bought presented rather more fundamental problems, however. In 1951, the average weekly wage of the male adult manual worker stood at £8 6*s.* By 1961 it had risen to £15 7*s.*, an increase only slightly dented by the moderate inflation of the later 1950s. Rising real wages fuelled the increase in the purchase of consumer goods that was such a feature of this period.

One study noted that, from 1950, League attendances fell approximately 1 per cent for every 1 per cent increase in consumer expenditure.[16] Two items, motor cars and television sets, were to become increasingly important in the context of football. The number of private vans and cars rose from 2.3 million in 1950 to 3.6 million in 1955, 5.6 million in 1960 and 9.1 million by 1965. TV sets, a rarity in 1950, were to be found in 75 per cent of households by 1961.[17] Alongside this, important changes took place in the housing market: between 1945 and 1970, the number of properties in owner occupation rose from 16 per cent to 47 per cent of the housing stock, while the number of council houses showed a similar rise from 12 per cent to 30 per cent.[18]

Many people thus had both a better home environment and a higher level of commitment to their domestic space. The house was ever more likely to represent an alternative focus to the football ground for male energies, with DIY joining gardening as a major hobby in this period. Television's threat came not from its football coverage, which was fairly minimal in this period, but simply from the fact that it offered a Saturday afternoon's entertainment in rather more comfortable surroundings than the average football stadium. It was actually the radio that was deemed to be the greater threat to attendances in terms of actual football coverage. Live commentary had become widely accepted in the war and the League's broadcasting ban went almost by default once peacetime soccer started. From 1951–52, the *Radio Times* was no longer allowed to give advance notice of its commentary match, in order to allay fears about the impact on crowd size.[19]

The exact impact of increased car ownership is not absolutely clear. By the late 1960s and 1970s, increased access to private transport was most certainly a factor diminishing attendance at grounds in the lower divisions as fans were able to travel longer distances to watch big city sides. It is unlikely, though, that either the level of car ownership or the quality of the pre-motorway road network was high enough to exert influence much before the mid-1960s. It is significant that even quite successful teams located a long way from attractive rivals seem to have shared in the decline in spectator numbers. Plymouth Argyle, for example, saw their average attendance drop from 23,000 in their 1958–59 Third Division championship season to 14,000 in 1961–62 when they finished fifth in the Second Division. The clubs most at risk in the early car age were probably those within easy commuting distance of the big London clubs. In most cases, the car's challenge came simply from the opportunity it provided for trips to non-sporting locations and for Saturday afternoon exhibitions of male mechanical skill. James Walvin has suggested that a further powerful challenge in the post-war era came from 'changes in female expectations and demands . . . In the changing climate of a prospering Britain, more and more men were no longer able, as their forebears had been, simply to do as they wished. Many took heed of their womenfolks interests; many wanted to spend their free time in the company of their spouses and companions.'[20] This is an interesting and fertile line of enquiry. However, it is possible that some women were merely experiencing the transfer of male energies from a public to a private sphere, deeds with tenon saw, hi-fi and wall-papering brush competing with or replacing tales of dipping volleys and chipped free kicks, as the symbols of the distinctiveness and specialness of male culture.

In regard to the many who did still attend, the existence of reliable attendance records coupled with the fact that crowd size was far less influenced by such variables as unemployment does allow for a rather more scientific study of the exact rhythms and patterns of attendance than has been possible for earlier times. One detailed study by the FA in 1949–50 showed First Division average attendances running at about 40,000 until early October, when, presumably as a result of deteriorating weather and the first signs of consistent poor form at some grounds, crowds began to fall. They dropped steadily throughout November and December, reaching their nadir on 12 November, a 'wet and stormy day' and on the last Saturday before Christmas. The Christmas matches saw a huge rise, with the average reaching 46,000, followed by a rapid return to the mid-winter levels. Finally, as both better weather and championship and relegation issues loomed, crowds recovered, and by April, almost reached their early season levels. The study claimed that these patterns were repeated across the League, although it suggested that the Third Division North recorded a rather more constant level of support.[21] These figures demonstrate a fair degree of rationality among supporters, not least in the desire to avoid getting pneumonia. Similar rational considerations emerge from the analysis of the attendance record of specific clubs. Arsenal, for example, enjoyed an average gate in the 1949–50 season of 49,001, but crowds varied quite dramatically from match to match. Between 8 October and 5 November, the match with Everton drew 53,000, 66,000 came to see Blackpool, then thanks to Stanley Matthews probably the biggest draw in the English game, but only 40,000 came to watch lowly Fulham on a very wet day. The absolute bedrock of the team's support were the 27–35,000 who still attended toward the end of the season as Arsenal's championship challenge faded. Weather, the quality of opposition and the home team's form clearly had a considerable impact on the crowd size. In London at least it is also likely that big clubs not only had a certain level of the floating support that all clubs enjoyed, but that they also attracted genuine neutrals, or even fans of other sides, anxious to see a particular visiting player or team.[22]

Facilities at most grounds improved but little over the period. Many grounds were covered on only one or two sides, catering services remained limited and toilet facilities positively medieval. At some games, the sheer weight of the crowd rendered the latter almost irrelevant anyway, and the oral tradition of most big clubs contains stories, often embellished, of bladders being skilfully emptied along well-directed funnels improvised from rolled-up newspapers. Grounds were built to accommodate numbers, not to provide comfort, and only at the very end of this period did some clubs begin to consider the need to use ground improvement as method of fighting falling gates. The only major change that fans saw was the

The Hawthorns, home of West Bromwich Albion, in 1954. A typical English ground, best appreciated on sunny days. (*Football Association*)

arrival of floodlights, used mainly in friendlies against foreign opposition at first, but legalised for League and Cup games from 1956 as the League and the FA gradually dropped resistance to something which initially been seen as a gimmick.[23]

Crowds were generally well behaved at this time, sheer numbers rendering misbehaviour inside the ground quite difficult at least in the immediate post-war period. The FA dealt with only 22 incidents in the 1948–49 season, which, even allowing for the fact that many others occurred which did not reach their attention, seems remarkably small in a season when total attendances passed 41 million. Referees' reports, again a source that tended to under-record misbehaviour, documented only 138 incidents between 1946 and 1959. Although sections of the press, against a background of national concern over delinquent youth culture, appear to have given a rather more sensational coverage of these isolated incidents from the late 1950s, reporting in general still stressed the good order and nature of the English crowd.[24] The rituals of terrace life seem to have been much as before, cup ties in particular leading to a colourful and carnivalesque atmosphere. It is possible, though, that crowd culture was becoming a little less varied and a little more decorous. The habit of singing certainly appears to have been less common than in the pre-war period. Supporters' clubs continued to do heroic work, and still for minimal reward in terms of a share in the control of the game's destiny. In 1956 the passage of the Small Lotteries and Gaming Act gave the FA little option but to allow football clubs to organise lotteries and supporters' clubs played a major role in this new avenue of fund-raising, often vital for smaller teams. Arguments frequently broke out between supporters' clubs and the football club over control of these funds, and a number of managements began their own separate lotteries in order to maintain authority.[25]

Football and the media

The period between 1946 and the early 1960s saw few fundamental alterations in the relationship between football and the various branches of the media. Rather, it saw an acceleration of pre-war trends which eventually reached full fruition in the 1960s and beyond. Broadcasting continued to play a vital role in placing the game within a national framework and culture. As already noted, radio broadcasts of League games became a feature of Saturday afternoons from the moment the competition was re-established, and at the same time the game's profile was raised by the establishment of sporting 'magazine' style programmes. The most important of these was the Light Programme's Saturday night *Sports Report*, which began in 1949. Although covering a range of sports, football results, match reports and interviews usually took up the bulk of the programme and provided the main interest for the majority of listeners. Its informative, non-sensationalist approach served as both an acknowledgement and a reinforcement of the game's importance. Television showed little football until the mid-1960s beyond the Cup final (ITV were allowed simultaneous rights of coverage alongside the BBC from 1961) and internationals. The BBC showed a limited amount of League highlights from 1955 but in the following year, First Division clubs voted against accepting an offer from independent television, valued at £40,000, for live coverage of the second half of some 35 matches. Ironically, given their role in the 1980s, the opposition was led by Liverpool and Everton. The fear of lost turnstile revenue outweighed any other factors at this stage. In 1960, the League agreed a £47,000 package for the coverage of 26 live games, but only the second half of one game, Blackpool *v*. Bolton, was ever shown, The clubs objected to a deal which had been negotiated without their knowledge and live League coverage had to wait for another 23 years.[26]

Even its limited coverage, however, allowed a glimpse of the enormous potential influence that TV would one day wield. The clearest testimony to its latent power was its impact on the timing of the Cup final. Traditionally, the final was played at the same time as a full League programme. In 1950, the one million plus TV audience cut sufficiently into League attendances for Sunderland to propose a ban on the live transmission. Although such draconian action was avoided, in 1952 the final was moved to the last Saturday of the season, when few sides had matches. The estimated 10 million who watched the 1953 Cup final made further action inevitable and, from 1954, the game was moved back yet another week to avoid all clashes.[27]

The 1953 Blackpool–Bolton final, the so-called 'Matthews final', in which the 38-year-old helped inspire a dramatic Blackpool recovery which turned a 3–1 deficit into a 4–3 victory, also demonstrated that television, perhaps even more than radio, could elevate football into a national ritual and place it at the heart of public affairs. That so many, even those who were not close followers of the sport, experienced the novelty of watching a national hero win an honour which had previously eluded him not only gave this game in particular a privileged place in football history, but gave the sport in general an enhanced status.

Despite the ever greater contribution of the broadcasting media it was still the press that continued to play the major role in publicising the game and constructing its image. Local papers, with their Saturday specials and daily coverage of local teams, remained central to the process, offering their standard mixture of gossip, constructive criticism and enthusiastic celebration of achievements. For many supporters the local paper provided a largely reassuring view of football's landscape in comparison with the increasingly cynical version offered in the popular national press. By the later 1940s, the new sporting journalism was becoming a commonplace in Fleet Street, with the *News of the World* and the *Daily* and *Sunday Express*, in particular, following the path that the *People* had illuminated. Alan Hoby, Trevor Wignall and Desmond Hackett were among the key figures here. Although much of their time was devoted to simple match reports, it was their feature writing that perhaps had the greatest impact. Much of it focused on supposed corruption within the game, mainly related to the exposure of strategies for circumventing the maximum wage, and on the problems of the national side and the conservatism of the football authorities. While players took much criticism, directors and football administrators were in many ways the favoured targets. Extra spice was added by the willingness of the papers to give space to football personalities on and off the pitch to make their own accusations and defences. Even relatively innocent stories were often embellished with almost salacious headlines. An item by Wolverhampton manager Stan Cullis, headed 'I plotted behind Billy Wright's back', simply referred to the fact that Cullis had discussed moving his captain from wing half to centre half with the England manager, before raising the issue with the player.[28]

The exact impact of this style of coverage is not easy to discern. At one level, it hardly boosted the game's image. As Simon Inglis has written, 'Had an outsider based his assessment of the league in the mid 'fifties upon the popular Sunday papers, he might well have concluded that all footballers were rowdy, dishonest, greedy and corrupt, while most club chairmen and League officials were either lazy, ignorant fools or insanely ambitious profiteers.'[29] Such dramatic coverage may even have been responsible for turning some supporters away from the game. However, newspaper readers were probably able to detect the difference between the occasional genuine crisis and the impression of the permanent one which the papers proclaimed. For all its hyperbole, however, the popular press probably did help create a climate in which change could occur.

The considerable public sympathy for the players in 1960–61 when the maximum wage and retain and transfer issues finally reached a head surely owed something to press coverage which at the very least had shown that the existing system was unworkable and corrupt. While the popular press needed the game and fed hungrily on it, it was, in a distinctive way, capable of giving something back.

The post-1945 era also saw an increased interest in the game among the so-called quality press, both cause and consequence of football's enhanced position in the national culture from the late 1930s. In the process, a new breed of football journalist emerged, typified by Geoffrey Green, *The Times* football correspondent from 1946 to 1976, Brian Glanville, J. L. Manning and Hugh McIlvanney. Interestingly, it was often to this group, rather than the 'populists', that the BBC turned for much of its expert comment on programmes like *Sports Report*, thus increasing their sphere of influence. It is not necessarily the case that this new area of coverage brought the game a new public, although it may have helped remove prejudice in certain households. What it certainly did was to raise the status of the game by placing it more firmly in a prestigious area of the public domain, and by giving it an intellectual veneer that was to prove vital in the troubled decades that lay ahead.

Some of these writers were also to play a part in the football publishing sub-culture that expanded so dramatically in this period. The 1940s and 1950s saw a great growth of footballing literature at every level. Green, Glanville and others took the opportunity to write on various aspects of the game's history and politics, a number of the resulting titles being published under the *Sportsman's Book Club* imprint. Another major element here was provided by the professional footballer's autobiography. Until this point, autobiography was largely the province of the amateur sportsman, although the mould had been cracked a little in the mid-1930s by, among others, Yorkshire cricketer Herbert Sutcliffe. From the later 1940s, however, there was a spate of such books, with one leading bibliography of sporting literature listing titles by 36 players (and/or their ghost writers or collaborators), published between 1946 and 1960.[30] Several players, including Denis Compton, Tommy Lawton, Stanley Matthews and Billy Wright managed to produce several, nominally separate, works. Many of these books were also serialised in the press. Here was powerful testimony to the raised status of the professional player within British society.

Football continued to be at the heart of much comic book literature.

The post-war period saw an increasing preference for the comic-strip over the more literary style of the earlier period and it is appropriate that among these strips a new style of fictional football hero was born. As ever, these cultural products should not be burdened with undue interpretative weight. They were written and read within a clear set of rules that demanded certain outcomes and moral lessons, and they were always aids to private fantasy rather than commentaries on the contemporary game. Nevertheless, changes within the repertory of characters and stories suggest that public perception of the game and its participants was changing. Although the *New Hotspur*'s Danny Lorimer and Lampy Flack, the *Hornet*'s Bernie Briggs and the *Tiger*'s Roy Race got themselves into some amazing scrapes and participated in some amazing matches – the phrase 'real Roy of the Rovers stuff' remains a footballing cliché – they were often rather more of the reader's known universe than pre-war heroes.[31] They were certainly still chivalric heroes, scrupulously honest in all things. However, they were often from a more humble background than their predecessors, albeit still more likely to be small businessmen than proletarians. Lorimer ran a one-man briquette business from which he would emerge, exhausted after a night's labour, to score crucial goals for Mancaster United, while Briggs was a scrap metal dealer, with a motor-bike in his bath. Caricatures then, and wonderful vessels for stories of the victory of honest toil and simple virtue over snobbery and pretension, but of a markedly different breed from the gentlemen-amateurs who had so often featured in the 1920s and 1930s. The authors of comic book literature could not quite see their way to removing the residual stigma from the professional player, but they came ever closer to doing so.

The period saw two substantial additions to football literature: *Charles Buchan's Football Monthly*, launched in September 1951, and the weekly *Soccer Star* (originally *Raich Carter's Soccer Star*) first published twelve months later. Both were targeted largely at boys and young men but they probably had some readership outside this group. In one sense they were both very traditional in their content, the mixture of club and player profiles, gossip and, in *Football Monthly's* case, feature articles marking them out only a little from the earlier *Athletic News*. However, they can probably lay claim to being the first modern football magazines with *Football Monthly* attaining a circulation of some 350,000 by the late fifties. They were devoted exclusively to the game, used a contemporary journalistic style and idiom and made great use of photographs, *Football Monthly* in particular specialising in full-page colour portraiture.

Similarly, unlike the previous generation of soccer publications aimed at young men, such as the *Football Favourite*, they carried virtually no fictional element. *Football Monthly* tended to carry a number of fairly lengthy, issue-based pieces in its early years, although it was studiedly uncontroversial. Even something as dramatic as the maximum wage controversy was completely ignored until the matter had been settled, by which time a contributor felt safe in giving the PFA broad support.[32] Overall, both magazines gave a highly sanitised view of the game, acknowledging only controversies that related to the playing of the game and showing football as a very safe and uncomplicated world within a wider one, which was, of course, never allowed to intrude.

The media in all its forms, then, gave a number of often contradictory images, showing football to be anything from a progressive and positive force in English society to a site of corruption and decay. Individual fans, players and administrators juggled these views and used them as they saw fit. In a crucial sense, though, at this time in football's history it may well have been that all publicity was relatively good publicity. Although attendances were falling, the game was in the public's mind to a hitherto unknown extent and the media's constant interest in the game showed that football's place in society was secure, even if it was less often expressed by attendance at a match. Moreover, the balance between the game and the media was still largely in the former's favour. Football benefited from much of the publicity it received, while still being able to deflect some of the worst of it. Private lives were rarely exposed before they came into public view via the law courts and a type of honour code existed. Cliff Bastin (admittedly an ex-player, but also a *Sunday Pictorial* journalist) and his co-writer, Brian Glanville, chose to be remarkably circumspect about even the events of twenty years earlier in his 1950 autobiography: Tommy Black, the Arsenal player whose foul led to a Walsall penalty in the historic 1933 cup tie and to his subsequent transfer from the club, was never actually named in their detailed account of the game.[33] As the century progressed, however, that balance became harder to maintain, and it became easier to see the 1940s and 1950s as a seedbed for a later revolution in media–football relations.

Finally, it is worth noting that sections of the footballing authorities, and certainly the Football Association, showed an increasing awareness of the need for some public relations mechanisms in this period. Some of the FA's publications have already been discussed, but there were other signs of an ever more astute cultivation of respectability and credibility.

William Turner, 'The Night Before the Cup-tie', one of the works at the FA's exhibition of 1953. (*Williamson Art Gallery and Museum, Birkenhead*)

In 1952–53, for example, the FA marked its ninetieth birthday celebrations with a fine art competition which attracted an extremely healthy collection of paintings and sculpture.[34] Similarly, the FA chose novelist H. E. Bates to write a memorial article in its *Yearbook* following the Munich disaster.[35] As the events of 1960–61 were to show, the Football League, however, was a little less attuned to the public relations revolution.

Players

The money flowing from the unprecedented boom in football's popularity in the late 1940s led to an equally unprecedented number of people earning their living by playing the game. By the end of the decade, there were some 7,000 professional footballers in the country, about 3,000 of them, mostly with League clubs, on full-time contracts.[36] Most of them were still drawn from working-class families and came disproportionately from the industrial areas of the north and midlands: as late as 1963, 40 per cent of League players came from the north-west, the north-east and Yorkshire.[37] At one level, their social standing and status seemed to be in the ascendant. Increased media coverage gave star players an ever higher profile and the opportunity for earning quite substantial amounts outside the game from journalism, endorsements and a variety of public engagements, including modelling in the case of Birmingham City's Eddy Brown.[38] Soccer tragedy played its part, too, in placing players firmly in the public gaze, never more so than in February 1958 when the Munich air disaster gripped the nation, or in March 1959 when Birmingham and England player Jeff Hall died of polio.[39]

Despite these developments, or indeed, perhaps because of the glimpses of greater possibilities that many of them offered, the period to the early 1960s was marked by much player dissatisfaction. Its major cause related to the hardy perennials of the maximum wage and the retain and transfer system. The maximum wage climbed reasonably steadily over the period as a result of constant union pressure. The threat of strike action in November 1945 brought a rise to £9 a week along with the restitution of pre-war win and draw bonuses, while a National Arbitration Tribunal raised it once again to £12 in 1947. The same tribunal also insisted on a £5 *minimum* for players over 21, which represented a significant victory for players at the game's margins. Further rises in 1951, 1953 and 1958 eventually saw the maximum reach £20.[40] However, these increases were far less satisfactory than they appeared on paper. First, as had always been the case, the majority of players were not receiving the maximum, probably only 30 per cent being in receipt of it at any one time. Many reserve team players with top clubs and first teamers with Third Division sides were earning below the national average industrial wage by the early 1950s. At the same time, even the best paid saw a substantial erosion of the differential between their earnings and those of the typical members of the industrial community that had marked the pre-war period: comparable rates of approximately £8 and £4 in 1939 had been replaced by those of £20 and £15 in 1960. The earning capacity of their counterparts in the film and music industry gave them a further source of unfavourable contrast. The players were also aware of football's relatively healthy economic state, at least among the largest clubs who would have to meet the heaviest increases. While in 1955–56, the 92 clubs showed a net profit of only £69,428, a very small return for such a big industry as later reformers were to point out, the First Division clubs showed a combined profit of £107,000. Again, the abolition of Entertainment Tax in 1957 was expected to release some £900,000 back into the game, while the Football League's belated realisation that the pools represented a valuable source of income led to a ten-year deal with the leading companies in 1957. The League and the Scottish League were to receive ½ per cent of pools stake money, or a minimum of £245,000 in return for the companies' use of the fixture list.[41]

Obviously, some players were actually receiving substantially more than the maximum, as directors found endless interesting ways of circumventing the rules which they supported so enthusiastically in public. Illegal signing-on fees and bonuses were among the most frequently used tactics, but presents to players' wives (handbags at Preston in 1954), use of club houses and cars, provision of household goods and so on were also popular ways of compensating for the maximum.[42] While few players seem to have rejected this largesse, they clearly found it demeaning and, occasionally, it proved downright disastrous. In 1957, Sunderland were fined heavily, and several directors banned for life, after the discovery of a web of illegal payments which stretched back for some years. Five of the club's players, believed to have benefited or to be in receipt of relevant information, were called to a League enquiry where, on the advice of the Union, they refused to speak. As a result, they too were banned *sine die* and it was some time before the Union was able to extricate them from this difficulty.[43]

At least *some* progress had been made on the issue of wages. However, the League consistently refused to discuss the retain and transfer system. The period was littered with stories of wage cuts which players could not prevent, refusals to accept transfer requests and unrealistically high transfer fees being placed on the heads of ageing players, thus denying them the opportunity for mobility at the end of their careers. At some clubs, these tangible economic grievances were embellished by directoral displays of arrogance and high-handedness. This is not to suggest that club boardrooms were inhabited solely by unthinking autocrats; many directors were thoughtful and civilised in their approach to players. Many professionals, however, were still addressed brusquely and by surname only, if indeed they were addressed at all. The fact that Barnsley's Harry Hough was a strong trade unionist, whose club chairman, Joe Richards, was also chairman of the Football League, might have made him the target of especially cold treatment, but he was probably not the only player who could claim that his chairman only spoke to him twice in twelve years. On one of those occasions, Hough's transfer request was rejected with the comment 'You go where I tell you.'[44] In an age when footballers were becoming

Cornelius 'Neil' Franklyn. His move to South America ended an outstanding international career.

ever more conscious of their special 'technocrat' status and when older notions of discipline and hierarchy were under challenge in some quarters of the wider society, such attitudes hardly improved the industrial relations climate.

A small number of players were tempted to escape these restrictions and play abroad. From the late 1940s, a trickle of players left for Italy, including Eddie Firmani who went in 1955 for a financial package which was reputed to include a £5,000 signing-on fee, a weekly salary of £100 and a rent-free flat.[45] More dramatically, in 1950–51 the Colombian club Bogota persuaded Stoke's Neil Franklin to break contract in order to join the club. Three others, George Mountford, Franklin's Stoke team-mate, Charlie Mitten of Manchester United and Everton's Billy Higgins, followed suit. Mitten claimed to have been given a £2,500 signing-on fee, £50 per week and generous bonuses and living expenses. Most of the players returned quickly, unable to settle, and, *pour encourager les autres,* Franklin was banned from English soccer for a year and suspended from the England side indefinitely for his breach of contract.[46]

More typically, players took what they could from the domestic game with varying degrees of acceptance and contentment. As ever, collective action proved a far from generally favoured option. As John Harding has argued, even the more rebellious players 'rarely if ever turned to the Union to help solve their problems. Instead, the tendency had been to escape, trick or cheat the system – never to confront it.'[47] Others simply denied that footballers had any cause for complaint. Gradually, however, a momentum for concerted action developed, leading to the attainment of major and enormously significant changes between 1961 and 1964.[48] From the end of the Second World War, the Association Football Players' and Trainers' Union had been led by Jimmy Guthrie, an ex-Dundee and Portsmouth half back. Guthrie's aggressive, radical, high-profile stance achieved rather more for the Union than is sometimes appreciated. Not only did he help win improvements to the maximum wage as well as other benefits, but he also gave the players a level of publicity and a platform which laid much of the base for future success. Unfortunately, he could be abrasive and autocratic, characteristics which led to his being banned from a number of grounds by directors, and, more importantly, to his eventual rejection by the Union in January 1957.

The new chair, 33-year-old Fulham inside forward Jimmy Hill, was in many ways the ideal candidate to realise Guthrie's erratically accumulated capital. He was well known to the public as a good, albeit not exceptional, footballer; he was articulate and was extremely confident in his dealings with the media. At a less cerebral but equally important level, he gained a useful notoriety as the country's only bearded footballer, one journalist linking his facial hair to his club's location in an artistic London quarter by christening him 'the beatnik with a ball'.[49] In 1958, in a moment of linguistic inspiration, the Union changed its rather antiquated name to the Professional Footballers' Association, a title redolent with connotations of worthwhile aspiration and respectability. From this rather innocent-sounding body there came a serious and determined trade union campaign.

In April 1960 the PFA formulated four principal demands: abolition of the maximum wage, the right of players to a proportion of their transfer fees, a new retaining system and new contracts. By June 1960, an official dispute existed with the League, and a long series of negotiations began. The League made a number of limited concessions before finally agreeing to abolish the maximum wage on 9 January 1961. At a series of mass meetings, the players showed remarkable loyalty and discipline by refusing to settle unless the retain issue was also dealt with; a strike notice was issued to take effect from 21 January. Finally, on 18 January, a settlement *appeared* to have been reached, which removed the worst elements of the existing system. Players were to be transfer-listed if they refused the terms offered but, crucially, they now had to be paid an agreed rate while listed. The strike threat was lifted.

In fact, the battle to end the retain system was decidedly not over but, even at this stage, the PFA had made impressive gains. Obviously, the public relations skills that the Union demonstrated (and which the Football League singularly lacked) played a key role here. The decision to invite journalists to a mass meeting at Manchester in January so that they could sense the strength of feeling and witness the rejection of the offer of 9 January was a typically bold ploy. Again, the willingness of respected star players to back the Union was crucial. Stanley Matthews's support in particular gave the cause almost a national sanctity. The TUC's call to its members to boycott any games that should go ahead in the event of a strike (part of Guthrie's heritage, for he took the union into the TUC in 1955) was another important factor. Ultimately, though, the PFA's success rested on the broad public support that existed for the players' case, something that the Football League simply could not ignore.

It was not until 3 June 1961, and only after most League clubs had initially voted to reject the deal that their representatives had negotiated, that the League AGM voted to make a new offer which agreed to most of the players' demands. Crucially, however, they still refused to abolish the retain system and the dispute rumbled on. By the summer of 1961, strike action was no longer a serious possibility. The winter's militancy had largely evaporated, particularly among the star players who had quickly benefited from the abolition of the maximum wage. The focus now shifted to the law courts. The PFA had long been preparing a case, the origins of which actually preceded the battles of winter 1960–61.[50] In the summer of 1960, George Eastham, one of the country's most promising inside forwards, had walked out of football after failing to secure his release from Newcastle United. After a great deal of bad publicity, Newcastle eventually relented and, in November 1960, he joined Arsenal. The

PFA persuaded Eastham, for whom the issue was now effectively over, to allow his case to go forward as a test case to challenge the legitimacy of the retain and transfer system. It was June 1963 when the case finally reached court, but in the following month, Mr Justice Wilberforce, deeply impressed by the quality of the evidence put forward by PFA secretary Cliff Lloyd, declared that the system was 'an unjustifiable restraint of trade'. The PFA had now to force the League to acknowledge the judgement and act upon it. As ever, some voices within the League were far from willing, but wiser counsel eventually prevailed. In April 1964, a new system of contract was negotiated. While complete freedom of contract was not to arrive until 1978, the agreement reached vastly improved the players' situation. In essence, every contract was now to be freely negotiated, and was to contain agreed details of all bonuses and other benefits. Clubs were to have first option on the renewal of the contract at a no less advantageous rate. If clubs did not wish to exercise that option, they could grant a free transfer. Further renewals were, of course, possible. If a transfer took place, the contract was to be honoured until the transfer was complete. Disputes over contracts and transfer fees were to be dealt with by an independent tribunal.

The changes won between 1961 and 1964 were to have great significance, not just for the players, but for the game as a whole. For a few star players, this was the beginning of a road to truly spectacular wealth, although the full extent of this change was not yet fully realised. Fulham and England captain Johnny Haynes's £100 a week, granted almost as soon as the maximum was abolished, seems quite modest (7½ times the average manual wage) compared with the £15,000 a week (roughly 60 times the average) reputedly paid to a handful of leading players in 1995–96. Many clubs tried to operate unofficial maxima for a long period. Interestingly, two of the League's top sides, Liverpool and Manchester United, paid probably the lowest First Division wages in the early 1960s, Busby threatening to sack Denis Law in 1966 for asking for a substantial increase.[51] Nevertheless, such a revolution in earning capacity was to have a profound effect on football's economics, as will be demonstrated in the next chapter. The abolition of the maximum wage initially heralded little for the rank and file players. Indeed, many would have preferred a substantial raising of the maximum combined with unlimited bonuses, which would have spread earnings a little more evenly. Nevertheless, wages did rise, while the new contractual arrangements removed long-standing grievances. Even the most humble player had a hand in negotiating his contract, was paid at an agreed minimum at all times and was now very rarely held against his will.

The whole dispute underlines a number of points both about power relationships in football and about the culture of the male middle-class business community which ran the game. First, its resolution was a clear sign that significant shifts of power within the game could only come about through sustained action at an institutional level. One of the running themes of this book has concerned 'ownership' of the game and arguments have been noted that, for example, boisterous crowd behaviour or the 'culture of professionalism' can be seen as representing important 'symbolic' mechanisms for the capture of the game by the working class. While there may be validity in such arguments, the substantial and tangible shift towards the interests of the players described above was earned by a clear and organised challenge, by substance not symbols.

At the same time, the reaction of many club directors to the whole issue is extremely instructive. Obviously, it is not possible to characterise a whole class of individuals, but the clubs' attitude to industrial relations seemed to have been marked by a meanness of spirit and imagination. Individual boards operated a system whereby not only did they break the rules to protect their own interests and thus cheat on their fellow League members, but they also refused the reforms which would have removed the need for such dishonesty because those reforms would have weakened the overall powers of the directors vis-à-vis the players. It is not too fanciful to argue that football symbolised the world of industrial relations as the businessmen who largely ran the clubs would have liked it to be. It was one in which their word was law, in which outside bodies had little or no control and in which the labouring classes experienced reforms as gifts, not as rights. Similarly, rivals were only to be supported when mutual interests were threatened. Football was a microcosm of what society as a whole might have looked like without the influences of mass democracy and political and social reform. The problem for many professional footballers was that they had to inhabit the microcosm.

Football and society

In many ways the story of soccer's social and political significance up to the early 1960s is very much the same story as before. It continued to be a powerful vehicle for the expression of local identity in success and indeed, sometimes in failure. Preston North End's relegation from the

Blackburn celebrates its club's promotion from Division Two in 1958 with a civic reception, brass band included, which would have been recognisable to a late Victorian fan. (*Blackburn Public Library*)

First Division in 1961 was acknowledged by a mock funeral at nearby Bamber Bridge, where an estimated 30,000 people saw a coffin accompanied by two bands carried from a local pub to a corn mill and back. Blackburn Rovers fans entered into the spirit by sending a wreath of carrots, onions, cauliflowers and radishes.[52] In an age of generally full employment, the tensions between north and south were less marked than they had been in the 1930s and were to be again from the 1980s, but they could break through, particularly in areas where economic strength was less secure. This was demonstrated by local reaction to Gateshead's failure to win re-election to the Football League in 1960. The club, which had joined the League as South Shields in 1919 and changed name and location in 1930, was certainly rather harshly treated by its fellow League clubs. The end of the 1959–60 season saw them finish at the bottom of the attendance table, with an average of only 3,412, the seventh time in eight seasons they had finished among the four poorest-supported clubs. Their playing record, however, was far from disastrous, this being only the second time the club had applied for re-election. In fact, they garnered

Tom Finney's farewell speech at Deepdale, Preston, in April 1960. Finney's retirement and the manner of it, symbolized many of the changes that were transforming the professional game. (*Lancashire Evening Post*)

only 18 votes and were replaced by Midland League Peterborough. It is hard not to believe that the other clubs' dislike of lengthy trips for poor financial reward informed the vote. The *Newcastle Evening Chronicle*, although bitterly critical of the poor level of local support for the club, saw it as a conspiracy by 'a cosy clique of southern clubs', who, like the reluctant industrialists that the region was trying to attract, saw the north-east as 'up in the wilds'.[53]

The 1940s and '50s saw little debate over football's role in the structuring of political culture and class relationships, a demonstration of both the game's now secure place within English society, and the strength of faith in mass democracy in an age of full employment and consensus politics. Although there were individual complaints about the game's social impact, neither right nor left seems to have been threatened by it. That is not to say that the game did not continue to reflect and shape attitudes, and those seeking to extend the discussion over the game's political function could usefully pursue it into this period. Although I do not intend to investigate those arguments in detail here, it is interesting to consider one distinctive issue. Nicholas Fishwick has noted that from the 1930s, even those popular newspapers that were 'solidly conservative politically' were 'taking populist, anti-establishment stances when it came to football.'[54] Obviously, for many fans, attacks on administrators or directors remained exactly that, evidence of disputes and power struggles within the game. However, it is at least worth considering that press reporting and representation of these issues reflected or even influenced the wider political culture. Consumption, via the media, of arguments criticising the football establishment might have served as a substitute for radical political and industrial action; industrial and commercial elites were perhaps more easily challenged in the sporting than in the political and industrial context. At certain times, of course, 'sporting radicalism' might alternatively have fed into political radicalism, if indeed, such a phrase can really be applied to the mainstream political climate of this period. The PFA successes in 1961–64 can be viewed as a victory for 'progressive' forces over an established elite, and it is not inconceivable that the Labour Party benefited from the groundswell as they fought to defeat another apparently outmoded elite (albeit of a rather different social class) in the run-up to the 1964 election.

Epilogue

On 30 April 1960 27,000 people attended Preston's Deepdale ground to see Tom Finney's final appearance as a professional footballer. At the beginning the crowd sang 'Auld Lang Syne' and, at the close, Finney went to the centre circle and addressed the crowd over the public address system. The fans listened quietly, a number of them in tears.[55] These events symbolise the passing of an age in a number of ways. First, the whole style of the event, with the singing and the speech, belonged to a mode of civic culture and spectator behaviour that had emerged in the late nineteenth century and was coming to an end; it would have appeared anachronistic perhaps even by the late 1960s. Again, it demonstrated the strength of the bond that could grow between player and fans in the period before the abolition of the maximum wage, a point further reinforced by the letters of gratitude tinged with sadness that flooded into the local press. Certainly, Finney's exceptional talent earned him special affection and players at all levels of League football were to win enormous popularity among supporters in the years ahead. Nevertheless, here was a level of fan-player bonding that was rarely to be seen again. Perhaps most striking of all, Finney stayed with his home-town club for the whole of his career, despite the fact that, as a result, he failed to win a single domestic football honour. Admittedly, he did consider his future with the club on two occasions, while his local plumbing business (because of which Finney chose to remain on a semi-professional contract) provided another factor holding him to the town.[56] However, it is surely inconceivable that such loyalty could have been displayed by a leading footballer in the post-1961 climate. If Tom Finney had been born in 1942 rather than 1922, it is hard not to believe that he would have played most of his football with Everton, Liverpool or Manchester United.

7

The Glamour Game, 1961–1985

In social and economic terms, the timespan from 1961 to 1985 does not form a coherent block: fundamental changes in all aspects of English society somehow place a distance of far more than 24 years between the ages of Macmillan and Thatcher. In footballing terms, too, it could be argued that the late 1970s and early 1980s formed a distinct and often troubled period of its own. However, there is a certain neatness about this particular quarter century which makes it a useful focus. A new era was ushered in from 1961 by the changes in the game's economic structure following the abolition of the maximum wage and another foreshadowed as a result of the crisis that hit the game in the mid-1980s. This chapter is essentially concerned with those aspects of football's history that relate to the organisation, management and playing of the game in this period, while the following one concentrates upon relationships between the game and the wider society.

Running the game

Despite the many changes and problems facing professional football from the 1960s, the Football League remained remarkably static. Major reforms were certainly suggested. In 1961, the League's secretary, Alan Hardaker and president, Joe Richards, presented their 'Pattern for Football'.[1] Its main proposals included a League of 100 clubs, divided into five divisions of twenty, including two regional fourth divisions, and with a four-up, four-down promotion and relegation structure throughout. Automatic relegation faced any side seeking re-election twice in succession. Designed to increase spectator interest, and thus improve club finances (most sides would have remained in contention for promotion or relegation for a long period), to reduce costs for smaller clubs and to make the re-election procedure simpler and fairer, the plan proved too dramatic for some League chairmen. At the 1963 AGM it failed by just eight votes to win the necessary three-quarters majority, which was ironic given that the plan also included a proposal to reduce the necessary majority for change to two-thirds.

In 1968 the government-appointed committee headed by Sir Norman Chester, Warden of Nuffield College, Oxford, found that the fruits of their two-year deliberations were equally unattractive to the League's chairmen. A restructuring of the League coupled with an emphasis on community involvement and the need for salaried directors featured among the committee's proposals. Fifteen years later, Chester was persuaded to head another committee, this time convened by the League itself, but once again its major recommendations were rejected.[2] Implementing major change was clearly difficult, rendered so by a peculiar mixture of institutional opposition to external criticism, a refusal to acknowledge current and potential problems and genuine respect for existing structures and traditions. When 'restructuring' next took centre stage in 1985, supporters of a break-away 'Super League' could hardly be blamed for cloaking their own and their clubs' ambitions in the language of a radicalism born of long and deep frustration with the League's conservatism.

The changes that did occur were largely piecemeal. The 1960–61 season saw the introduction of the League Cup, a competition suggested originally by Hardaker in the late 1950s partly as a compensation for the reduction in League matches which would result from the 'Pattern for Football' scheme, partly to encourage loyalty to the League in the face of clubs' appetite for floodlit friendlies. It was initially greeted with something less than enthusiasm, with many leading clubs refusing to take part, a situation which helped Second Division Rotherham reach the first (two-legged) final and Fourth Division Rochdale the second. By the later 1960s, however, it was gaining acceptability, a process completed by the decision to make the final a single match played at Wembley; the first Wembley final added further appeal when Third Division Queens Park Rangers beat First Division West Bromwich in 1967. A number of other tournaments were added over the period, but few lasted save the Third and Fourth Division cup competition instituted as the Associate Members Cup in 1983–84. Constantly renamed as a result of sponsorship deals (it was the Auto Windscreens Shield in the 1995–96 season), its early games have often drawn derisory attendances but the Wembley final has proved a hugely popular and profitable event.

The reform of the re-election procedure gradually moved forward over the period. Although four sides, Bradford Park Avenue (1970), Barrow (1972), Workington (1977) and Southport (1978) were voted out, the League was increasingly sensitive to claims that the procedures discriminated against non-League clubs.[3] Nevertheless, despite reforms introduced in 1977, designed to place the strongest non-League applicants before the League AGM, no League club lost its fight for re-election after 1978. More importantly, from its formation in 1979 the new Alliance Premier League (later the Gola League and currently the GM Vauxhall Conference) was effectively treated as a fifth division, although it was not until 1987 that automatic promotion and relegation between the League and its feeder was established, thus introducing a genuine pyramid structure.[4]

Other changes were scattered across the period. One of the most popular was the introduction of substitutes in 1965, initially restricted to one per side and only to be used in cases of injury. One of the least popular came at the very end of the period when in 1981, the Football League allowed the use of plastic pitches. Only four clubs took up the option and the last one was removed in 1993.[5] A further set of reforms was mainly designed to encourage increased attendance. A three-up, three-down promotion system was adopted from 1973, while the 1981–82 season saw the introduction of three points for a win, believed to be a stimulus to attacking football. A similar motive had underpinned the replacement, from 1976, of goal average by goal difference when deciding the divisional placing of teams tied on the same number of points. The introduction of the three-up, three-down system led to the greatest level of mobility between divisions that the League had ever seen. While seeking to take nothing away from their remarkable achievement, Swansea City's rise from Fourth to First Division in five seasons from 1977–78 was the result of a third place in both Third and Second Divisions, while alternatively, Bristol City's plunge from First to Fourth in consecutive seasons between 1980 and 1982 was precipitated by their occupation of the third First Division relegation place. Many of the sides forced to endure the single club promotion system of the Third Division South and North for over thirty years could have been forgiven for wondering what might have been and none more so than Accrington Stanley, forced to resign from the League with debts of £62,000 in March 1962, yet Third Division North runners-up as recently as 1955 and 1958.

The FA, for its part, continued to shed some of its Victorian intellectual heritage. Sunday football was given its blessing in 1960 and a cup tournament established for Sunday amateur sides in 1964–65. In early 1974, FA Cup and League games were allowed to be played on Sundays as a short-term expedient to help clubs cope with the disruption caused by the 'three-day week' that resulted from a conflict between the government and power-workers and miners. It was not until February 1981 that the FA officially sanctioned Sunday Football League fixtures and a further two years before FA Cup ties could be played on the Sabbath. The FA was also increasingly inclined to accommodate the women's game. In response to pressure from European football's governing body, UEFA, a joint consultative committee of the FA and the newly formed Women's FA was established to oversee certain aspects of the women's game in 1972.[6] Most strikingly, in 1974, the FA ended the distinction between amateur and professional, finally abandoning the hopeless task of trying to police the payments made by nominally amateur sides.[7]

Significantly, the FA and the League continued to enjoy an often tense relationship. Some of this stemmed from the clash of strong personalities, notably those of Hardaker and Rous.[8] However, there were genuine differences, both between the leading protagonists and their organisations. The unwillingness of clubs to release players for England international duty was a constant source of irritation to Rous and the FA. Hardaker, on the other hand, found Rous's arguments for a European 'super league' both threatening and unconvincing, while FA directives often angered League members. Indeed, in 1964–65, 87 League clubs threatened to leave the FA after being asked to ensure that their amateur players were paid nothing beyond legitimate travelling expenses. That such a relatively minor issue drew such a dramatic response is indicative of how much bad feeling existed. The FA withdrew their request but another stone had been laid in the path that eventually led to the rupture of 1991.[9]

The game

By the mid-1960s, the first real generation of modern 'tracksuit' managers and their coaches were now firmly in control of events on the pitch and their influence led to significant changes in the way the game was played. England's success in the 1966 World Cup using a 4–3–3 line-up gave managers and coaches a model which many adopted for some years. By the 1980s styles ranged considerably from the possession-oriented passing game used to great effect by Liverpool, to the various 'long-ball' games whereby the ball was delivered into the opposition penalty area as rapidly as possible.

From the early 1960s, football became ever more concerned with defensive strategies. The period from about 1955 to 1962 had been notable for the number of high-scoring sides. In 1956–57, Tottenham and Manchester United became the first First Division sides since 1936–37 to score over 100 goals in a League season, a feat which was repeated on eleven more occasions in the next five seasons. Wolves scored over 100 goals in four successive seasons from 1957–58 to 1960–61. The following table charts the subsequent decline of goal-scoring.

Table 3. *Goal-scoring in First Division, 1960–76*

Season	*Champions*	*Goals scored*	*No. of other sides scoring more than 70 goals*
1960–61	Tottenham	115	14
1961–62	Ipswich	93	12
1962–63	Everton	84	10
1963–64	Liverpool	92	11
1964–65	Man. United	89	8
1965–66	Liverpool	79	7
1966–67	Man. United	84	6
1967–68	Man. City	86	6
1968–69	Leeds	66	2
1969–70	Everton	72	2
1970–71	Arsenal	71	1
1971–72	Derby	69	2
1972–73	Liverpool	72	1
1973–74	Leeds	66	0
1974–75	Derby	67	0
1975–76	Liverpool	66	2

This trend was repeated throughout the League. No side scored 100 goals between 1966–67, when Third Division Queens Park Rangers managed 103, and 1975–76, when Lincoln City won the Fourth Division with 111. The 1975–76 season was to be something of a turning point in this regard and by 1985–86 Liverpool could score 89 goals in winning the championship, with four other First Division sides scoring more than 70 goals. However, goal-scoring levels were never again to reach those of the period 1955–62. In this sense, the game had changed for good.

It is hardly surprising that the new generation of managers and coaches emphasised the importance of improved defensive strategy, a central tenet in many club philosophies from about the 1965–66 season.[10] Their analyses of performance data offered considerable evidence that League position depended ultimately on defensive rather than attacking qualities, a point

Peterborough United in 1961. Elected to the Fourth Division from the Midland League in 1960, they won the title at the first attempt, setting a League record for any division by scoring 134 goals. Terry Bly (back row, second from right) scored 52 of them. (*Football Association*)

underlined in spectacular fashion by Newcastle United, relegated in 1961 despite scoring 86 goals.[11] 'Modern' football emerged at the point when a First Division team knew that it could no longer win 10–4 at home only to lose subsequent away game 2–5 and 0–4, as Spurs contrived to do in autumn 1958. A series of tactical shifts resulted, demanding that virtually all players tackled opponents and denied them space in midfield. The inevitable corollary was the emergence of the 4–3–3, 4–4–2 and 4–5–1 systems which imposed limits on both sides' attacking options. Ultra-defensive methods were most commonly adopted in away matches where they negated home advantage; few managers were prepared to risk alienating their own support by using such methods to any extent on home soil. All this is not necessarily to say that soccer was a worse game, although some defensive exhibitions could be painful to watch. It was, though, a very different one and it bore the stamp of highly professional planning, training and discipline.

From the late 1950s there was much discussion of the 'spirit' in which the game was being played. Many observers claimed that, as financial rewards rose, so players became more 'cynical', more prone to challenge referees, to waste time, steal distance at free kicks and indulge in deliberate petty fouling. The decline in goal-scoring was also often cited as evidence for their case by those arguing that the game had lost direction. The age of 'gamesmanship, the art of cheating fairly', was, so it was claimed, upon us.[12] Gamesmanship, even if it could be satisfactorily defined, can rarely be *measured* in any reliable way, rendering the necessary comparison across time virtually impossible.[13] It should be stressed that it had always been present in some form. A journalist reporting the 1928 Cup final praised a Blackburn Rovers full back for 'his long kicking, his sure tackling and his efforts to waste time when Huddersfield were fighting for the equaliser.'[14] The nature of the timewasting is not made explicit, but the tone of the report, which does not appear to have been ironic, suggests that it was deemed a fair tactic in a crisis. Many whose work in football spanned the period from the 1920s to the 1960s did, however, believe that 'sharp practice' had largely come 'with the new generation'.[15] If this was the case, it does suggest interesting changes both within the game and in English society. Stephen Wagg has claimed that from the 1950s, as life in general 'came to be seen in more competitive terms' and as British business dropped 'much of its pretence to gentlemanliness', football followed suit. He further suggests that the new technocratic vocabulary of the 'professional' doing his 'job' justified these breaks in the spirit, and sometimes the letter, of the law.[16]

Whatever the validity of this interpretation, a more positive reading can be offered. It is also possible that the new professional ethic led to a different attitude towards violent play. We are in very subjective terrain here and largely dependent on the later memories of pre-war players whose testimony is prone to colourful exaggeration. Harry Storer, for example, a notorious 'hard-man' of the 1930s, was reported by a colleague as suggesting that the 'dirty players of today should be wearing brassieres'.[17] However, the claim was regularly made in the 1950s and 1960s that really dangerous play had declined. The rise of gamesmanship was perhaps a response from a new generation of professionals who respected their colleagues too much to allow the excessive use of dangerous foul play, and sought compensation in other methods.

There can be little doubt that the game became less overtly physical. Statistical evidence would at first sight suggest otherwise, with the number of sendings-off and cautions in professional matches rising from 942 in 1970–71 to 3,968 by 1981–82. However, such figures are as much an index of shifting attitudes among the game's administrators as they are an objective measurement of wrongdoing. This is demonstrated by the enormous increase in punishments in particular seasons, as the League and the FA sought to respond to specific, highly publicised incidents. In 1972–73, for example, the number of cautions increased by 27 per cent as a result of a clamp-down on the sliding tackle, while a campaign against the 'professional foul' in 1982–83 led to a 36 per cent increase in sendings-off.[18] Rather than players becoming more violent, the parameters of what constituted acceptable behaviour were altering as the game fell ever more under critical public scrutiny. It is also quite possible that refereeing styles were altering. In an age in which many commentators demanded clear public displays of discipline in all public arenas and where, in the football world, links between violence on and off the pitch were always likely to be made, officials were forced to adopt a more 'formal' approach. In this instance, social forces as well and perhaps as much as sporting ones dictated footballing style.

Football's geography

The Football League almost completed its gradual colonisation of England in the 1960s and '70s. Three counties gained their first ever League representatives as Oxford United, Cambridge United and Hereford United replaced, respectively, Accrington Stanley (1962), Bradford Park Avenue (1970) and Barrow (1972). The other two entrants in this period, Wimbledon (1977) and Wigan Athletic (1978) came from rather less propitious areas in terms of potential growth, the former sandwiched between Fulham and Crystal Palace, the latter rooted in a Rugby League stronghold.

The key issues to be discussed here, however, relate to the geography of success and failure. What follows is an examination of two prominent features of the period from 1961, the increasing strength of southern teams and the dominance of big city sides. The oft-heralded 'rise of the south' has been a major point of discussion in this book, and in some ways the later part of the period under review provides evidence which demonstrates its existence in fact rather than assertion. The following table illustrates the geographical structure of the First Division between 1960–61 and 1987–88, the season in which southern and metropolitan representation reached its zenith.

Table 4. *Geographical location of First Division clubs, 1960–88*

	1960–61	1968–69	1978–79	1987–88
East Anglia	0	1	2	1
Textile Lancashire	5	1	1	1
London	5	5	4	8 *
Manchester	2	2	2	1
Merseyside	1	2	2	2
Midlands	6	6	7	3
North-east	1	2	1	1
Southern	0	1	1	4
Wales	1	0	0	0
West	0	0	1	0
Yorkshire	1	2	1	1

* Includes Watford

Since the Second World War, clubs from London and the south had usually comprised about 30 per cent of the First Division's strength, but from the 1980s, this figure rose to 50–60 per cent. At first sight this important shift appears to fit conveniently with a simple economic model of the period, emphasising the strength of the southern economy in comparison with much of the rest of the country. However, it is not entirely clear just how this increase in First Division representation connects with southern economic success. A number of the sides that rose from the lower divisions in the late 1970s and 1980s appear to have secured at least some of the necessary finance from imported directors and chairmen or from a single local figure rather than from a general attraction of capital from the wider local business community. Elton John's money certainly helped Watford rise from the Fourth Division in 1977–78 to second place in the First in 1982–83, while Robert Maxwell, having saved Oxford United from near bankruptcy in 1982, used his money to help the club move from the Third to First Divisions in consecutive seasons from 1983–84. At the same time, few of the new southern arrivals in Division One succeeded in attracting particularly big crowds; hence it is not possible to speak of clubs making rapid progress because of wealth generated at the turnstiles by an economically buoyant local population. It may well be the case that southern clubs, located as they were in closer proximity to convenient sources of capital, tended to have an easier time raising money than their northern counterparts. Economic advantages might also have been translated into cultural ones: London and the south perhaps proved a more attractive location for players than some northern destinations. However, clear links between a general southern prosperity and the rise of its football teams are hard to secure. Only a detailed club-by-club analysis, focusing not only on social and economic issues but on such things as the quality of scouting networks, and, in particular, examining whether southern clubs had an especial ability to draw on the emerging pool of black players, will reveal the roots of these changes.

In terms of actual playing success at the highest level, northern and to a lesser extent midland clubs still tended to dominate the game. Admittedly, southern clubs enjoyed considerable cup success. Extending the period under review a little, between 1960 and 1995 the FA Cup went south of Birmingham on 17 occasions and the League Cup on 9.[19] In the sterner test of the Football League championship, however, only Arsenal (1971, 1989, 1991) Ipswich (1962) and Tottenham (1961) were successful. Moreover, many of the southern sides obtaining or regaining First Division status since the 1970s have either not held it for long (Brighton, Charlton,

Although never able to win a major honour in the 1950s, Preston North End were one of a number of Lancashire clubs able to compete at the highest level. Here, Tom Finney scores in a First Division game at Deepdale. (*Lancashire Evening Post*)

Millwall, Oxford, Portsmouth, Watford), have oscillated between the First and Second Division (Crystal Palace, Luton) or have largely survived, but have only occasionally threatened or achieved major success (Queens Park Rangers, Southampton, Wimbledon). Football's power has ultimately continued to lie somewhere further north.

The second glaring fact of the post-1961 period has been the dominance of big city at the expense of small town clubs. Between 1962 (Ipswich) and 1995 (Blackburn), no side representing a town with a population of below 200,000 won the championship: Jack Walker's massive financial investment in Blackburn, of course, makes them highly untypical of other so-called 'town' clubs. Indeed, only two towns with populations of below 300,000, Derby and Nottingham, saw championship success in the same period. More fundamentally, not only have town clubs failed to win major honours, they have generally failed even to compete at elite level. This point is well illustrated by the fate of the five Lancashire clubs, Blackburn, Blackpool, Bolton, Burnley and Preston, that were in the First Division in 1960. The table offers a snapshot of their respective positions immediately before the abolition of the maximum wage and in the mid-1980s.

Table 5. *Some Lancashire 'town' football clubs, 1958–85*

	Season	*League position*	*Average attendance*
Bolton	1958–59	4th, First Division	27,659
	1984–85	17th, Third Division	4,951
Blackburn	1958–59	10th, First Division	30,544
	1984–85	5th, Second Division	9,648
Blackpool	1958–59	8th, First Division	20,860
	1984–85	2nd, Fourth Division	4,907
Burnley	1958–59	7th, First Division	23,733
	1984–85	21st, Third Division	4,117
Preston	1958–59	12th, First Division	22,435
	1984–85	23rd, Third Division	3,793

The 1985–86 season saw Preston finish 91st and they were forced to apply for re-election. Even more dramatically, in the 1986–87 season only a victory in Burnley's final game stopped the Lancashire club from earning the doubtful honour of being the first side to suffer automatic demotion to the Vauxhall Conference. Interestingly, Burnley's plight seemed to shock many people into a realisation of just how seriously threatened the county's deeply rooted soccer culture was. Over 13,000 people attended Burnley's crucial last match and the whole saga helped spark a revival in Lancashire

Burnley play Orient (light shirts) in May 1987, needing a victory to avoid relegation from the Football League. The club's plight helped focus attention on the problems of 'town' clubs in the north of England. (*Halifax Courier*)

soccer in the following years, fuelled to no small extent by a revived sense and awareness of tradition.

This, however, is to run ahead. The decline of these clubs was not quite as constant or as steady as this simple table suggests. It is also obviously the case that not all of the clubs suffered equally, or at the same time. Burnley won the championship in 1960, were runners-up in the FA Cup and League the next year and their youth development policy kept them an intermittently effective force until the mid-1970s, when financial over-extension on ground development precipitated a rapid and perilous decline. Blackburn Rovers, on the other hand, avoided the extreme fortunes of their neighbours, spending most of the period in the Second Division. Such variations also question the often-made assumptions positing a strong link between the decline of the Lancashire cotton industry and the decline of Lancashire football. While local industrial decline hardly helped, it is probable that factors mainly specific to football, rather than the general economic climate, were central here.

As has been demonstrated in Chapter 2, population differentials have always had some bearing on patterns of soccer success. However, once football's economic structure had been transformed by the abolition of the maximum wage and the wholesale reform of the retain system, the size of the population base required to attain that success increased considerably. Big city clubs had always enjoyed an advantage in this area, but it was far less valuable in an age of controlled wages and tied labour. In a free market, they reigned supreme. Their potential support base was the rock on which secure finance and thus playing success could be built. Clubs from the middle-sized Lancashire towns (and elsewhere) were able to survive for much of the sixties on an accumulated capital of historic achievement, which kept attendances buoyant and proved attractive to many players. However, from the late sixties and seventies, ease of transport to nearby Manchester and Liverpool, combined with the ever growing gap between the playing records of city and small town clubs, accelerated the loss of support. Smaller clubs were trapped in a spiral of decline. Once they began to slide into the Third and Fourth Divisions, the consequent collapse in attendances made the gap between the town and city clubs impossible to bridge. The once great names of English football were increasingly simply nurseries for wealthier clubs. Only the arrival of very wealthy benefactors could change this situation.

So far, the phrase 'big city club' has been used very loosely, and in a way that perhaps carries the implication that size of population alone guarantees success. It is instructive to examine the term more closely. First, 'big city' is defined here, rather arbitrarily, to denote places with populations of above 400,000, namely (alongside London) Birmingham, Liverpool, Sheffield, Manchester, Leeds and Bristol.[20] Even the briefest of surveys demonstrates the obvious point that not all clubs from big cities have been 'big' clubs in recent decades. Bristol has indeed failed to produce a major side. The strength of the rugby tradition in the area, the fact that fan loyalties are split between two sides in a city where the population is perhaps not quite large enough to sustain such a division, the city's slightly isolated position, which might make it harder to attract and retain players – all these factors have contributed to Bristol's 'underachievement' as a football city.

Similarly, a number of London clubs rooted in suburban or what were once somewhat isolated working-class districts have never really established themselves as leading sides. Crystal Palace, Fulham, Brentford and Millwall all fall into this category.

Most interesting of all is the fact that even a number of city sides that have spent long periods in the First Division since the 1960s and which are thought of as 'big' clubs actually have remarkably limited records of achievement. The reality is that only a very small number of big city sides have been consistently successful in the post-maximum era. The following table, obtained by 'awarding' clubs two points for winning one of the three major domestic trophies and one for being runner-up, illustrates this forcibly.

Table 6. *Success in major domestic tournaments, 1960–61 to 1994–95*

1.	Liverpool	59
2.	Manchester United	34
3.	Arsenal	23
4.	Tottenham	21
	Everton	21
6.	Leeds	18
7.	Nottingham Forest	14
	Aston Villa	14
9.	Manchester City	11
10.	West Ham	8
11.	Chelsea	7
12.	Ipswich	6
	Leicester	6
	Norwich	6
	Sheffield Wednesday	6
	West Bromwich Albion	6

Clearly, some sides with huge potential derived from both actual and possible support base simply have not been able to fulfil this potential. Chelsea, probably professional football's greatest underachievers, Sheffield Wednesday and perhaps even Aston Villa, despite their championship and European Cup successes in 1980–81 and 1981–82, might all have expected to have achieved rather more than they have done. So, too, might sides who do not even appear on this list, most notably Birmingham City, winners of a solitary League Cup title in 1963, and Sheffield United, whose last major honour came with the FA Cup in 1925.

All this raises fundamental questions about the exact ingredients for modern football success. Why should Liverpool, Manchester United and Arsenal be so much more successful than, for example, Chelsea, Sheffield Wednesday and Manchester City, clubs with which they would seem to share many of the same social, demographic and economic advantages? Simple weight of historical tradition seems to have played a vital role. With the exception of Leeds United, and to a lesser extent Tottenham,

Tottenham Hotspur players celebrate their 5–1 victory over Atletico Madrid in the 1963 European Cup Winners Cup final which made the club the first English team to win a European tournament. (*Football Association*)

the most successful teams of the post-1961 period have long traditions of success, dating back to the pre-1914 period in the case of Liverpool, Everton and Manchester United, and the 1930s in the case of Arsenal. The resultant sense of a club's 'greatness', which combines an almost mystical allure with the realistic expectation that these are clubs which are likely to continue to experience success, has proved a powerful incentive for the attachment of fans and the recruitment of players. On the other hand, once-powerful or potentially powerful big city clubs which have experienced long periods without consistent success (Aston Villa, Chelsea, Sheffield United, Sheffield Wednesday, Manchester City) have generally maintained fan loyalty, but have not always been able to recruit or hold key managers and players. Their success since 1961 has thus been either very limited or, as in the case of Manchester City between 1967 and 1971 and Chelsea from 1965 to 1972, confined to a relatively short period.

The crucial ingredient, however, remains the ability of individual managers and coaching staffs to get the best results from their players. Population-base, money and tradition are important factors but on their own they are not enough to guarantee success. As any fan is aware, managers can literally make, re-make or break a club. Four (very different) managerial records stand out in this period. Matt Busby's reign at Manchester United from 1945–69 saw the building of three separate championship-winning sides. The famed Liverpool dynasty, embracing Bill Shankly, Bob Paisley, Joe Fagan and Kenny Dalglish, brought the club unrivalled and continous success between 1959 and 1991. Don Revie succeeded in forcing Leeds United into the game's elite, an achievement for which he has not always been given due recognition. Perhaps most striking of all was the success of Brian Clough in taking Derby County in 1972, and then Nottingham Forest in 1978, to championship honours. Clough's record in becoming only the second manager after Herbert Chapman to take two different clubs to the League championship is all the more remarkable because, in this age of big city/elite club dominance, it was achieved with essentially unfashionable clubs. The importance of managerial expertise is further illustrated by the high turnover of managers used over the period by less successful city clubs as they searched impatiently for results, statistics which make an interesting commentary on the boardrooms at some clubs. While Liverpool had only six managers between 1959 and 1995 and Manchester United and Arsenal seven, Aston Villa had thirteen, Chelsea and Sheffield Wednesday had fourteen and Manchester City sixteen.

Players

By the 1970s perhaps as many as 1.5 million boys and men played football at some level or another. As ever, though, only the tiniest fraction had the ability, dedication and good fortune to become League professionals. As the recession gripped Britain in the early 1980s and clubs shed labour in an attempt to cut costs, that fraction became smaller than ever, with an all-time low of only 1,575 players registered with League clubs in 1983 compared with 4,000 in the boom years of the late 1940s.[21] The Conservative government's Youth Training Scheme (YTS), introduced in 1983, and bitterly criticised in many quarters as a mechanism for the delivery of cheap labour and social control rather than useful training, actually proved invaluable in this climate. Unable to afford traditional apprenticeship schemes, most clubs made enthusiastic use of YTS trainees. Whereas in 1983 the 24 Fourth Division sides could boast only 33 apprentices between them, by 1989 Crewe Alexandra alone had 21 trainees. The PFA claimed that 50–60 per cent of YTS trainees went on to gain full contracts, including among their number future stars such as Paul Gascoigne, David Platt and Matthew Le Tissier.[22]

The majority of players continued to be drawn from working-class backgrounds, and the 'traditional' areas of recruitment continued to provide an especially significant share of the professional football community.[23] Although labour restrictions controlled the number of foreign players in English football, a small but influential number did arrive from the late 1970s, most notably the Argentinians Osvaldo Ardiles and Ricky Villa, who joined Tottenham in July 1978. By October 1978 PFA pressure had persuaded the government to provide work permits only to those who were 'established' performers.[24] This regulation and the failure of some of the imported players to establish themselves delayed the mass arrival of the overseas player for another twenty years.

One of the most striking features of the period was the gradual emergence of black players in English football. There had been a marginal but almost continuous black presence from the earliest days. West African athlete Arthur Wharton, played for Preston as an FA Cup goalkeeper in the 1886–87 season, and later for Rotherham Town. His successors included Walter Tull of Tottenham and Northampton, who was killed in action in the First World War; Jack Leslie of Plymouth Argyle, a prominent player in the 1920s and 30s; and in the 1950s, Roy Brown, Lindy Delapenha and Charlie Williams.[25] Their colour was a source of interest to journalists who invariably lapsed into language that reflected and reinforced contemporary stereotypes of Afro-Caribbean habits, culture and physique. In 1953, for example, *Soccer Star* referred to Delapenha, then playing for Middlesbrough, as 'lithe like a snake . . . the coffee-coloured king of the wing' whose play was blessed with the 'spirit of the calypso'. Interestingly, a recent club historian remembers him more prosaically as 'stocky and particularly effective in the rough and tumble around the penalty area.'[26] In such a context, the trickle of black players entering the game in the 1960s carried a great burden, for any failings perceived in their play tended to be translated into criticism of black players in particular and black temperaments in general. The supposed inconsistency of West Ham's

Bradford City's Cec Podd in 1971. Born in St. Kitts, he was one of the first of the new generation of black players that emerged in the English game in the 1970s. (*Bradford Telegraph and Argus*)

Bermudan forward Clyde Best, and the belief that Leeds United's black South African winger Albert Johanneson lacked fighting spirit, are key cases in point.[27]

By the early 1970s, the first significant number of black players born or raised in Britain as the children of post-1945 immigrants began to establish themselves in professional football. Their emergence was underscored by England's selection of defender Viv Anderson in 1978, the first black player to be thus honoured. They were, and remain, drawn almost exclusively from Afro-Caribbean backgrounds, Ricky Heppolette, an Anglo-Asian who played for Preston, Orient and Peterborough in the

1960s and 1970s being almost the only exception. A complex network of factors involving both the values of the various south Asian communities and white perceptions of those communities has held back the development of an Asian professional football tradition.[28] The Afro-Caribbean community, however, proved a fertile source of players from the 1970s and provided approximately 15 per cent of English League professionals by 1995. These players have usually been nurtured by clubs in London and the midlands. Although the Afro-Caribbean community was increasingly well represented in English professional football from the late 1970s, it is still possible to see evidence of stereotypical attitudes towards their skills and commitment retarding their progress. One important study has demonstrated that as late as 1990, black players were far more likely to be found in the First rather than the lower Divisions, a feature which suggests that aspiring black players have to be especially good to be noticed. Moreover, the study also notes that they were most frequently found in playing positions associated with speed and mobility rather than thought and concentration.[29]

The racial tensions in British society were rather less subtly displayed on the terraces from the 1970s. Against the background of a rise in the influence of the far right and an unstable economic climate, black players emerged in sufficient numbers for them to be perceived by some fans as a threat rather than a novelty. The classic pattern saw black players attain popularity with their own supporters, often rendered conveniently 'colour-blind', but being subjected to a variety of taunts and abuse away from home. Players coped in their own ways, with some of the 1970s generation defusing tension by, albeit often reluctantly, conniving with a slightly jokey acknowledgement of their presence. This saw, for example, West Bromwich Albion players Laurie Cunningham, Cyrille Regis and Brendon Batson collude with manager Ron Atkinson's description of them as the 'Three Degrees', a reference to a black pop trio of the period.[30] While most managers picked players on merit and the PFA along with a number of clubs and supporters' groups worked hard to combat the problem, the existence of serious racial abuse was rarely acknowledged by the game's authorities or by much of the media. Brendon Batson, a PFA official from 1984, noted that TV commentators often studiously ignored the abuse only too audible to viewers at home.[31] It was only in 1993, by which time black players along with an increasing number of European and South American players were a significant element within the game, and football was working overtime to foster a respectable image, that a sustained national anti-racist campaign was launched.[32] Significantly, even then the main thrust came from the Campaign for Racial Equality and the PFA. There are, of course, positive notes to be sounded. Outside of their often considerable footballing achievements, black players have served as crucial role models for younger black generations, and their presence in many English sides has probably helped contribute to the less often noted process whereby many white people have quietly come to terms with the realities of a multi-cultural society.

Irrespective of race, colour or creed, professional footballers experienced considerably improved financial rewards in this period. As well as the benefits which accrued from the abolition of the maximum wage in 1961, the players' bargaining position and earning potential increased yet further in April 1978, when something very close to freedom of contract was established.[33] Much of our available information refers only to *basic* wages and does not illustrate the often substantial additions to income generated by testimonials, bonuses and transfer fee shares, or measure the value of the sponsored cars, clothing and other goods and services which players often enjoyed. Within these limitations, the evidence suggests that all players benefited considerably from the changes in the contractual system, but that pre-existing differentials between star players and the rest grew ever wider. This process became apparent immediately the maximum wage was abolished, as the table below illustrates.

Table 7. *First team players' average annual earnings (estimated) 1960–64*[34]

	1960	*1961*	*1964*	*% increased, 1960–64*
First Div.	1,173	1,540	2,680	56
Second Div.	1,093	1,132	2,003	45
Third Div.	1,034	1,130	1,475	29
Fourth Div.	937	965	1,304	28

These differentials were maintained across the period. Statistics gathered in 1983 suggested that a significant minority of all First Division footballers earned more than £15,000 a year, while only 36 out of the Fourth Division's 497 players earned more than £10,000, with many earning well below that. In terms of the relationship between footballers' wages and those of the community in general, differentials widened very considerably in the players' favour, at least for those in the top two divisions. In 1983, the average gross earnings for a male manual worker were £140 a week (£7,280 a year) and for non-manual male workers, £190 a week (£9,932 a year). The general level of reward, though, was not as spectacular as was sometimes assumed. In 1985, 70 per cent of all players earned below £15,000, a salary at that time earned by, for example, some headteachers, senior academics and established members of the medical profession; 90 per cent of players earned under £20,000.[35] All but a few of the best paid First Division players were moving into a very comfortable middle-class lifestyle and not into the super-rich bracket.

The reward for the leading players could be enormous. The level of wage increases in the immediate post-maximum period varied from club to club. Fulham and England captain, Johnny Haynes, became the country's first £100 per week player in January 1961, thus trebling his wages overnight. However, Haynes was a big star at a small club, and chairmen with large star contingents could not afford to be as generous as Fulham's Tommy Trinder. As late as 1965–66, for example, most Manchester United stars were earning £50 a week.[36] The momentum for high wages in fact became stronger in the 1970s and 1980s. High earnings made in the game, of course, show only a part of the picture. With opportunities for work in advertising and the media burgeoning, and high earnings providing the launchpad for business ventures, a number of players could, even by the late 1960s, earn more in two or three season than many had earned in a long career before 1961.[37] Some established fairly traditional business ventures, others, notably George Best, invested in clubs and boutiques and developed a lifestyle hitherto more closely associated with pop singers or film stars. Some succeeded in holding on to or increasing their earnings, others, for a variety of reasons, proved less successful. In the late 1980s, John Charles, who had admittedly earned much of his money in Italy, found it necessary to accept the proceeds from a charity match in order to help clear debts, while Albert Johanneson died penniless in a Leeds council flat in 1995, his later life dogged by drink problems.

Improvement in material conditions was also accompanied by an enhanced status within the wider public domain. Stanley Matthews was knighted in 1965, Alf Ramsay in 1966 and Matt Busby in 1969, the first footballing knights to be drawn from anywhere other than the game's administration.[38] A reasonably generous allocation of OBEs, CBEs and other minor honours were also granted to leading internationals and long-serving players. Recognition was granted rather more frequently through the magazine features, modelling engagements and TV and radio appearances which increasingly supplemented the long-established news-

Stanley Matthews, with daughter and wife, receives a C.B.E. in 1957. Honours began to accrue to professional footballers for the first time from this point. (*Football Association*)

paper reportage and post-match interviews. Players were often photographed or filmed in the company of figures from show business, thus helping to make footballers 'personalities' in their own right, while the line between sport and show business was blurred by the development of TV shows like the BBC's *Quiz Ball* in the 1960s and the recording of pop songs by the national and leading club sides. Most of these songs, such as the England World Cup squad's 1970 number one hit 'Back Home', Chelsea's 'Blue is the Colour' (1972) or Tottenham's 'Ossie's Dream' (1981), were thunderous chorus songs in the tradition of 'Roll out the barrel', which allowed players to enjoy a little fun and notoriety without burdening them with artistic pretension, or stripping them of the cheery laddishness that was still seen as the essence of footballing culture. While clubs and the media were anxious to promote a good public image by publicising the presence in the game of graduate footballers such as Steve Heighway, Brian Hall and Steve Coppell, the footballer as sophisticate was not one of the preferred public relations options.[39]

One small but significant example of the footballer's rising status is provided by the approach to player biography in football programmes. Programmes became far more substantial in the later 1960s and as editors sought to fill the extra pages, they increasingly moved away from viewing footballers as mere athletic specimens. Until the early 1960s, players, and visiting players in particular, were often described in the language of a livestock show. Geographical origin, height, weight, position and other interesting characteristics relating to special skills were the main things deemed to be of interest. From the later 1960s and certainly by the 1970s, home players were the subject of question and answer biographies which focused on their taste in music, food, women, films and so on. Visiting players were rarely the object of such detailed attention, but they became a little more than mere bundles of vital statistics.

Clearly, there were moments when the general improvement in the players' image was threatened. The uncovering of a match-fixing ring in 1965, which saw ten players including three England internationals imprisoned and banned from the game for life, was hardly a good advert, especially as it was apparent that the problem went back several years and probably involved many others who were not brought to account.[40] Nevertheless, scandal was hardly unknown in football's history, or indeed, in public life in general, especially in the 1960s, and the damage was limited.

All these changes must have restructured relationships between players and their public to some extent. Fans had long stopped meeting their heroes on tram rides to the ground, but as players moved into more 'desirable' housing areas and as more of their meetings with fans took place via the media, a certain distance inevitably resulted. The nature of the fan-player relationship ultimately depended on the individual concerned. Liverpool captain Phil Thompson's decision in 1981 to take the European Cup to his local pub rather than to the ground where the nation's press awaited showed that the warmest of personal links could still exist.[41] Stephen Wagg, who has pioneered the sociology of the modern player, sees the changes in relationship as truly far-reaching, arguing that through their public utterances and autobiographies, leading players have 'become standard bearers for the new consumer capitalism, catapulted, many of them, far from their working-class origins into the wide, blue, new-bourgeois yonder and sending back scraps of simple, commercialist dogma for their public to feed on.'[42] Certainly, many players were projected as powerful role models for an acquisitive, consumerist lifestyle.

This has been a key function for the entertainer from at least the nineteenth century, but has become of greater significance than ever in the economic context of the later twentieth century. Wagg is surely also right to see the professional footballer as, with a few notable exceptions, someone who rarely publicly challenges the social, economic or political *status quo*. The actual influence that players had in this area is much harder to measure. Fans were, after all, likely to be equally aware not only of the wealthy star but of the player who spent everything and ended up in a one-bedroomed flat, or of the career cut short by injury or ill-advised transfer.

The huge changes of the period brought problems as well as rewards. Traditional pressures were now often increased by media attention and financial considerations, leading to players bearing considerable levels of stress. The best known are the high-profile but highly untypical cases of players like George Best, a prodigy at 17, his career at the highest level effectively finished at 28. Others suffered in less dramatic ways. 'I did finish the season feeling rather sorry for modern footballers, their lives so regulated by those background coaches, missing out on so much of their normal growing up years, continually under tension, both physical and mental, and most of all, getting such little pleasure out of playing football.'[43] Hunter Davies may have been a little too pessimistic here in his perceptive study of Tottenham Hotspur's 1971–72 season, but a similarly cautionary note must be sounded in any consideration of the professional game.

The PFA's role was inevitably changed by the very improvements in wages and conditions which they had done much to engineer. Certainly, any residual militancy had long evaporated by 1973 when the Union was expelled from the TUC for placing itself on a government register of trades unions in defiance of TUC policy.[44] Nevertheless, through a combination of high profile financial rescue work and the provision of a variety of more mundane but important services, it managed to earn a greater degree of sustained influence than it had ever achieved before. In the early 1980s Gordon Taylor, who replaced Cliff Lloyd as secretary in 1981, spent a considerable amount of time attempting to protect the future of players at the many clubs threatened by bankruptcy in this most unstable period. Indeed, on no fewer than fifteen occasions the PFA either paid wage bills or made loans to help clubs through financial disasters. There was, too, a continuous involvement in less spectacular but equally vital work, including attempts to improve players' educational opportunities and the taking of a major role in the administration of the YTS scheme. The PFA, while hardly resembling a traditional model of trade unionism, found a mode of operation that seemed to suit the needs of the professional footballer, hardly a typical trade unionist, in a much altered age.

Women's football was placed on a slightly firmer footing with the establishment of the Women's Football Association in 1969; by 1979 it had 278 affiliated clubs.[45] However, there was still a long distance to travel before the game gained any credibility with men or popularity with women. Indeed, until the later 1980s it was regarded as little more than an easy source of comedy. *Football Monthly Digest* published a lengthy piece in 1973 which, while accepting that a modestly developed women's game was a feature of contemporary recreation, used real issues about access to the game and age old arguments about the limits imposed on women's sporting prowess by their biology as a basis for satire.[46] Starting gently enough with anticipation of a future story involving of the transfer of 'Georgina Better from Manchester Suffragettes to the W. I. Athletic', the article worked through the need for 'pram parks . . . flanked by nurseries' and for referees to come to terms with 'hair pulling, eye gouging and biting', before considering the problems imposed by 'menstrual instability'. The reader was asked to imagine

> the starlet in full flight of her monthly cycle and vulnerable to the professional taunts by opponents endowed with the feminine perception to recognise her discomfort and exploit it to the full . . . One can visualise the ladies' dressing-room wall equipped with a chart logging the dates that opposition players arrive at this unfortunate juncture so that maximum capital can be gained from the situation.

The cartoon wife who either interferes with her husband's football pleasure, or who fails to grasp its essence ('I suppose you double what they've got there if you want the final score' says one such character on seeing the half-time scores), was another comic device which stressed that ultimately football, on and off the field, was still a decidedly male republic.[47]

8

We'll Support You Evermore? Football in the Media Age, 1961–1985

WRITING IN 1984, the sociologist Stephen Wagg argued that, 'By most criteria the main significance of football in contemporary British society is as a television show.'[1] Although the relationship between football and television forms only a relatively small part of this chapter, Wagg's perceptive statement identifies the central fact which governed relationships between football and society in the period from the 1960s to the 1980s. Quite simply, more people experienced the game through television, and indeed the media in general, than through attendance at live matches. This shaped perceptions, loyalties and attitudes in a number of crucial ways. At the one extreme, the game's leading sides gained an increasingly glamorous image and a growing band of adherents. At the other, images of a sport blighted by hooliganism lowered the game's status and standing. In 1985 the negative images overcame the positive and soccer was plunged into crisis.

Crowds, hooligans and fans

The social composition of the football crowd changed remarkably little over the period. The only exception was that the game attracted a higher proportion of males under 20 at the end of the period than at the beginning, a point which will prove of some significance when considering the issue of hooliganism.[2] Beyond that, even towards the end of the 1980s, some 80 per cent of all fans were drawn from the working class and those in adjacent 'routine non-manual' occupations.[3] Minority ethnic groups continued to be under-represented, comprising only 1 or 2 per cent of the typical crowd, the vast majority of which was still male. There were occasional murmurs relating to the need to attract more women, but these usually occurred only when magazine editors were short of material. In May and June 1968, *Charles Buchan's Football Monthly* ran a special 'female fans' letter page and accompanied many of the published missives with photographs, an 'honour' rarely if ever bestowed on males. Several correspondents acknowledged that their initial attendance, typically with a father, brother or boyfriend, had been a little reluctant, but were at pains to underline their subsequent commitment to the game. One suggested that clubs 'turn their gymnasiums into nurseries' on match days, another commented that 'you never hear of girls wrecking trains'. In the attendance boom of 1968, however, such thoughts, quite commonplace in later, more troubled times, generated little interest and the feature disappeared with the new season.[4]

The most striking thing about attendances in the period 1961 to 1985 was that they continued to fall. Total League attendances declined from 28,619,754 in 1960–61 to an all-time low of 16,488,577 in 1985–86.[5] Within that broad picture there were interesting counter-trends. There were, for example, seven seasons between 1962–63 and 1976–77 in which attendances actually rose, with the most marked and sustained increase occurring in the late 1960s. England's success in the 1966 World Cup is generally held responsible for this rise, which saw attendances top 30 million in the 1967–68 season for the first time in almost a decade. Only after 1977–78 did the decline in numbers become continuous, with 9.7 million supporters abandoning the game by 1986.

It is also noteworthy that some sides were far more successful in holding crowds than others. First Division attendances held up far better than those in lower divisions, declining by only 30 per cent between 1960–61 and 1985–86 compared with falls of 50 per cent in the Second, 48 per cent in the Third and 64 per cent in the Fourth. These differentials were rooted partly in genuine fan discrimination, partly in the power of images generated by the often intense TV and press coverage given to the leading clubs. Patterns of support for specific clubs are also revealing. In general, most sides saw support rise and fall in more or less direct correlation to their success on the field. Arsenal, for example, saw an average League attendance of 43,776 in their 1970–71 'double' season fall to only 26,945, as they slipped into 17th place in 1975–76, before recovering to 36,371 as they reached a respectable 7th and won the FA Cup in 1978–79. However, a small number of sides retained a surprising loyalty in adversity, most notably Newcastle and Sunderland, who both regularly featured amongst the ten best-supported sides in the League despite lengthy spells in the Second Division. Yet again, claims of north-eastern loyalty and southern fickleness receive some support from the historical record.[6]

The most remarkable attendance record of the period, however, belonged to Manchester United. The club had always been extremely well supported, with their position in the attendance table often higher than their actual League placing. However, in the 1950s and early 1960s, United's attendances more or less followed the standard pattern, with crowd size broadly reflecting playing success. The great watershed occurred in 1966–67, when their championship success in a year of generally rising attendances saw average gates leap from 38,769 in the previous season to 53,854. In the next season, which saw them finish second in the League and win the European Cup, numbers rose still higher to 57,552, the highest average attendance that any English side has ever achieved. From that point on, United continued to garner massive support. In the 22 seasons between 1964–65 and 1985–86 they were the best-supported side in the country on 19 occasions, suffering a mere 1 per cent fall in attendance over a period when the First Division as a whole suffered a drop of 29 per cent. Significantly, all this was achieved despite a playing record that was, particularly in the 1970s, often modest. Even a disastrous run between 1972 and 1975 which saw 18th place followed by relegation and a season in the Second Division barely influenced levels of attendance.

Something far more than simple local loyalty was at work here, for United were clearly attracting supporters from all over the north and, indeed, from other parts of the country. To a degree hitherto unknown, fans were paying to be associated with a team, almost with a product, as

George Best moves through the Benfica defence in the 1968 European Cup Final. (*Popperfoto*)

much as for results on the field. Although the Munich tragedy had given the club an aura which differentiated it from all others, this does not appear to have been the crucial factor in earning United its privileged position as England's first modern 'glamour' club. Although crowds were often very large in the immediate aftermath of Munich, United generally experienced standard patterns of fluctuating attendance in the post-Munich seasons. Indeed, the Munich story may have only begun to exert a powerful influence on the club's image once that image had already been shaped from the late 1960s.

The club's peculiar standing seems to have stemmed from three factors at work in the crucial 1966–67 period. First, the club had benefited enormously from the publicity that surrounded their European Cup exploits. Their 5–1 demolition of Benfica in Lisbon in March 1966 gained enormous publicity, capped by the *Daily Mirror*'s front page photo of George Best in a sombrero, captioned 'El Beatle'. Many regard this as one of the defining moments in the emergence of the footballer as true media star and United could only benefit from the player's new notoriety. Again, United's championship success in 1967 came at a time when, owing to England's World Cup success and the rapid growth of televised football, the game was at a unusually high point. Above all, United were an outstanding team, Best, Bobby Charlton (a particularly popular World Cup hero) and Denis Law providing three very different but potent types of footballing hero. In an age of increasingly defensive football, United's ability to win the championship with 84 goals, when most of their nearest rivals could only manage some 20 fewer, brought excitement and romance to Old Trafford and other English grounds.[7] The events of 1966–67, then, secured Manchester United a popularity and status that any future setbacks only rarely diminished. The unpleasant corollary for United was that the influx of new support included a small but much publicised hooligan element, although, ironically, for some young fans this only added to the club's appeal.

Most other clubs could only look at Old Trafford in envy as they struggled to explain the gaps on their own terraces. A range of explanations for those gaps has been put forward. A number of them emphasise changed patterns of demand. By 1961, 91 per cent of British households had a television set and it is hardly surprising that TV, and especially televised football, was seen as central to the decline in attendances.[8] Certainly, it was possible to suggest various ways in which TV coverage threatened the live game. One argument was simply that once people could enjoy football from the comfort of their living-room they found attendance at live matches less appealing. Another propounded the view that TV brought supporters of lower division sides higher quality play than that normally laid before them (the quality often enhanced by judicious editing), encouraging them either to desert the terraces altogether, or to go in search of a 'glamour' side.[9] Alternatively, some stressed TV as myth-breaker rather than myth-maker, arguing that televised football made what was once a fortnightly treat altogether too commonplace, thus discouraging attendance at 'live' games.

It is likely that, in these various ways, and simply by offering an alternative form of Saturday entertainment, TV did exert some influence on falling attendances. However, it must again be stressed that football's 'missing millions' had begun to desert the terraces long before televised football had become a major feature of the sporting environment. It is also worth noting that, at certain moments in the age of televised soccer, gates rose; the period immediately after the World Cup success in 1966 is an obvious example. Similarly, moving ahead momentarily, attendances have risen every year since 1986–87 despite the fact that TV coverage of football has increased considerably over the period. TV may have been partially responsible for these increases if only in the sense that, at moments when the game enjoyed a positive image within the national culture because of the success of either the national side or a leading club side, television has been able to reinforce that image and make attendance seem a sensible option. At yet other times, live and TV football have suffered together, the audience for both falling from the late 1970s, for example. It seems that several complex relationships exist between televised soccer and attendance patterns rather than one simple and essentially damaging one.

Overall the strongest demand-side explanation, and probably the most convincing of all explanations, lay in the simple fact that many people continued to find other things to do against the backdrop of an overall rise in living standards and a concomitant increase in consumer choice. The restructuring of the traditional weekend was a significant contextual factor here, the increasing trend towards finishing work on Fridays placing the football match in the middle of the break rather than allowing it to act as an appealing and symbolic beginning. Increasing levels of car ownership continued to play a major role, too, allowing all manner of other attractions to draw people from traditional locations, including football grounds. As noted in an earlier chapter, increased access to private transport also allowed fans to adopt a neighbouring big city club at the expense of their local one.

While relative affluence was undoubtedly responsible for many of the game's missing fans, the hardships of those who could not enjoy its pleasures should not be overlooked. From the late 1970s, unemployment certainly exercised an influence on attendance patterns. Official unemployment figures show a rise from some 700,000 in January 1975 to just over 3 million in early 1981.[10] Of the 9.7 million fans deserting the game between 1977 and 1986, more than six million were lost in the three seasons between 1980–83, with attendances falling by 2.7 million in the 1980–81 season when unemployment reached its height. Even some leading clubs suffered as a result. Merseyside was badly affected by the recession and Liverpool experienced a 16 per cent fall in attendance in 1980–81, at a time when the First Division's aggregate loss was only 6 per cent. As in the 1930s, fans showed considerable discrimination as they husbanded potentially scarce resources. While Liverpool's key League matches and European Cup ties drew near-capacity crowds, less important games saw attendance levels plummet.[11] As high unemployment became one of the central facts of British society, some clubs were allowed to offer discounts to the unemployed, but for a significant minority of fans the decline of English manufacturing industry meant deprivation in leisure as much as in many other areas of their lives.

Supply-side factors also loom large in the discussion of falling attendances. The fact that fans had to pay increasing amounts of money for the privilege of entering poorly appointed grounds has been seen as important by a number of observers. Basic admission prices rose steadily over the period from the 2*s.* 6*d.* levied in 1960–61 to 3*s.* 6*d.* by the mid-1960s and 40 pence by 1972. From that point, as inflation rose and as attendances fell almost continuously, clubs raised their prices in order to try and offset lost revenue. By 1983, minimum admission to First Division grounds stood at between £2 and £2.50.[12] For many, this often meant only a marginal real increase in entry costs, but it was a serious problem for the low-paid and the unemployed. Many fans also found themselves paying more to attend grounds which were poorly maintained and equipped. While from the 1960s, some clubs, notably Manchester United, Tottenham and Sheffield Wednesday, had invested considerably in new grandstands, or had consciously set out to attract middle-class fans via the provision of executive boxes and generally improved facilities, many grounds had changed little from the inter-war period.[13]

Football fans, however, should not be viewed as orthodox consumers and many accepted traditional facilities and showed little enthusiasm for fundamental change. As the 1980s and 1990s were to show, many fans most certainly did not want to be seated as some visionaries thought they should be. Moreover, directors contemplating new stands and other major alterations were fully aware of the unpopularity of their counterparts whose expenditure on bricks and mortar instead of players had led to relegation or poor results. [14] Although poor conditions must have deterred some individuals, fans' low expectations and their grudging acceptance of football's economic realities suggest that the 'facilities' argument should not be seen as a major factor influencing attendance. Significantly, it took Parliamentary legislation in the form of the 1975 Safety of Sports Ground Act, itself rooted in a major disaster at Glasgow's Ibrox Park in 1971, to make many First Division clubs look closely not just at safety but at the whole issue of facilities. Many lower division sides, short of money and excluded from the Act, simply ignored the problem. [15]

The nature and quality of the game itself has proved another fertile area in the attendance debate, much of it centred around the belief that the increasingly defensive nature of the game was a major disincentive for fans. The *Football Monthly Digest* was not alone in seeing a crucial link between the loss of three million supporters in the 1972–73 season and the fact that goal-scoring levels had fallen to a record low. [16] While the magazine may have been correct in seeing more systematic and predictable defensive ploys as a deterrent to regular attendance, it was on far less secure ground when assuming that the sheer number of goals scored shaped attendance patterns. At one stage, it compared the 1160 First Division goals scored in 1972–73 with the 1724 in the prolific 1960–61 season. However, it did not point out that 1960–61 had seen the biggest single drop in attendances in the post-war period. Looking at this in the longer term, there is in fact no clear link between goals scored and levels of attendance. Attendances peaked in the late 1940s when the goal-scoring rate was not so much higher that it had been at the time of the 1925 offside reform. They then fell throughout the 1950s at a time when the number of goals scored actually increased season by season. [17] Similarly, the 1966–70 and the post-1986 increases in crowd size both occurred at a time when goal-scoring rates were relatively low.

This is not to argue that fans lacked discriminatory powers. On the contrary, attendance was usually lowest at games featuring poor sides (when home goals are often likely to flow) and highest against more demanding opposition. Success, though, was the ultimate aim and although fans preferred it to be achieved through exquisite goal-laden football, they would often settle for less. When Gillingham won the Fourth Division title in 1963–64, scoring a miserly 59 goals in their 46 games while conceding only 30, they gained the Division's highest average crowd of 9,902. An average of only 5,656 had seen the team two seasons earlier, when their record of 73 goals for and 94 against brought them twentieth place.

Probably the most convincing supply-side explanation focuses on the impact of hooliganism and the accompanying change in terrace culture. As ever, the links are not straightforward. An increase in hooligan activity was being noted at a number of London grounds, particularly Chelsea's, from about the beginning of the 1967 season, at a time of rising attendances. Again, a number of sides with reputations for poor fan behaviour, including Manchester United, had little trouble holding their attendance levels. Moreover, as will be discussed shortly, the hooligan problem was not necessarily on the scale that some people assumed. However, there is much to suggest that fear of *potential* hooliganism along with a dislike of an often far more aggressive terrace culture was a factor in cutting crowds. The oral testimony of lapsed supporters, evidence that historians would do well to collect more systematically, is suggestive here.[18] The increasing proportion of the football crowd under the age of 20 is also viewed by most informed commentators as evidence that older supporters were abandoning what had become a less pleasurable environment. There can be no doubt that over-dramatic media coverage played a significant role in shaping older fans' views, but reality was also sometimes unpleasant. A menacing atmosphere on public transport, the presence of large numbers of police and the large-scale chanting of obscenities, which many traditional working-class fans found thoroughly offensive, acted as a powerful deterrent. The racism apparent at many grounds was yet another unappealing factor for many. Consideration of trends after 1985 also sheds helpful light on these issues. It is surely striking that attendances rose from 1986 as the hooligan issue, at least inside grounds, posed ever less of a problem. Furthermore, that rise began in the lower divisions, especially the Second, where the atmosphere had often been less threatening.[19] From the early 1970s, in the context of increasing choices on offer away from the football ground, hooliganism, as both myth and reality, was a highly damaging phenomenon.

It is now time to investigate the topic of crowd behaviour in rather more detail. Disturbances within football grounds had gradually increased from the late 1950s and the Football Association was moved to express some concern in late 1961. The problem was not deemed especially serious, however, and Everton's decision to erect retaining fences behind their goals in 1963 surprised the press.[20] However, by 1967, the problem was a source of considerable attention and concern. In the atmosphere of growing public unease, irritating but relatively innocuous and often previously condoned forms of behaviour, such as loud shouting in the street, jostling and gesticulation, could all be perceived as 'hooliganism' and lead to ejections and arrests. Given the definitional problems that arise from this, no attempt will be made to measure 'hooliganism' across the period from this point. Suffice it to say that both a range of behaviour that earned the term 'hooliganism' and a vigorous public debate over the nature, causes and cure of that behaviour was a constant feature of football's culture from the late 1960s onwards.

Writing about modern hooliganism is, to say the least, problematic. The subject has become in the words of one writer, 'almost a minor branch of the social sciences', and, like most such branches, it houses a number of competing and conflicting schools of interpretation.[21] At the same time, capturing its essence demands an endless balancing act setting myth against reality, manipulated and manufactured public order 'scare' against tangible phenomenon. There is, for example, absolutely no doubt that the scale of the problem was exaggerated by a number of groups for a variety of reasons. As a result there was over-reaction within the wider community. Manchester United's visit to York in December 1974, for example, virtually closed the whole city, with shops erecting protective barricades. Some town centres were almost permanently paralysed on Saturday afternoons, as became apparent when the supposed threat receded. When Luton Town banned away supporters from their games in 1986–87, a local shopping centre reported a 40 per cent increase in customers and a secretarial college felt it safe to re-open.[22] Yet even these exaggerated fears must be acknowledged and, indeed, respected: fear of what might be can be more damaging than actuality, especially for certain vulnerable groups. Moreover, real problems – running battles between rival fans, pitch invasions, vandalism inside and outside grounds – did exist and could have frightening consequences. What follows is a necessarily brief attempt to sketch the main elements of 'hooligan' behaviour and culture, but one rooted in the acceptance that the 'hooligan' is a very slippery figure.

First, it is extremely difficult to draw a clear division between 'ordinary fans' and 'hooligans'. Only a tiny minority, exemplified by those closely involved with the so-called 'super-hooligan' gangs or 'firms' in the early 1980s, adopted hooligan activity as a dominant leisure pursuit. Many hooligans were in fact regular, committed supporters who were drawn into violence, either real or ritualistic, at certain times but who could drift away from it just as easily. There was a continuum along which people placed themselves at different stages of their lives, at different games and even at different times within a game. A scarf-bedecked, chanting youngster standing at the away end who had been forced to run through the town centre by police on horseback with all the other 'hooligans' might be a genuine fan, desperate to avoid trouble, but acting the part because it was expected of him.[23] Alternatively, 'ordinary fans' could join in behaviour which although not necessarily defined as hooliganism was most certainly equally anti-social. The racial abuse, such as the shouting of insults, monkey-chants and the throwing of bananas, that appeared from the mid-1970s was not (and is not) the sole preserve of hooligans.

Hooligan style and behaviour did not remain static. Each successive generation adopted and/or established a distinctive contemporary style of dress. Skinheads predominated in the late 1960s, but by the middle of the next decade terrace gangs were typified by long hair, flares, and scarves attached to every possible limb. By the 1980s, smarter, less conspicuous styles, partly fashion statement, partly attempt to avoid the ever more sophisticated police surveillance, became the norm, leading to the label 'soccer casuals' being used by, and of, many gangs. From about 1979, some groups took on a virulently racist mentality. This was encouraged by neo-fascist organisations that saw the terrace as a promising recruiting ground following their failure to make progress in the 1979 General Election. The resultant extreme nationalism had already been prefigured when English supporters began to travel in Europe in the 1970s in support of their club sides. It became ever more overt as, with club enmities temporarily cast aside, significant numbers of young English fans followed the national side abroad from the early 1980s.[24]

Most commentators claim that the vast majority of those involved in hooligan activity were young, white males drawn disproportionately from socio-economic groups 4 and 5. A survey of 497 convicted hooligans carried out in 1968 showed that 41.4 per cent were from an unskilled or labouring-class background, and a further 22.5 per cent were from semi-skilled backgrounds, while a Leicester University survey of 519 individuals across the whole period from the 1960s to the mid-1980s reveals an almost identical picture.[25] Many attempts to explain hooliganism have acknowledged that membership of a relatively poor and deprived section of the working class had a bearing on behaviour, but the significance of this social profile is interpreted in different ways. Important pioneering work by sociologists Ian Taylor and John Clarke, both influenced by the neo-Marxist sub-cultural theory much favoured by those exploring 'deviant' youth culture, treated hooliganism as a 'proletarian resistance movement'.[26] This approach emphasised the novelty of hooliganism and saw it as a conscious attempt by a deprived section of the working class to reclaim a game in which a strong tradition of active, involved spectatorship was increasingly being channelled into passive forms of consumerism as television and certain elite clubs set out to market the game as spectacle. Taylor and other writers working in this tradition, especially Stuart Hall, also emphasised the extent to which sections of the media and the state apparatus manipulated the hooligan issue in order to win support for authoritarian political programmes.[27] The central planks of some these arguments now appear rather unsafe. Historical research has shown the extent to which such an interpretation exaggerated the novelty of the hooligan phenomenon and subsequent events have demonstrated just how tentative the 'bourgeiosification' of the game had been by 1969. This casts some doubt on the 'resistance' argument, as does the probability that many hooligans were drawn to the game for the first time during the surge of enthusiasm that followed England's World Cup success in 1966, and came to it with little sense of its history and culture. It is much harder to discount the notion that the 'hooligan card' has been skilfully played by right-of-centre politicians and some journalists. Above all else, Taylor and other early workers in this area deserve recognition for making an attempt to provide rational explanations for something which the popular media and the football authorities dismissed with far too easy reference to such terms as 'animals' and 'thugs'.

More recently, an alternative sociological interpretation has been propounded by Eric Dunning and his colleagues at the University of Leicester.[28] While largely rejecting the notion of hooliganism as resistance movement, they, too, stress the social background of most hooligans. Drawing on the notion of the 'civilising process' associated with the work of Norbert Elias, they claim that hooligans have largely been found in a strata of society which has been generally far from receptive to the 'revolution in manners' which, developing over centuries, has taught codes of behaviour placing great store on order and decorum. They argue in particular that hooliganism is rooted in 'a long-established sub-culture of aggressive masculinity' that is predominantly, although by no means solely, associated with poorer working-class males. It is a sub-culture that celebrates very narrow, rigid and exclusive notions of locality, community and nation, notions that involve an ambivalent mixture of contempt for, and fear of anything or anybody that is "different", "foreign", "strange".'[29] In a sense, then, hooligans are seen to carry the mind-set of many supporters to great extremes.

The 'Leicester School', to whose work I have barely done justice here, has been extremely influential in recent years although some critics, especially some of those working in an anthropological tradition, have claimed that their work exaggerates the levels of actual violence involved and locates hooliganism too narrowly in a specific social strata.[30] There is, though, much common ground between the contending schools on the issue of press coverage of the hooligan phenomenon. While it would be foolish to accuse the press of creating the problem, sensationalist coverage and a tendency to focus more on the crowd than the game have resulted in self-fulfilling prophecy and exaggerated the extent of the problem. The British media's coverage has been compared unfavourably with that in other countries. In the late 1960s, for example, sections of the press moved rapidly from a traditional celebration of the amiable boisterousness of English crowds to a rather panicky condemnation of terrace culture. This gave the game a negative image and aroused the interest of at least some young men whose propensity to violence might otherwise have found other outlets. The Danish media, however, chose to celebrate the carnivalesque atmosphere but decry actual incidents of violence. They coined the term 'roligan' to distinguish the noisy but safe supporter from his more threatening counterpart. This had the benefit of stopping whole sections of football crowds from being tarred with the hooligan brush and may well have limited the problem of disorder. The British press, much of it ever anxious to incorporate the football hooligan into the catalogue of youthful 'folk devils' that seemed to reflect the declining moral fibre of a post-imperial nation, never really gave such a strategy a chance.[31]

As with the media, the football world, with a few exceptions, showed little willingness to consider the hooligan phenomenon coolly and rationally. The problem was always 'society's', as if soccer existed in a self-contained cocoon. 'Hooligans', the term usually ill-defined, were invariably labelled as 'adolescent head-cases' or similar and those who sought to explore their behaviour dismissed as 'head-shrinkers' or worse still, 'experts'.[32] Here was a powerful expression of the insularity and anti-intellectualism that seemed to pervade football's ruling bodies. Perhaps this was merely a reflection of a wider current in English society. However, the sporting establishment does appear to have felt its manhood threatened by the need to engage with any type of liberal agenda.

By the late 1980s, high-profile, high-technology policing, rigorous fan segregation policies and, above all, some fundamental shifts in terrace culture had made crowd disorder a far less frequent occurrence, at least inside English grounds. This was perhaps a good thing for academics as well as the game of football. Hooliganism has probably taken up more of the time of those engaged in exploring modern soccer than any other topic. At one level, this is absolutely appropriate. The hooligan sub-culture is of itself an important social phenomenon, while its impact on both the game and those in close proximity to major grounds was traumatic and damaging. Yet again, attempts to control it led to considerable although often insufficiently acknowledged issues relating to individual civil liberties. Large numbers of young supporters who had no criminal record, and no intention of earning one, found themselves herded into compounds or forced to jog long distances from railway stations to grounds because they had chosen to follow their team away from home. In some of the larger police operations, home supporters who did not even wish to stand on the same section of the terrace as the younger 'hooligan' element were searched for weapons before entering the ground.[33] An identity card system was only narrowly avoided in the late 1980s and the innocent, as well as the guilty, fell under the gaze of closed circuit television. Football was, then, both a major site of conflict between the state and a section of working-class youth and a forcing ground for styles of policing and surveillance that received powerful support from certain law and order lobbies. In all these ways, the hooligan phenomenon lay close to the centre of England's social and political culture at this time.

Whatever its importance, the danger is that we will lose sight of the fundamental point that hooligans, even broadly defined, made up only a tiny element of the several hundred thousand people who regularly went to professional matches and the millions of others who followed football. By the early 1980s, the arrest rate at football matches was at the very low level of slightly less than 5 per 10,000.[34] Obviously, such figures do not capture the sometimes unpleasant atmosphere at some games or the gestures, taunts and 'staring-outs' that were quintessential products of terrace life from the early 1970s. Similarly, it has to be acknowledged that the hooligan problem of the later twentieth century was of a greater order than its earlier major manifestation in the late nineteenth and early twentieth centuries. The hugely increased extent of away travel made this almost inevitable. Nonetheless, most fans were innocent of any 'crime' beyond the shouting and swearing that has long been the essence of active support. At many clubs, particularly in the lower divisions, a hooligan culture was either almost unknown, or on such a small scale as to be almost comical, provided its occasional eruptions could be avoided. Even at those grounds where the 'ends' were somewhat fuller and more volatile, young fans added much to the colour and atmosphere within which the game was played.

Excessive concentration on hooliganism also obscures the fact that older styles of active support, albeit tailored to modern patterns of popular culture, existed throughout the period and tempered the more aggressive elements of terrace culture. The most famous example was provided by Liverpool's Spion Kop. Housing almost 30,000 fans under a roof which amplified noise levels to a frightening extent, the Kop became probably the most celebrated football 'end' in the world. It was during the club's 1961–62 Second Division promotion season that fans began to develop the collection of rhythmic chants that were soon to become the common currency of English and, indeed, European football crowds.[35] By 1963–64, Koppites had taken to singing both the original and bowdlerised versions of the string of Merseybeat songs that so dominated British and American popular music at this time. In particular, 'You'll never walk alone', originally from *Carousel*, but revived by local group Gerry and the Pacemakers in autumn 1963, became Liverpool and English football's greatest terrace anthem. The Kop was mythologised by Liverpudlians and by outsiders in search of 'authentic' working-class values. Both groups often ignored its less savoury features. Garth Crooks was only one black player who recalled being taunted by some of its inhabitants and Liverpool, like all major clubs, had a hard-core hooligan element.[36] Overall, however, throughout the period, the Kop genuinely does seem to have been a place of wit, colour and sportsmanship. It was, too, not the only place where these virtues were to be found. That football eventually recovered from its bad press in the 1980s was to a considerable extent made possible by this reservoir of humour, passion and only moderately impolite behaviour.[37]

The media

The period from the late 1960s was a crucial one in the history of the relationship between soccer and the media. As attendance levels fell, the media, in all its forms, took on an ever more important role in shaping public perceptions of the modern game. Moreover, TV was to become a major economic force within the game by the 1980s. As has already been noted, the 1960s began with many leading clubs suspicious of television and fighting hard to prevent live coverage of League football. Over the next two decades, attitudes changed as a result of the new economic and cultural climate within which football operated and TV moved from fundamental threat to central pillar.

Radio still had a vital role to play in football culture, but from the mid-1960s TV increasingly took over as the key broadcasting medium. That period saw the establishment of the TV soccer format that was to remain in place for almost a decade and a half. In 1964 the BBC launched 'Match of the Day', which gave viewers 55 minutes in place of the half hourly excerpts that had previously sufficed. Transmitted initially on the four-month-old BBC 2 channel which most people could not yet receive, its early games drew tiny audiences, only 75,000 watching the inaugural transmission of the Liverpool–Arsenal game on 22 August.[38] However, by the early 1970s when it was available in colour, its audience averaged 12–13 million, with the Football League earning £100,000 for the transmission rights. ITV began Sunday afternoon broadcasting of highlights in 1965, with its 'Big Match' attracting 9–10 million by the early 1970s.[39] Football, losing the power to draw spectators in the flesh, still possessed the power to colonise the weekend to a remarkable extent, with 10 to 15 times the number of live supporters following the game at home.

In 1978 media politics and soccer economics combined to generate major changes to this relatively unproblematic arrangement. London Weekend Television's Michael Grade, anxious to force his company into the lucrative Saturday evening slot occupied by 'Match of the Day', offered the Football League a fee worth three and a half times that currently paid to them by the BBC. Independent Television's 'Snatch of the Day' was only prevented by the BBC mounting a successful legal action. The two rivals eventually agreed a new deal in 1979, which saw them share the Saturday slot on alternate weeks across the season. The four-year deal signed by the two was worth £25,000 per season to each League club as opposed to the £5,000 paid up to that point.[40] In an age when football's finances were uncertain, TV money was more than gratefully received and its position as a critical source of revenue secured. Admittedly, the League had perhaps acted unwisely by allowing the creation of a cartel which reduced its bargaining position in the medium term. It was the existence of such a cartel that placed the satellite companies in such a powerful economic and 'moral' position when they began bidding for rights in the late 1980s. Overall, though, this was a defining moment in the history of the relationship between football and television.

By 1983, when the deal was due for re-negotiation, both ITV and BBC were arguing that the decline in the audience for televised highlights necessitated the introduction of live coverage. Although clubs were divided on this, the Football League was anxious to secure sponsorship from a major company for the 1983–84 season and realised that such a deal would be impossible to broker without an agreement on TV coverage. As a result, it was accepted that alongside the recorded highlights, ten matches should be shown live, five on BBC on Friday nights, five on ITV on Sunday afternoons. For the first time, television schedules were affecting the construction of the fixture list to a really significant extent. The two-year deal was worth £4.6 million, with a further £300,000 set aside for compensation, should gates be adversely affected.[41] The first ever live transmission of a complete League match took place on Sunday 2 October 1983, when Spurs defeated Nottingham Forest in front of a White Hart Lane crowd of fractionally above average size. By 1985, some club chairmen came to see TV as source of untold wealth. As a result, a four-year deal recommended by the League's TV negotiating committee and valued at £19 million was rejected by the clubs on the basis that a far more lucrative one could have been struck. The 1985–86 season was the first to kick off without TV coverage for thirty years.

There is not space here to explore the impact of televised soccer upon its audiences in any detail. Arguably the most important outcome of televised soccer was that it did much to boost the image of a relatively small number of sides. Although the obsessive concentration on the game's supposed elite that typified the period from 1988 was avoided, certain clubs did draw the cameras with rather greater frequency than others. In that sense, TV sketched the foundations for a 'super league' long before the idea gained common currency. This process also meant that younger fans coming to the game through TV rather than attendance at live games were likely to be drawn to a small number of successful clubs. Local bonds were often thus weakened or severed.

The intimate relationship between soccer and the press remained as strong as ever in this period; indeed, at least in regard to the popular tabloid press, it strengthened still further. The amount of news space devoted to sport by the *Daily Mirror*, for example, increased from 24 per cent in the period 1947–51 to 53 per cent by 1968–75, with soccer always the dominant element.[42] Sport had become absolutely central to circulation battles. This, coupled with the impact of television, clearly influenced the nature of newspaper coverage. Now that key matches and key players were watched by millions who would have depended previously on match reports for their view of the game, the press had to find new angles and approaches. The cult of the personality, already encouraged by the changes set in train from as early as the 1930s, was hugely enhanced as a result. The broadsheet press, especially *The Times*, continued to give extensive coverage to Rugby Union and other amateur sport, but, by 1970, professional soccer had finally eclipsed its amateur counterpart in terms of the share of attention it received. The World Cup of 1966 was important here: the *Sunday Times* launched Michael Parkinson's distinctive football column during the build up to it. Interestingly, soccer finally found a fully secure place in these prestigious papers just as its place in national affections was about to come under threat. The respectability and credibility that the quality press gave the game in the next two decades may have been an important factor in its capacity to fend off crisis for so long. Soccer writers in this area of the press continued to develop a distinctive range of styles which enriched the nature of football journalism. In 1970, for example, Tom Freeman described Manchester City's Maine Road pitch as 'like a playground for rhinoceros . . . to expect players like Lee and Bell to struggle above four inches of mud is to put dancers in army boots.'[43] The many aspiring writers who sought to give soccer a worthy literature found helpful role models here.

Soccer continued to support a considerable body of specialist literature and to feature strongly within more general publications such as boys' comics. From the late 1960s, some comics adopted a style of humour bordering on the surreal; the adventures of an insect team, Antchester United, graced *Plug* and then *Beezer* in the 1970s and early 1980s. Playing at Antfield, managed by Matt Bugsy and including one Gnat Lofthouse on their playing staff, they drove one opposition manager whose team had lost 36–0 (a reference to the highest score ever recorded in senior football) to commit 'insectiside'. In such unexpected ways, football's past history and traditions were kept alive for a new generation, alongside its present preoccupations and triumphs.[44] In the much-changed climate, some of the traditional magazines struggled to find an appropriate voice. A notable victim was *Charles Buchan's Football Monthly,* its solid and cheerfully uncritical approach much less appealing in an age where younger readers in particular were likely to have been exposed to more sensationalist elements of the tabloid press and to the satirical tendencies so strong within popular culture from the early 1960s. As a result, the magazine metamorphosed into the *Football Monthly Digest* in 1973, a pocket-sized volume that claimed to be 'pungent and provocative'. Although it carried some penetrative features and adopted a more jokey style than its predecessor, as when it referred to Derby manager Brian Clough as having 'a haircut stolen from a fifties "B" picture', it lasted only one season in this new format. The editor blamed its demise on escalating costs resulting from the 1973–74 oil crisis, but its end probably owed much to *Football Monthly*'s rather dated image in the years immediately before the change of title and approach.[45]

A number of new titles did emerge over the period. At one extreme came *Football League Review*, launched in August 1966 as a Football League publicity and promotion vehicle, a testimony to the Football League's gradual acknowledgement of the need to adopt a less opaque public position.[46] Although for sale at 5 pence, it was mainly distributed as a free supplement in club programmes and, at its peak, was used by over sixty clubs. Renamed *League Football* in 1972, it survived until December 1974 when it was deemed too expensive for publication to continue. Its aim was to show the Football League as a happy and interdependent family, working hard at covering the full range of League sides and their backroom staff. At the same time, every opportunity was taken to deflect criticism of football personnel. In November 1971 the rhetorical question 'Are directors really "petty dictators"?', was unsurprisingly answered in the negative. Players, too, were defended, the *Review* criticising schoolmasters for claiming that bad behaviour was rife in schoolboy football because young players aped their professional heroes. In a typical display of the populist conservatism which marked the magazine's occasional forays into the margins of the political arena, it reminded teachers of both the high standards maintained by most players and of the possible bad example teachers had set by taking industrial action in pursuit of a recent pay claim.[47] The rather odd mixture of glamour, broad coverage and self-justification made for a sometimes patchy and awkward read which at times revealed as much about the Football League's self-perception as it did about the deeper social and economic realities of the game. It did serve a useful public relations function, however, sensibly rebutting many wilder journalistic comments. It was, therefore, unfortunate that the League chose to end publication at the very moment when football was edging toward troubled times and its authorities most in need of regular contact with fans.[48]

Foul was a very different proposition, described aptly by one historian as providing 'a critical, radical if unfocused voice' during its relatively short life between October 1972 and October 1976. Launched by Cambridge University undergraduates, it was the first sporting manifestation of the 'alternative' press that had blossomed among younger, better-educated audiences from the 1960s. Its title parodied those of the glossy, star-oriented magazines such as *Shoot* (1969), which were a feature of the early 1970s. Its criticism of entrenched interest groups within the game, as well as the style in which that criticism was expressed, owed much to the satirical magazine *Private Eye*. There was, too, something of a student rag magazine flavour, as when it advertised an imaginary Leeds United pantomime entitled 'Piss in Boots' starring Norman Hunter as 'Widow Wankey', or when Manchester United defender Jim Holton's broken leg was greeted with the message 'enjoy your winter break'.[49] In a sense *Foul* had much in common with the fanzine movement from the late 1980s, although it adopted a rather more consistently radical tone than many of its successors. It is interesting that, like *Football Digest* and *League Football*, it failed to survive the mid-1970s. As noted already, high inflation as well as escalating raw material costs made this a difficult time for small magazines in general, and there were individual factors influencing the closure of each magazine. *Foul*, for example, finally folded in the face of a label action. However, the fact that all three were relatively short-lived suggests that the social and economic pre-conditions for the sustenance of reasonably 'literate' football magazines were simply not in place. The 'fanzine revolution' took place in a much more propitious climate, typified by a youth culture with a strong inclination to small-scale modes of cultural production, low inflation and major developments in the field of cheap reprographic technology.

However, it was still the case that serious, even intellectual studies of the game, could find an audience. Certainly, football failed to find a novelist able to do what David Storey had done for Rugby League in *This Sporting Life*. However, playwright Peter Terson focused on the problems of hooliganism in his play *Zigger Zagger*, written for the National Youth

Theatre in 1968, while a number of journalists produced considered and serious studies of the game.[50] Central here were John Moynihan's *Soccer Syndrome* (1965), Arthur Hopcraft's *The Football Man* (1968), regarded by many as a classic of sporting literature, and Hunter Davies's *The Glory Game* (1972), an intimate portrait of Tottenham Hotspur's 1971–72 season. 1976 saw the publication of Eamon Dunphy's *Only a Game?* Eventually to make his career as a journalist, Dunphy gave an insider's view of football that was at times painfully honest in its laying bare of both the author's character and those of the people he worked with. As such it remains one of the most revealing sporting autobiographies ever written. Such honesty broke with the normal conventions of celebrity autobiography and, by so doing, created the potential for a new genre. Few, however, had the skill or, in the age of the soccer superstar, the courage to write in this vein. Blandness still typified much sporting literature, but Dunphy's work and these other exceptions to the rule provided the crucial foundations for the literate products of Nick Hornby and other members of the so-called *soccerati* in the 1990s.

Football as a business

For most of its history, professional football set its face firmly against commercialisation. While a few individual directors did well from catering or building concessions, most individual rewards were modest and most clubs made either a small profit or a small loss each season. Numerous external observers expressed surprise and sometimes frustration at the lack of 'dynamic objectives . . . and modern business practice' in the typical boardroom, not all of them fully comprehending the limited place that clubs allotted to notions of profit-maximisation.[51] Similarly, the FA and the Football League showed a strong anti-commercial stance. The late twentieth century was to see a sea-change in attitudes. 'Football clubs,' said Tottenham director Irving Scholar in 1988, 'are an Aladdin's cave but the riches inside are untapped.'[52] While the real revolution in football's business culture took place after 1985, the period immediately preceding saw its prefiguration: the cave's explorers were queuing outside.

For much of the 1960s and 1970s the pace of change was slow. Against the backdrop of fairly constant levels of support, most clubs saw commercial ventures as increasingly valuable but expected them to generate only a modest income. The majority of clubs settled for the traditional advertising revenue raised from hoardings and programmes and hired commercial managers to run various fund-raising draws, lotteries and club shops. These sold mainly low cost items such as programmes, key fobs, pennants, bobble hats and the occasional extras such as the 13-inch garden pixies ('very attractive . . . in the club colours of red and white') which Exeter City offered its devotees in 1971. Interestingly, as late as 1971–72, Tottenham Hotspur, pioneers of the changes that were to take place in the 1980s, were sufficiently squeamish (and wealthy) to refrain from having advertising boards within the ground.[53] In similarly modest vein the Football League experimented with sponsorship arrangements, although these were initially short-lived. 1970 saw the introduction, for one season only, of both the Ford Sporting League, which awarded money to clubs according to their goal-scoring and disciplinary records, and the Watney Mann Invitation Trophy. This eight club pre-season knock-out competition, which survived until 1973, was the first ever sponsored domestic football tournament involving League clubs. It was also the first ever tournament to use penalty shoot-outs to settle drawn ties.

From the late 1970s and early 1980s, economic necessity gradually forced the football world to develop far more sophisticated and lucrative commercial strategies. Falling attendances, spiralling transfer fees and the concomitant escalation in wage rates and signing-on fees spelt potential disaster. In 1979–80, a number of relatively modest players changed hands for over £1 million and wage rates ran ahead of prices by 25 per cent, only for attendances to fall by 11 per cent in the next season. Over the next few seasons a number of clubs came desperately close to bankruptcy. In reluctant acknowledgement of the shambolic state of football's financial structure, the first, often slow steps, were taken towards salvation. Queens Park Rangers had been the first side to ask the League for permission to display a sponsor's logo on club shirts in March 1977. The request was initially turned down, but rescinded within six months, provided that Rangers and other like-minded sides changed their shirts for televised games.[54] That decision marked a significant moment of acceleration in the process of commercialisation. In 1981 Arsenal signed a three-year deal with JVC worth £500,000 and, by the early 1980s, few sides lacked sponsors, ranging from major companies injecting significant amounts of money to individual fans funding a single item of kit. In 1981, the League allowed clubs to appoint one paid director, an acknowledgement of the increasing commercial complexity of the modern game.[55]

From 1973–74, amateur leagues were attracting sponsors, with cigarette manufacturers Rothmans taking the lead. The resultant naming procedures led to a rather incongruous marriage of commerce with neo-classical idealism in the form of the Rothmans Isthmian League and the Rothmans Hellenic League. It was only a matter of time and financial pressure before the guardians of the game's major tournaments found the financial rewards on offer irresistible. The first such competition to find a sponsor was the League Cup, renamed the Milk Cup from 1982 as a result of the National Dairy Council providing £2 million backing over a four-year period. In May 1983 it was finally agreed that the Football League was to be sponsored by Japanese electrical goods manufacturers Canon, which gave the League £3.3 million over three years.[56]

A further set of new business practices were tested out at Tottenham. In 1982 Irving Scholar took over a club in a dire financial position following a ground-rebuilding programme. As already suggested, Scholar sought to transform soccer economics by treating the game as a business. In October 1983 Tottenham Hotspur was floated as a public company and Scholar began what one writer termed 'a new path of rampant commercialism'.[57] Eventually, a series of poorly judged investments saw Scholar over-extend himself and lose control of the club in 1991. New economic possibilities, however, had been suggested.

These changes stemmed from a combination of factors relating to the game's economic position, the impact of TV exposure and wider shifts in economic practice stimulated by the 'Thatcherisation' of British society. As already noted, at one level clubs sought greater involvement with sponsorship simply because of the financial shortfall caused by falling gate revenue and rising costs. High-profile TV coverage, particularly after the ban on televising shirt logos was lifted in 1983, made such sponsorship ever more profitable.[58] It is hard to believe, however, that the changes would have run so deep without the powerful influence of the Conservative Party's free market ideology which encouraged or forced institutions, at every level of British life from state-run industries to schools and museums, to maximise their market potential. Beginning the process of unlocking Aladdin's cave would have been much harder in an economic environment that had not seen the privatisation of fourteen publicly owned industries between 1983–87 or, more modestly, the introduction of museum charges in a number of institutions. At the same time, football clubs began to attract younger directors whose business careers were being forged in this new climate and who were much more likely than many of their predecessors to pursue new paths and new methods. Although what one economist dubbed 'Mrs Thatcher's economic experiment' ran a little ahead of the one brewing in football, it set the tone for much of what was to follow in the game after 1985.[59]

Football, politics and society

As with earlier periods, it is interesting to explore soccer's role in shaping relationships between leaders and the led. There can be no doubt that, in an age when the management of public relations became an increasingly important political art, politicians of all colours were anxious to capitalise on the game's popular appeal. Marriages of personal passions and political opportunism litter the period. Harold Wilson's genuine love for the game, and Huddersfield Town in particular, was well known, as was Michael Foot's enthusiasm for Plymouth Argyle and, later, John Major's for Chelsea. Wilson's playing of this particular populist card was so adroit that there remains a well-established popular myth that England's World Cup success in July 1966 secured the re-election of his Labour government later in the same year. In fact, that election success had occurred three months earlier. Others with less of a grounding in the game were quick to learn of its value. In June 1976, Margaret Thatcher, then leader of the Conservative opposition, began an official visit to Liverpool at Anfield. This, according to the *Guardian*'s Peter Jenkins, was the 'equivalent in that city of laying a wreath at the war memorial.'[60] Suitably, her blue outfit was embellished by a red chiffon scarf.

Many of those interested in rather more than simple short-term political advantage continued to be exercised by the game's capacity to shape wider political mentalities. The issue took on new importance in this period, and especially from the later 1970s, as mass unemployment, racism and growing disenchantment with a two-party system took centre stage in political debate. As already noted, some neo-fascist groups saw the terrace as a potentially rich recruiting ground and they may have had some, albeit limited, success in their endeavours. Alternatively, some on the left sensed that the football crowd represented a powerful demonstration of the latent power of the working class, a power that had great potential if suitably directed. Writing in 1990, for example, Anthony Easthope remembered how strongly he had once sensed this, especially when a million people filled Manchester in May 1977 to celebrate United's defeat of Liverpool in the FA Cup. The crowd,

> took over the whole city and could have had the factories, the offices, the police stations and Granada TV for the asking. But we didn't. After

> the players disappeared into the Town Hall everybody went quietly home leaving the city – and the political arena – empty for Maggie Thatcher to do what ever she wanted.

Thirteen years later he had decided that 'the people's game does not encourage working-class activism – it is a substitute for it.' As ever, football disappointed many socialists.[61]

Within the narrower confines of the game itself, it is as difficult as ever to see much evidence for any significant popular control of football. Certainly, individual sets of fans could exert influence at critical moments, as when Oxford United and Reading supporters mounted effective opposition to Robert Maxwell's plan to amalgamate the two clubs as the Thames Valley Royals.[62] However, by the early 1980s it was obvious that clubs needed the support of individuals with considerable disposable wealth if they were to prosper. Moreover, the game's altering business culture represented another force tending to take power away from fans. Unless one is prepared to witness football hooliganism as a resistance movement, it is very difficult not to conclude that, by 1985, football was further from being the 'people's game' than it had been at any time since the 1870s.

The various 'sub-political' identities that have been charted throughout this book continued to surface in various ways throughout the period to 1985. The fierce small-town local pride that had been so effectively reflected and shaped by soccer may well have been a less prominent feature, at least by the 1970s. It had by no means died, as was to be exemplified by the highly impressive displays of support for lower division clubs at the Wembley Freight Rover and play-off finals from the late 1980s. However, football does not seem to have had quite the capacity to move communities in the way that it had in previous periods. Indeed, the outpourings of carnival spirit that have been generated by fans of smaller clubs *en route* to Wembley represent almost a hankering after a lost 'Golden Age' of community. The decline of local patriotism was partly a function of the shifting patterns of footballing allegiance, as potential supporters of small town clubs preferred instead the allure of the successful city clubs, either losing interest in the local side altogether or maintaining only a rather erratic affection. Some commentators saw here, too, 'a sickness of modern society', in the shape of a trend towards the worship of success and a denigration of failure.[63] Celebration of the 'local' was, however, arguably a decreasing force within society from the 1960s, as social mobility and concomitant shifts in population, coupled with the growth of national and international influences upon popular culture and popular consumption, gave it an ever more 'dated' flavour.

The local and the regional still had some place in the footballing context. This was especially the case in those cities where football success became a powerful symbolic compensation for economic decline and poor image within the national culture. The most dramatic example is provided here by Liverpool. In the 1960s, the success of the city's two major sides had been part of a wider flowering of Liverpool's popular culture, as the 'Mersey Sound' became the most significant force in western popular music. By the 1980s a different kind of notoriety attached itself to the city as it suffered greatly from economic hardship and often ill-informed press comment on the battles for political control of the city, particularly those between supporters of 'moderate' Labour and the Trotskyite Militant Tendency. The success of both Liverpool and Everton in this decade allowed for the generation of potent self-images which helped sustain a city in hard times.[64] Like all such images they blended reality and aspiration. Apart from emphasising the quality of the two sides, Liverpool especially, the Liverpudlian (and indeed many outsiders') view of the city's soccer culture built up a web of positive imagery. It stressed the wit and knowledge of the supporters, with Anfield's Kop a byword for the best in this sense; the good relations that existed between fans of the city's two clubs in an age of football hooliganism; the loyalty of players and managers to their clubs; and the two clubs' unspectacular public relations style in a period of growing media 'hype'. Merseyside soccer was presented almost as the epitome of the best values to be found in the working-class community, a valuable symbolic weapon with which to fight a government that preached the value of individualism, and its southern middle-class supporters.

There were also enemies nearer home. Rivalry between supporters of Liverpool and Manchester United reached a new intensity in this period. This was fuelled not simply by the long tradition of rivalry between the two cities, but by their mutual success on the field in the 1960s, coupled with what was deemed by some Liverpool supporters the excessive and undeserved media attention lavished on United in the next two decades. Such antipathies meant that, as ever, any sense of *regional* identity tended to be gained and experienced through identification with a specific locality rather than any really significant level of identification with other communities in that area. Within these parameters, regional identities did flourish at times. 'North–south' tensions continued to operate in this period, coming into especial prominence in the 1980s when the issue of southern economic and political dominance moved back into political centre stage. Sporting expressions of such tensions were not quite so overt as they had been in the 1930s, possibly because southern sides had not succeeded in matching Arsenal's success of that decade. Nevertheless, they did surface and southern supporters were as likely as their northern counterparts to promote them. The late 1980s, for example, saw a brief vogue among some visiting London fans for the waving of ten pound notes at home supporters with the accompanying shout of 'loadsamoney' in confrontational acknowledgement of the supposed existence of 'two nations'.

1985 – 'Annus *horribilis*'

By the early 1980s, professional football was clearly losing the central place that it had long held within the national culture. Even those whose job it was to provide positive public relations found it ever harder to do so. Tony Williams, the editor of the 1984–85 *Rothman's Football Yearbook*, argued that, at times, the game seemed set on a 'course of self-destruction'.[65] Historian James Walvin spoke for many fans when he acknowledged that, since the 1970s, the game that had once meant so much to him no longer held the same attraction. Violence, obscene chants, racial abuse, the sometimes 'bizarre' behaviour of well-paid managers and players and the sensationalist tone of much press coverage were some of the features that he listed as the cause of his disenchantment.[66]

A further problem for the game was that it was experiencing difficulties at a time when many institutions which had strong associations with working-class culture were under threat. Broadly speaking, between the 1920s and the 1970s, football was invariably depicted as a game which showed the working class in their best light; they were tolerant, cheerful, well-behaved, humorous. From the late 1970s and early 1980s, as the consensus politics rooted in full employment began to disintegrate, football became an easy target for those who sought to stigmatise working-class culture in order more easily to undermine its political institutions, and to designate the very term 'working class' as irrelevant and old-fashioned. The massive socio-economic changes of the 1980s, most notably the decline of manufacturing industry, the halt of the 'forward march' of organised labour, the huge reduction in (and stigmatisation of) public housing and the accompanying rise of owner-occupation, as well as the continued rise

Bradford Park Avenue left the Football League in 1970. Some were tempted to see their rotting ground, pictured here in 1980, as symbolic of the English professional game in the early 1980s. (*Bradford Telegraph and Argus*)

of popular consumerism, led at times to the very term 'working-class' being stripped of its positive overtones and being endowed instead with connotations of backwardness, conservatism and irrelevance. Institutions and movements as diverse as the Labour Party, the brass band and the working men's club all enthusiastically embraced the need to lose what was often termed the 'cloth cap' image. Football, especially when some of its (often decaying) grounds were troubled by a minority of largely young, working-class males, was hardly an attractive proposition in such a culture. This was compounded in various small but significant ways by the ease with which certain aspects of football culture elided with other aspects of contemporary life which many found threatening. In 1984, for example, when noting the 'industrial brawling which was often indistinguishable from mayhem on the terraces and outside grounds', the editor of the *Rothman's Football Yearbook* linked aspects of the miners' strike of 1984–85 with football hooliganism.[67] Again, observers unsympathetic to both strikers and football fans may well have had their views reinforced by the miners' adoption of the football chant ''ere we go, 'ere we go, 'ere we go' as their rallying cry. The 'enemy within' inhabited the sporting as well as the industrial landscape.

In 1985 crisis point was reached. Many supporters will have happy memories of that year, of good football played in a pleasant atmosphere. But, in general, in the first six months the reputation and status of professional football reached its nadir. In February, the Football League's rejection of a £19 million TV deal not only left the nation without televised football for the following season and precipitated events which threatened the future of the League, but made some of the game's leaders appear grasping and short-sighted. Attendances continued to fall, the 1984–85 season recording the first ever aggregate of under 18 million. In March, a TV audience was treated to the spectacle of a full-scale battle between Luton and Millwall supporters, while on the last Saturday of the season a fan was stabbed to death at a game in Birmingham. That was overshadowed by events the same day at Bradford, where a Third Division championship celebration turned into English football's (then) worst ever disaster, when 56 people died and hundreds of others were injured in a horrific fire which started among rubbish under an old, poorly maintained wooden grandstand. Ironically, major renovation was due to begin the following week. Finally, but perhaps most crucially, on 29 May, 39 Juventus fans were crushed to death at the European Cup final in the Heysel Stadium in Brussels as they attempted to flee from marauding Liverpool supporters. Both the ground and the policing arrangements were pitifully inadequate for such an event, but it did not diminish the real hurt felt by many football supporters. The *Guardian*'s Frank Keating, a highly respected sports journalist who always gave the impression of caring deeply for the sports he covered, wrote words which illustrate just how keenly this event was felt. 'One more corpse was carried from the Brussels stadium last night. Soccer itself – draped in the Union Jack. It deserved to be spat on.' Another paper referred to the game as 'a slum sport played in slum stadiums watched by slum people'.[68] Football could only recover if it found some fundamentally new ways of presenting itself.

9

Seats in All Parts: Re-inventing Football, 1985–1995

THE EVENTS OF 1985 gave all the contending schools of football reform the opportunity to fuel their respective proposals from the public mood of despair and disgust. Existing trends, whether towards greater commercialisation, supporter involvement or a new role for football clubs in the wider community, were accelerated and the game began the long climb back towards respectability. En route, the football world experienced greater structural and cultural change than in any period since the late nineteenth century. What follows is inevitably a rather selective treatment. At the risk of simplifying a complex picture, it concentrates largely on what is surely the major theme of football's recent history: the attempt by those within football, the media and the wider business community to reshape the game in a more obviously commercial direction and the response to these changes by fans not always sharing this set of priorities.

Reform from above

i. Restructuring the Football *League*

Football's image gradually recovered in the immediate post-Heysel period and Barclays Bank's sponsorship of the Football League from 1987 represented an important stage in the process. The deal, worth £4.55 million, was at that point the largest single sponsorship agreement in the history of British domestic sport. It was probably bank's name rather than its money that mattered the most.[1] If such a firm was prepared to be involved, albeit in order to boost customer appeal among younger males, then football's health was perhaps not as bad as many suggested. The introduction of both the 'play-off' system and automatic relegation and promotion between the League and the GM Vauxhall Conference in 1986–87 helped stimulate public interest, as did a particularly enjoyable

Cup final in the same season. Coventry's success in overcoming favourites Tottenham and the ecstatic manner with which the city greeted its heroes struck a necessarily romantic, almost nostalgic chord. In the wider arena, England's relative success in the 1990 World Cup finals and the lavish attention heaped by the media on their star player, Paul Gascoigne, proved another significant moment of rehabilitation.

Such improvements in the game's fortunes were not enough to prevent major structural changes from taking place. From as early as 1981, it was apparent that a number of the wealthier First Division clubs saw existing League philosophy as a barrier to both their sporting and financial aggrandizement. By 1985, a 'reform' strategy had been adopted and a clear leadership group had emerged in the form of chairmen of the so-called 'Big Five', Arsenal, Everton, Liverpool, Manchester United and Tottenham. It had already been agreed in 1983 that clubs should be allowed to keep the full revenue from home games, rather than observe the practice dating back to the First World War of giving a percentage to visiting sides. Particular objectives for future reform included a change in the structure of the management committee to give elite sides a greater voice; a reduction from three-quarters to two-thirds in the majority required for policy changes; a redistribution of TV and sponsorship money in the interests of the larger clubs; and a reform of the system whereby all clubs paid 4 per cent of their gate receipts into a pool for equal distribution across the 92 clubs.[2]

Over the summer of 1985, concern among leading clubs that crucial revenue would be lost as a result of both the collapse of the TV deal and the ban imposed on English clubs after the Heysel disaster precipitated action. On 30 September, the 'Big Five' unveiled plans for a break-away 'super league' which, at different times in the debate, might have involved anything from 10–20 leading clubs. It is not clear whether this was a high-profile negotiating gambit designed to pressurise the other clubs into accepting major changes, or whether it was believed that such a league could be a success at that stage. Whatever the motive, after long and acrimonious negotiations, the withdrawal threat was dropped on 28 April 1986 after League members agreed to major reforms that served the interests of the biggest clubs. The agreement included the introduction of two-thirds majority voting, the restructuring of the management committee, the reduction of the gate levy from 4 per cent to 3 per cent and redistribution of all sponsorship and TV money. From now the First Division sides were to take 50 per cent, those in the Second 25 per cent and members of the Third and Fourth the remaining 25 per cent between them.[3] Although the increase in sponsorship and broadcasting revenue within the game cushioned the blow for the lower division sides, there was little doubt about who gained the most from such a deal. The gap between rich and poor in British football was set to become wider, just as it was in British society at large.

The 'settlement' turned out to be short-lived. In the summer of 1988, ironically the League's centenary year, the break-away threat was resuscitated when ITV offered to sponsor a super league as part of a virulent battle with the nascent satellite TV industry. A split was again averted, although TV revenues were once again reapportioned to give First Division clubs a 75 per cent share. However, the 'super league' was now too established a part of football politics for it to be easily discarded. The publication of the Taylor Report in 1990 following the Hillsborough disaster of the previous April, and, in particular, its insistence on what would inevitably be extremely expensive all-seater stadia, focused the attention of the elite clubs. Finally, in June 1991, after months of negotiations with the chairmen of leading clubs, the Football Association published its *Blueprint for the Future of Football*. A central plank of this far-reaching document was a scheme for a Premier League. The FA, long unhappy with what it regarded as the parochialism and conservatism of the Football League and concerned that the League was planning to spearhead a major reform of the English game, decided to assert its dominance of English football in the most dramatic fashion. Over a hundred years of social, geographical, personal and political tensions had come to a head. In the summer of 1991, the First Division sides gave official notice of their decision to defect *en bloc* to form what began on 15 August 1992 as the FA Premiership. From 1993–94, the brewing firm Bass began a four-year, £12 million sponsorship of the Premier League, while Endsleigh Insurance took over sponsorship of the League.[4]

The successful establishment of a break-away league stemmed from the fact that it was proposed by an outside body, the Football Association, rather than by a group of rebel clubs. This gave the scheme far more credibility, partly because, at least initially, it allowed the secession to be cloaked in national as well as self-interest. The FA's initial proposals had emphasised the benefits accruing to the English international side if an elite league of just 18 clubs, the number proposed in the original discussions, was introduced. Clubs would thus lose eight games per season, leaving the leading English players fresher and fitter for international commitments. Whatever the FA's intentions, this plan was rapidly diluted when it became clear that few of the chairmen of the existing First Division clubs were willing to be excluded from these lucrative developments, even in the interest of the national side. The new league thus began with 22 clubs with an agreement that it should be cut to 20 in 1995. The notion of the Premiership serving English national interests has been further eroded by the influx of overseas players from the early 1990s.[5] Quite simply, independence from the League offered leading clubs the irresistible chance to benefit from ever larger TV and sponsorship deals without the obligation of supporting poorer clubs in lower divisions.

This was hardly surprising. The entire 'super league' debate and the reforms that flowed from it had been predicated on the belief that the richest clubs earned most of the money and were entitled to keep the largest share of it. On the day before the meeting to decide the League's fate in 1988, David Lacey wrote the obituary of 'the idea which has sustained [the Football League] for a hundred years . . . While the League might remain intact so far as the fixtures and tables are concerned, the notion of a national competition embracing clubs big and small, rich and poor, on a basis of mutual aid and sympathy has been mortally wounded in the last few days.'[6] The philosophy utilised by the supporters of a break-away chimed in extraordinarily well with the wider free market philosophy of the 1980s. The individuals who had run League clubs in earlier decades were, of course, for the most part as thoroughgoing believers in capitalism as the new generation. However, they had a rather different view of football's economics and emphasised the interdependency of the League's individual members. Such an attitude was easier to hold in the period before sponsorship and television income began to complicate the picture. That it was held at all, however, owed at least something to a world-view that was far less in evidence from the 1980s, as 'rationalisation' and the search for 'efficiency' became the economic watchwords. It is no coincidence that the age of the new economic liberalism saw football's traditional structures transformed. Unsurprisingly, the gap between a small Premiership elite and the 'rest' has increased since 1992. Nevertheless, it must be said that the Premiership, skilfully marketed, rich from TV money and increasingly attractive to leading foreign players, has played a central part in reviving soccer's fortunes.

ii. Television

From the moment of ITV's 'Snatch of the Day' in 1978, television had played an increasingly central role in football's economics and politics. The arrival of satellite TV in the late 1980s added a dramatic new element to the plot.[7] In May 1988, it was announced that a major deal was likely between the FA, the League and British Satellite Broadcasting, a company due to commence transmission in 1989. Immediately, ITV, through senior executive Greg Dyke, set out to 'strangle the satellite threat at birth'.[8] Its strategy was to offer an exclusive deal to ten leading clubs (the 'Big Five' plus the biggest clubs in each ITV region) in the knowledge that a satellite contract which did not include these clubs would be commercially worthless. As already noted, a break-away league would be sponsored if necessary, although ITV was content for the League to remain intact, provided that the company gained these coveted fixtures. Eventually, after an extraordinarily ill-tempered and complex struggle, ITV won the contract for the entire Football League, valued at some £52 million over four years. Although this huge increase in TV revenue (a £23 million increase on the abortive 1985 offer) was of obvious benefit to the game, the implementation of the deal gave a significant boost to the process of elite club aggrandizement. ITV remained convinced that a small number of clubs held the key to television advertising revenue and deliberately focused on them. In 1990–91, for example, while the 'Big Five' enjoyed 34 appearances between them, five other First Division clubs received no coverage at all. In a less statistically oriented analysis, but one echoed by many fans, Chelsea chairman, Ken Bates, later observed that 'we saw Arsenal and Liverpool more times than fucking "Coronation Street"'.[9]

By May 1992, when the deal was due for renewal, a number of clubs were anxious to settle this particular score with ITV. Their chances were much enhanced by the arrival in the equation of British Sky Broadcasting, a satellite channel formed by the merger of BSB and Rupert Murdoch's rival Sky TV. In a charged and sometimes chaotic atmosphere, an ITV offer of £262 million over five years was defeated by a rival bid from BSkyB worth £304 million.[10] It is perfectly feasible that BSkyB would have made an even higher bid if necessary. The logic behind this was straightforward. Capturing sport in general, and football in particular, was central to BSkyB's business strategy. While it was obviously hoped that the soccer deal would boost advertising income, it was initially seen as a way of rapidly increasing subscription rates. Winning exclusive coverage of Cricket's World Cup earlier in 1992 was thought to have been responsible for 100,000 additional satellite dish purchases and subscriptions. It was believed that a soccer deal would not only lead to a similar boost, but that, once subscribing to Sky Sports, dish-owners would then buy subscriptions to their other services. Football was a route to other sections of the viewing public.[11]

The battle has continued for other prizes, big and small. In November 1995, BSkyB won a £125 million five-year contract for live coverage of Endsleigh League games and reached an agreement with ITV to share FA Cup coverage, while in June 1996, BSkyB won a renewed contract for coverage of the Premiership by offering £670 million over the four years from 1997.[12] What had been the impact of all this on football? BSkyB's imaginative and aggressive marketing strategies have undoubtedly helped place soccer much more firmly in the national consciousness than had been the care for some time. In economic terms, TV's injection of capital has proved crucial. Direct income from broadcasting typically provides some 8–10 per cent of a larger club's income, while money raised from sponsorship and merchandising activities would simply not have proved such a vital source of capital, both financial and 'psychic', without the exposure that television has brought. It is, however, the case that for some clubs the rapid injection of money may well have prevented a thorough review of deep-seated organisational and financial problems from taking place.

As regards its impact on football fans, the blessings of satellite TV in particular have proved to be somewhat mixed. Obviously, access to satellite TV carries a cost. By early 1996, a typical fee involved a charge of some £250 for equipment and installation coupled with a monthly subscription fee of about £16. Many, for a variety of reasons, were unwilling to meet these costs.[13] There was still certainly a considerable amount of English football on terrestrial TV, often in highlight form, while Channel Four rapidly built up an audience of some 2.5 million for their Sunday afternoon showing of live Italian Serie A games. Most of the football-watching population, however, have found themselves denied access to live coverage of top English club fixtures unless they have a dish-owning neighbour, friend or relative, or frequent one of the pubs or clubs quick to spot the potential of satellite TV sport. Moreover, for TV and live fans alike, satellite schedules which spread the fixtures over three days, and also sometimes over different parts of those days, have accelerated the fragmentation of the fixture list that terrestrial TV had begun from 1983. This has brought disruption to lifestyles as fans struggle to accommodate 4 o'clock Sunday afternoon kick-offs and similar breaks from tradition. However, BSkyB did at least guarantee some coverage of *all* Premiership clubs, thus ending the complete domination of TV soccer by a small number of clubs, while its often spectacular camera work and lengthy pre-match features have added much to the repertory of television coverage.

iii. Business

There have been three main avenues through which soccer clubs have engaged with the late-twentieth-century enterprise culture. Sponsorship, already well-developed by the mid-1980s, had become obligatory by the end of the decade. Even fictional football teams could not buck the trend, the Trustee Savings Bank paying £20,000 to the *Roy of the Rovers* comic in 1992 in return for ringing the Melchester Rovers ground with TSB hoardings.[14] Commercial redevelopment of grounds has presented another important route. The long-term trend towards imposing ground improvements which reached its apotheosis with the Taylor Report has provided an opportunity to marry necessity with business. A number of clubs have sold off spare land around their grounds to supermarkets and other businesses, while others have moved to new sites, selling existing grounds which were often in prime city centre locations. Since 1986, nine League sides (Bristol Rovers, Chester, Huddersfield, Middlesbrough, Millwall, Northampton, Scunthorpe, Walsall and Wimbledon) have taken this route and many others have plans to do so.[15] For Bristol Rovers and Wimbledon the failure to find or afford new grounds has led to largely unsatisfactory ground-sharing arrangements, but for most clubs such moves have proved invaluable. Scunthorpe United, for example, the first English club to build a new ground since the Second World War, sold their Old Show Ground to Safeways for £3 million in 1988, thus clearing a £2.5 million debt, as well as gaining £200,000 from a local council as part of a sponsorship deal.[16]

Obviously, grounds are assets which can only be sold once and the smaller clubs which have opted for this route may have bought only medium- or even short-term security. For a few elite sides, however, the business climate of the late 1980s and 1990s has allowed the sale of a renewable and ultimately much more potent asset even than land – their names. By the early 1990s, merchandising had become an vital part of the football economy. The core business has been in the replica strips which began to be worn by supporters in the mid-1980s, as sportswear in general began to gain status as a fashion accessory. With shirts selling at between £30 and £37 and full adult size kit at around £60 by 1995, this represented a lucrative market both for manufacturers and for clubs who received payment for their co-operation. By the mid-1990s, the range of products had increased dramatically, to embrace, for example, babygros (Manchester United's was emblazoned with the logo 'Here we grow!') and even, in Newcastle United's case, a school shirt, with the club name discreetly displayed on the pocket and its colours in a check pattern on the inside collar.[17] Links with wider areas of popular culture were increasingly sought in order to maximise marketing impact, as when in 1995 Manchester City launched a range of T-shirts modelled by the band Oasis.[18]

Manchester United, blessed with comfortably the most exciting and glamorous image of all English League clubs, has taken merchandising the furthest. Its potential was well illustrated by an advert in a supermarket Christmas catalogue offering football club mugs at £2.99 with the accompanying rider 'Manchester United, £3.99'.[19] In 1993–94, money from the merchandising of its own range of 1,500 types of branded goods increased by 180 per cent over the previous season to generate £14 million of the club's £44 million turnover; only £18 million came from gate receipts. It is a significant pointer to the future staffing structure of elite football clubs that, in 1994, the club employed 42 players and 31 coaches against 123 individuals connected with merchandising, catering and administration.[20] The scale of this operation has been a major factor reinforcing the already often intense dislike of United among many soccer fans, a state of mind which was celebrated in the summer of 1995 by the appearance of T-shirt bearing the logo '1994–95 was a great season. Man Utd won F**k All.' However, even some United supporters have expressed disquiet about a commercial policy which, among other things, appeared to have dictated the club's decision to change its shirt design six times in four years in the early 1990s. This level of commercial profitability, it must be said, is unlikely to be reached by many other clubs, with even their closest rivals probably making only about half as much from this source in recent seasons.

In one sense, soccer clubs had no option other than to embrace more aggressive commercial strategies from the late 1980s; without them, many would have faced bankruptcy and collapse. Indeed, a report by a leading firm of accountants at this time noted that 80 of the League's 92 clubs were technically insolvent.[21] Despite numerous scares, only Fourth Division Aldershot folded, their departure in March 1992 making them the first side since Accrington Stanley to leave the League without completing their fixture list. Although luck, sympathetic creditors and PFA money and negotiating skill saved a number of clubs, attempts to court sponsors and develop a more overtly commercial element proved valuable both as a way of raising money and of earning the confidence and favour of investors and bank managers. As the Manchester United example shows, however, for a number of clubs the 'commercial turn' represented a major change of strategy and a serious attempt to exploit the game's untapped potential.

To some extent this reflects the arrival in the game of a new breed of director. Tottenham's Alan Sugar is probably the best known of the 'new entrepreneurs' who have found their way into the game since the 1980s.[22] Almost an iconic figure of the late-twentieth-century enterprise culture, he rose from a working-class background to amass a fortune believed to stand at £600 million by 1987, through his computer and electrical goods company, Amstrad. On joining the Spurs board in 1991, he admitted knowing little about football and later claimed that 'initially, I considered it was purely a business decision. I looked at the United States and saw it as a template. You looked at the television rights, and you could see how sponsorship worked.' Sugar's most famous moment (infamous in some eyes) came during the negotiations over the Premiership TV contract in 1992. Amstrad were the main suppliers of satellite receiving dishes and his support, as Tottenham chairman, for the BSkyB deal placed £6 million on the value of Amstrad shares. Ironically, this was the exact amount he had put into Tottenham on joining the board in 1991.[23]

The commercial imperative introduced by Sugar, his predecessor Irving Scholar, Manchester United's Martin Edwards, Arsenal's David Dein and others does, then, represent a powerful element within the modern game. A few individuals and companies appear to have had predatory instincts. Marler Estates, purchasers of Fulham in 1986, were more interested in redeveloping the Craven Cottage ground than the club, which the company intended to amalgamate with Queens Park Rangers.[24] However, this is not to say that the majority of such individuals have been motivated purely by financial gain. While it would be foolish to deny the strength of commercial motivation in the contemporary boardroom, many businessmen-directors are still guided by very complex motives. They are doubtless more than happy that their business ventures receive stimulation in terms of financial reward or publicity and many seem to inhabit a culture which seems to make it impossible to work with any institution that is not run according to a certain notion of business efficiency. Nevertheless, many individuals have 'wasted' large amounts of money on fairly hopeless causes. Overall, the whole gamut of influences which drew the middle classes into the professional game from the 1880s – local pride, philanthropic impulse, the search for political and/or social status and power or simply love of the game – still seem to operate. Jack Walker, for example, whose millions returned Blackburn Rovers to England's footballing elite after he became the club's major shareholder in January 1991, seems to have been motivated mainly by a sense of loyalty to the town in which his wealth was made, and to a club he supported from boyhood. A number of other chairmen, including Sir John Hall at Newcastle, Leslie Silver at Leeds and Sir Jack Hayward at Wolves, all claim lifelong allegiances to their clubs, towns and regions, while Alan Sugar's growing affection for Tottenham has been publicly stated on a number of occasions. At the most basic level, owning a substantial share of a football club became almost a fashion accessory in the 1980s and 1990s, something which wealthy businessmen were half-expected to do. Perhaps the root cause here has been the search for the masculine 'clubbability' that football brings and that many had left behind as their business careers blossomed. Emotional as much as economic reward remains a major motivating force within the boardrooms of English soccer.

Football's recovering prestige and the increasingly entrepreneurial climate within the game has also stimulated business ventures within the wider community. The period since the mid-1980s has seen a considerable increase in marketing opportunities, with computer games and videotapes providing a particularly strong addition to the more traditional fare. The early 1990s also saw an especially buoyant climate for the production of soccer literature. Soccer magazines have certainly flourished, some of the older titles surviving in slightly refocused form designed to acknowledge changes in early teen sub-culture over the last decade. *Shoot*, for example, has evolved a slightly more sardonic style and shows an increased concern with fashion. *Sweet FA* (1993) is a rather more distinctive product of the late twentieth century, a soccer version of the hugely successful scatological comic *Viz*. Its characters have included Diego Marijuana, the Busby Babes (a family of United devotees living in Basingstoke) and Danny Maguire, the flesh-eating full back.[25] Of particular interest are the 'football glossies', *FourFourTwo* (1994), *Goal* and *Total Football* (both 1995). These titles represent a new type of football magazine based on styles and formats honed in other popular cultural arenas, especially popular music, fashion and film, in such journals as *Q*, *Loaded*, *Empire* and *Premiere*. Aimed at the twenty- and thirty-something markets so attractive to potential advertisers, they owed their existence to publishers' awareness that fanzines, the huge success of Nick Hornby's *Fever Pitch* and other products of the *soccerati* had partly created, partly discovered an audience that wanted rather more literate and thoughtful fare than had been traditionally offered.

While each of these journals has adopted slightly differing housestyles, the standard product was fairly well captured in the claim that 'the new soccer glossies have expropriated one aspect of fanzine culture – wit – while elegantly eschewing their angry clamour for punters' rights.'[26] They are certainly prepared to puncture or toy with the myths surrounding leading players and clubs in a way that would have been completely alien to *Football Monthly* or *Soccer Star*. One typical piece led with the question, 'Stan Collymore: £8.5 million genius or just a big moaning git?'[27] They have, nevertheless, nurtured the star system by focusing much of their attention on a relatively small group of Premier League performers whereas the older generation of journals were always likely to include features or photos of teams and players little known beyond Crewe, Barnsley or wherever. Overall, while offering some penetrative and informative journalism, they have been one of the forces which have given soccer a much more glamorous image in the 1990s, locking into the more sophisticated, affluent male sub-cultures whose constituents see themselves as far removed from the terrace stereotype of the late 1970s and early 1980s. The appropriation of the game by the 'glossies' has placed football very firmly into the mainstream of fashionable popular cultural consumption.[28]

A not insignificant amount of the game's new wealth has accrued to the players. A report by accountants Touche Ross showed that in the 1993–94 season, the wages of Premier League and First Division players rose by an average of 22 per cent at a time when inflation ran at only 3 per cent. As ever, the differential between the elite and the rest remained considerable and has probably widened, with salaries in the top two divisions accounting for 70 per cent of the game's £140 million wage bill. At least 11 sides had total wage bills of over £5 million in 1993–94 (these do include non-playing staff) and although it is difficult to give specific figures about the earning power of individuals, weekly salaries of £10,000 and above were clearly on offer to a handful of leading Premier League players by the mid-1990s. One Endsleigh First Division side was even able to pay its second-year trainees £200 a week along with signing-on fees that ranged from £1,600 to £4,000. At the other end of the scale, six clubs (albeit with much smaller staffs) paid out less than £600,000 on salaries.[29] Nevertheless, even lower division players are financially better off in the 1990s than at any previous time. For a small number of star players blessed with particular good looks, good bodies or interesting character traits, the period from the late 1980s has seen ever greater opportunity for lucrative product endorsement, modelling work and various forms of TV, radio and other public appearances.

Reform from below

i Serving the 'community'

While the drive to a more commercial culture was a major impulse within the game from the 1980s, it was by no means the only one. The belief that clubs should forge more formal links with the community and place their considerable resources at the public disposal had been suggested as early as 1968 in the pages of the first Chester Report. At a time when attendances were buoyant and modern manifestations of hooliganism in their relative infancy, little was done to implement such radical ideas. In 1978, in a rather different climate in terms of attendances and behaviour, the Labour government attempted to encourage clubs to develop community schemes through a £1 million grant scheme administered by the Sports

Bradford City started an Asian supporters' club in 1994. (*Bradford Telegraph and Argus*)

Council, but results and interest were limited.[30] Significantly, it was not until the deeply troubled mid-1980s that community issues began to be taken far more seriously. The PFA, anxious to develop its training and education role, was a pioneer here, launching a pilot scheme funded by the Manpower Services Commission which involved six clubs in the north-west. By 1989, over fifty clubs were involved in the scheme which saw the new figure of the club Community Development Officer organising coaching sessions in schools, encouraging football for the disabled, stimulating the women's game, establishing family enclosures, launching anti-racism initiatives and generally encouraging good behaviour on the terraces. By the mid-1990s, most clubs were involved in such schemes, now organised under the umbrella of Footballer's Further Education and Vocational Training Society. At least half of the participating clubs offered free training to albeit small numbers of the long-term unemployed, designed to lead to vocational qualifications in sport and leisure management.[31]

The whole apparatus of community involvement was greeted with cynicism in some areas. Football clubs were, of course, only one of the many institutions ranging from banks to universities which appreciated that the warm and positive connotations of the word 'community' offered considerable opportunities to secure both easy public relations successes and, more crucially, government and European Union grants. Similarly, for the larger clubs involved, community development could offer a skilfully deployed counter-weight to rampant commercial activity. Doubtless there has been an element of such thinking and it is true that many clubs only saw the need for such initiatives at a moment of crisis. However, there appears to have been much genuine commitment. Community programmes have played their part in improving the atmosphere at games and in bringing younger children, including girls, into football grounds. It is significant that Preston North End, one of the most committed pioneers of community involvement, have managed to sustain an attendance level well above their divisional average in recent years (8,469 in 1994–95 as opposed to the average of 3,700), as well as generating one of the noisiest and most carnivalesque atmospheres in the game. While many factors have contributed to this, including the efforts of supporters' groups, the fact that the club had worked hard in this area of football management has surely had an influence.[32] Overall, community programmes have helped clubs regain (or at least claim to have regained) some of the central place in local culture that they once occupied almost 'naturally', before later twentieth-century social and economic change wrought such fragmentation in patterns of community life.

In a small number of cases the community impulse was stimulated by an overt desire to harness football to wider political programmes. This was certainly the case in regard to both Millwall and Halifax Town, with Millwall receiving sponsorship from Lewisham Council from 1986 to 1990 and Halifax actually being largely operated by Calderdale Council from 1987 to 1991 in order to prevent the club's closure. Both Labour-controlled councils, and Calderdale in particular, sought to adopt new mechanisms which would make football clubs more the servants of the local community and less the hobby of members of the business community. David Hellewell, the main architect of the Halifax takeover, argued that, 'Boardrooms are full of chancers and ego-trippers. Why should they alone decide the fate of something with which the whole community identifies? All the expertise you need to run a football club exists within a local community.' He went on to outline plans for an elected board which would break the

It really is all over. The Halifax Town dressing room after their relegation from the Football League in May 1994. (*Halifax Courier*)

domination of 'white male businessmen over the age of 55'. A form of community directorship, albeit a very limited one, was eventually introduced.[33]

By the 1990s, however, Millwall had traded the Lewisham logo for one that celebrated Captain Morgan's rum, and Halifax Town had returned to private hands. These were interesting experiments, but ones which failed to bear full fruit or to be more widely followed. The clubs involved were essentially unfashionable, particularly Halifax, which eventually lost League status in 1994. Perhaps if Wolves, Middlesbrough or one of the other financially troubled larger clubs had entered into significant relationships with their local authorities (Wolves did sell their ground to the council in the 1980s), imitation might have been more frequent. More crucially, English football, unlike its European counterparts, had no significant tradition of local authority involvement and simple conservatism thus played a hand.[34] Moreover, in the 1980s and 1990s, an age of increasingly stringent central government control of local authority expenditure, it was difficult for local politicians to defend what was often simplistically referred to by its detractors as 'soccer on the rates', at a time when cuts in education and social service budgets were the order of the day.[35] Such issues were complicated in Halifax by the local Labour Party's decision not only to support soccer in what was a proud stronghold of Rugby League, but to offer municipal support to a ballet company. Labour's opponents had little trouble in undermining these projects by use of discourses which married ratepayer consciousness with a measured anti-intellectualism. Local authority involvement in the game is, of course, still very much a feature of the late twentieth-century game. Only a few miles from Halifax, Kirklees Council, in partnership with Huddersfield Town, Huddersfield Rugby League club and Alfred McAlpine Construction, invested £2 million in the Alfred McAlpine Stadium into which the town's two clubs moved in August 1994. This arrangement guaranteed the council a 40 per cent share in the stadium development company.[36] Such hard-headed partnerships between football, the public sector and private enterprise may well become more frequent. For the present, however, more radically oriented political projects look less likely to emerge.

ii Fans

In many, although most certainly not all cases, fans are watching football in vastly improved grounds. Some clubs were anyway anxious to upgrade their facilities either in order to improve conditions for existing fans or

The old. Huddersfield Town play their last game at their Leeds Road Stadium in April 1994. (*Huddersfield Examiner*)

The new. An evening match at the club's new, all-seater McAlpine Stadium, shared with Huddersfield Rugby League Club and a venue for major rock concerts. (*Huddersfield Examiner*)

to attract new ones, but many others were only forced into action by the Popplewell and Taylor Reports. The latter was particularly important, resulting in the decision that all Premier and First Division grounds should be all-seater by the start of the 1994–95 season. This edict, unpopular with many fans, saw the end of such famous terraces as Liverpool's Kop, Arsenal's North Bank, Chelsea's Shed and Villa's Holte End and may well have changed the atmosphere at big soccer grounds for ever. Most of the redeveloped grounds also included vastly improved refreshment and toilet facilities, as well as considerable investment in executive boxes and corporate hospitality suites, now seen as obligatory as a way of attracting both new customers and sponsors. The Football Trust, set up in 1975 to administer funds derived from a voluntary levy on the profits from 'spot-the-ball' competitions and, since 1990, money released by the Government from betting duties, has provided an invaluable source of finance for these improvements.[37]

The Taylor Report had argued that it should be possible for clubs to upgrade grounds without passing on significant cost burdens to those who had previously stood on the terraces. However, the most striking feature for those attending football matches since the 1980s has been the considerably increased expense. In 1984, all First Division sides had a minimum adult admission price of between £2.00 and £2.50.[38] By 1992, £8 had become the common minimum and by 1994, the move to all-seater stadia saw a rise to £12 at most leading clubs. Many clubs had also introduced a sliding scale by the mid-1990s, involving a series of tariffs set according to the supposed quality of the game, which could result in entry being set at over £20. Even in the lower divisions, charges of £7 for standing and £11 for seats had become the norm by 1995.

These often quite dramatic increases in price, however, can hardly be said to have depressed attendances. Having reached an all-time aggregate low of 16,448,557 in 1985–86, they rose steadily year by year to reach 21,856,020 in 1994–95, thus returning to the levels of the early 1980s and actually standing at only some 3 million below the figure for much of the 1970s. Interestingly, in the 1990s, attendances rose fastest in the Premiership where admission costs were the highest, the Premiership attracting 11,213,000 fans in 1994–95 in comparison with the 7,809,000 that represented the First Division's lowest ever total in 1988–89. Whether or not the price rises have had an effect on the *type* of supporter is less clear. It is hard to believe that poorer supporters have been able to meet price rises which dramatically outstripped wage and benefit increases and, at

The face of the football crowd as clubs would like to see it. A good sprinkling of women and youngsters at least. (*Huddersfield Examiner*)

the least, many fans have probably been forced to become very selective about their choice of match. Many fans, though, are simply too addicted to the game to give it up unless their finances are in perilous straits. There is some evidence that Premiership clubs at least are attracting a wealthier clientele, with a survey taken in the 1993–94 season suggesting that as many as 30 per cent of fans earned more than £20,000 per annum and 10 per cent more than £30,000; lack of directly comparable data from earlier periods does, however, render any comment about change over time decidedly problematic.[39] Similarly, there is strong evidence for an increase in the number of women supporters (although again comparison is difficult), with the same survey suggesting that women comprised on average 13 per cent of all Premiership crowds.

One of the major factors behind the rise in attendances has undoubtedly been the decrease in concern about hooliganism. The problem has certainly not been eradicated. Many of the worst incidents in recent years have been perpetrated by England supporters abroad. Such outbreaks usually owed at least something to the influence of organised far-right groups and often a great deal to an excessive and perverted extreme English nationalism. In the domestic context, hooliganism hovers in the background, rarely noted by the press at a time when football's image is generally good.[40] Crowd disorder has largely been contained, with the level of hooliganism *inside* grounds, as measured by the number of arrests, declining fairly consistently from 1987–88. The sheer weight of the police presence and their use of close-circuit technology and other devices has proved important here. Despite the often considerable bravery of individual officers, undercover operations have not generally brought particularly rich harvests, although, more prosaically, information from the police's National Football Intelligence Unit, founded in 1989, has sometimes been usefully deployed.

Clubs have also worked hard to minimise problems, using stewards to police the more notorious sections of grounds and in some instances, as in the case of Leeds United, taking strong action against racial chanting and other activities which drew in many beyond the specific 'hooligan' element. The most infamous scheme was that developed by Luton Town, victims of a major disturbance during a home game with Millwall in March 1985. As from the 1986–87 season, the club decided to ban all away fans, arguing that such a policy would not only stop visitors causing trouble but would keep away their own hooligan element by denying them a target. A membership scheme, involving entrance via electronic turnstiles, was introduced in order to implement this. The Luton chairman, local businessman and Conservative MP David Evans, argued that a hooligan-free Kenilworth Road ground could be developed as a major business and leisure centre. There were no arrests at the ground in 1986–87, compared with 102 in the previous season, and policing costs were cut by a quarter. However, the loss of visiting fans cost Luton £250,000 in revenue and made them extremely unpopular with many fans and commentators who believed that such a scheme punished all supporters for the faults of a few. A 'black market' in guest tickets developed allowing some away fans to get in and indulge in behaviour which, according to one season-ticket holder, 'would have meant certain eviction, or arrest' if only more police had been present.[41]

The Football League were not supportive of the plan, banning Luton from the League Cup in 1986 because of it.[42] One of its staunchest supporters, however, was Mrs Thatcher, whose attempt to defend Luton and her parliamentary colleague by trying to persuade the Football League to reverse its decision represented the first ever prime ministerial intervention into the affairs of the League. The Luton experiment gave her and her supporters the chance to revive pressure for a national football membership scheme, which would have demanded that any supporter attending a match carry an identity card. A membership system had been recommended in the Popplewell Report that followed the Bradford fire in 1985 and for the next four years the government pursued such a scheme enthusiastically. Their case was met in turn by articulate and well-informed opposition rooted in arguments which stressed both the practical and financial problems and the civil rights implications. A Football Spectators Bill passed the Commons in January 1989, leading to an often hilarious debate during the Lords Committee stage when an attempt was made to exclude women from the bill's provisions, on the grounds that they played little part in violence. At this point, some members genuinely seemed to believe that this would allow male hooligans the opportunity to indulge in a little deceitful cross-dressing in order to gain admission to the ground. A government minister acknowledged that this was unlikely, but noted that 'some gangs had become masters of disguise'.[43] The Hillsborough tragedy of April 1989 eventually ended hopes for the bill, opponents pointing out that a malfunction of the technical equipment essential to a membership scheme could result in an incident on an even greater scale.

The whole membership and ID card issue probably strengthened the professional game in the long run. Opposition to a government whose motives were part genuine, part populist gesture to the party's right-wing

Even all-seater stadia are not immune to hooliganism. West Yorkshire police face Birmingham City fans at Huddersfield in May 1995. (*Huddersfield Examiner*)

supporters mobilised many fans and forced to them to take concerted action, while also focusing the attention of clubs on the need for closer crowd control. As a result of compromises with the government and individual action, most clubs had introduced controlled admission areas and membership schemes by the end of the decade. Ultimately, the turn towards all-seater stadia and the relentless rise in admission prices in the 1990s clearly seem to have been viewed by many clubs as the most potent forms of crowd control.

Important as all this has been, as is so often the case in the history of popular culture the most important changes have come from *within* football fan culture, rather than being imposed from outside. Heysel was a factor here, forcing many to reconsider either their own behaviour or that of friends whose actions had been ignored or condoned. At the same time, shifts in youth culture from the late 1980s placed a new emphasis on cannabis and carnival rather than, or at least alongside, alcohol and violence and with the rise of face-painting, inflatables and even football rattles, the terraces took on a rather friendlier aspect.[44] This in turn encouraged some of the lost millions to return to the game and to bring their families with them. Streamers, balloons and 'ticker-tape' receptions followed and by the mid-1990s goalmouths in some grounds resembled the aftermath of an especially unruly school party. Interestingly, some clubs rapidly tried to limit such activities – in fairness, there are safety issues and stamping on balloons is not necessarily a skill worthy of a professional footballer – or to incorporate them into more slightly more organised, club-led pre-match activity. Even friendly crowds, it seems, must be tamed.

The football fan's re-discovered respectability has allowed for (and been encouraged by) the emergence of a burgeoning body of fan-centred football literature. Three major strands can be identified. Club histories with a strong statistical flavour have proved popular, especially those published in the Breedon 'Complete History' series. Oral histories, often focused particularly on fans' perspectives on terrace culture, form another blossoming sector.[45] Most striking of all, however, has been the success of works by the so-called *soccerati*, writers usually drawn from outside the game who blend often serious literary ambition with highly personal views of football's meaning and significance. The prototype for work of this type was *Saturday's Boys* (1990), a set of essays edited by Harry Lansdown and Alex Spillius, but the classic product was Nick Hornby's *Fever Pitch* (1992).[46] This immensely successful dissection of an obsessive passion for

Arsenal was very much part of the culture of the male-confessional that took shape at this time, against a background of discussion of male roles after the impact of feminism. Indeed, this whole body of literature, largely although not exclusively written by men, was partly a celebration, partly a gentle critique of male culture: revealingly, the Lansdown and Spillius collection was dedicated 'to our Dads for taking us in the first place'. In Hornby's case it was also a humorously honest acknowledgement of the way in which middle-class youths have sought new and more exciting proletarian identities through their association with football.[47]

A particularly distinctive feature of post-1985 soccer culture has been the emergence of what might be loosely termed the 'independent fan movement', which has coalesced around a new type of supporters' association and the fanzine.[48] The first of the new style supporters' groups was the Football Supporters' Association, a national body originating in Liverpool in August 1985.[49] A product of the post-Hillsborough debate, the FSA found an articulate public voice in the form of its chair Rogan Taylor, a Liverpool supporter with a doctorate in cultural anthropology and, from 1989, a post at the Norman Chester Centre. By 1989, 20,000 members had been attracted by the arguments he and his colleagues put forward in favour of allowing fans a much closer influence in club decision-making, improved facilities, greater community involvement, an end to racial chanting and a range of other policies which distinguished the FSA from the older style of supporters' clubs. In the immediate post-Hillsborough period, when Taylor gained a very high media profile, the FSA made the views of the 'ordinary' supporter seem ever more the stuff of common sense. Other national pressure groups also emerged, including Football Fans Against the Criminal Justice Act, formed to fight public order legislation (which was eventually passed in 1995) which was thought to threaten fans' rights to peaceful demonstration, an increasingly frequent tactic in the 1990s, and make arrest for sheer exuberance more likely. At club level there was also a large growth in the number of 'independent' supporters' associations, groups anxious to avoid the kind of intimate relationship between club and supporters which had traditionally helped draw the teeth of fan discontent. The independent sector was behind most of the campaigns against bond schemes (a device asking fans to buy often expensive bonds to help raise money for ground improvements), unwanted ground alterations, the sale of key players, the role of unpopular directors and the many other things which have annoyed football's fans.

One of the most successful campaigns was that organised by networks of Charlton Athletic supporters who fought a seven-year campaign to return their club to The Valley. The club's board had decided to abandon the ground in preference for a nomadic existence in September 1985, following wrangles over ownership and ground safety. In 1989, the local council confounded the problem by refusing planning permission to re-develop the ground. Using, among other weapons, a fanzine, *The Voice of the Valley*, and the Valley Party, a political party whose 60 candidates took 10 per cent of the vote in the 1990 local elections, a group of fans succeeded in winning planning permission in 1991. Then, when financial shortages looked certain to wreck the scheme, over £1 million was raised by supporters in return for free season tickets and a seat on the board. Charlton finally returned to The Valley on an emotional afternoon in December 1992.[50] In a shorter but equally successful campaign between 1991–93, the Hammers Independent Supporters' Association destroyed a desperately unpopular bond scheme launched by the West Ham board.[51]

Not all fanzines have played quite the role enjoyed by *The Voice of the Valley*, but they have been one of the most distinctive features of the modern game. The fanzine originated among music fans and was made possible by the growth of cheap printing methods and personal computers. The search for the Holy Grail of the first football fanzine has exercised some and York City's *Terrace Talk*, founded in 1981, is one of a number that have been put forward for the honour.[52] By the mid 1980s, perhaps half a dozen titles existed, but reactions to Heysel, the growth of the FSA and its local counterparts and the various problems facing football fans, led to a dramatic growth. The other crucial factor here was the publication *When Saturday Comes*, launched on very modest scale in 1986, but establishing a circulation of 40,000 by 1991.[53] Describing itself as 'a half decent football magazine', it has been a more radical and less consciously commercial product than the 'new glossies' discussed earlier. Its great contribution to the fanzine movement has been the publicity offered via its listings section and its provision of models for content, approach and writing style.

At one level, it is dangerous to talk of 'fanzines' as though they were a homogeneous category.[54] They adopt different approaches, languages and political flavours. A few, such as *The Football Pink*, aimed at gay supporters, and *Born Kicking*, a feminist fanzine, have definite political agendas. While some, such as the *Chelsea Independent*, proclaim a non-sexist, non-racist editorial policy, others show a sub-rag magazine approach to women. (Fanzines, though, are almost invariably overtly anti-racist.) Some give quite lengthy coverage to major issues facing the game, others prefer a lighter touch and often devote remarkable amounts of space to attacks on rival clubs. There are, though, very clear unifying threads, apart from an often unavoidably erratic publication schedule and an interest in the quality of beer awaiting in the oppositions' town centres. These include a great deal of irreverent humour; a broadly radical, anti-establishment position, certainly on footballing issues; considerable nostalgia usually directed at the 1970s and early 1980s, when the spectating careers of many of the writers and readers began; and, last but certainly not least, an intense commitment to their team, mirrored by an often equally intense dislike of particular opponents.

It is probable that the typical readership is similar to that attracted to *When Saturday Comes*, namely largely male, aged 20–30, relatively well educated and a regular attender at matches.[55] By the nature of their very local appeal, fanzines may well reach a rather younger audience as well, and, indeed, some are produced by teenagers. Although women and girls do read and contribute to them, fanzines seem to represent and construct a decidedly male culture and mental terrain. Indeed, males under thirty produce the vast majority of these publications.[56] What is most striking in this regard is the way in which, as with much of the writing of Hornby and others, they chart young men's search for authenticity and for cultural roots through football. This is most often expressed simply by the writers' desire to stress (often with justification) that they are the 'real' fans, loyal despite the weather or league position, paragons of virtue to be set against the new wave of family and middle-class spectators/consumers. Such thoughts were most focused in the often quite powerful attacks on the introduction of all-seater stadia, a development which fanzines almost universally opposed. Obviously, much of the opposition was rooted in practicalities including the inevitability of price rises, the problems of keeping warm and the dangers of sitting next to undesirable company that could no longer be avoided by a subtle move a few feet along the terracing. However, there was also a sense that the young, committed fan was both at the heart of the modern game and the defender of a proud heritage. They created the atmosphere which 'the middle and upper-class types who hire out executive boxes expected . . . to come free – we were as much part of the entertainment as the football was.'[57] Moreover, they watched football in the way that it should be watched (standing up) and as their forebears had watched it. 'The heart and soul of British football, going way back to when the game emerged from the grimy backstreets of the Industrial Revolution, is being ripped out and the clubs don't care . . . the clubs could see more money coming in from "better" clientele and they did not stand in the way of progress.'[58] Rather in the way that music, especially black music, has allowed young white men to escape the boundaries of their own culture and to experiment with more exotic ones, the terrace represented a space in which the middle-class fan could enjoy an experience that connected them to a wider culture, and the working-class one to an older notion of community which was increasingly diminishing in the 'outside' world.[59] The end of the terrace symbolised the end of a much larger and more profound cultural configuration.

Not surprisingly, broadcasters have been anxious to appropriate something of the fanzine style and a number of TV and radio programmes have emerged which have tried to give represent supporters' views or even to give them public expression. The best known, Radio 5's Saturday evening phone-in, *Six-O-Six*, was started in August 1990 with ex-music journalist Danny Baker as presenter. A Millwall supporter with a well-honed dislike of the football establishment, Baker proved an highly effective figure, consistently supporting the views of the terrace supporter and refusing to give air-time to those directors (and occasionally those fans) who 'phoned up with the party line'. Other broadcasting commitments led to his replacement by ex-Conservative minister David Mellor in 1992, who, having persuaded depressingly deferential callers to refer to him as 'David' and not 'Mr Mellor', succeeded in building on its success and helping make it, according to one recent observer, 'the most popular and credible football show on radio'.[60]

At the very least, the emergence of an active, participatory fan culture has often been the source of great fun and pleasure for both those who have constructed it and those who have consumed it. It has given the game a vibrant popular culture which, although having deep roots in the past, has been a very distinctive product of the late twentieth century. More than that, it has helped considerably to resurrect the image of the football fan, to 'defend the integrity and good nature of fans against the deviant discourses posited by the media, the police, the government and frequently the football clubs themselves'.[61] It can also claim a string of considerable achievements ranging from the success of Charlton supporters in The Valley campaign right down to tiny but important decisions regarding the removal of over-zealous stewards and the price of half-time tea. The 'independent fan movement', does, for all its failings and divisions, deserve a place among the many single issue pressure and direct action movements which have proved to be an often effective radical political and social force since 1979. They have given football fans far more influence than was engendered by any of the 'symbolic' victories claimed by some historians for fans in earlier periods.

Care must be taken, though, not to adopt too celebratory a tone, especially in regard to the fanzine. One stimulating article has argued that they have provided 'at least in part, a *successful* contestation with the increasingly insistent commercial tendencies in modern spectator sport'.[62] H. F. Moorhouse is surely correct to claim that such a view can lead to a romanticised and exaggerated view of fanzines' influence. 'Praising them for their "counter-hegemonic" thrust and the like is simply to hymn the powerless and to avoid confronting the exact forces which are changing the nature of soccer as a cultural product.'[63] Moreover, on a broader front, some fans are supportive of many of the changes in the game's marketing and style, while plenty of fanzine-reading members of independent supporters' associations can be found purchasing expensive replica strips and subscriptions to satellite TV. As ever, supporters cannot always be placed in neat categories and active minorities, whether 'hooligans' or 'reformers', cannot be seen as representing the norm. Because of this complex set of attitudes, fanzines and in fact fan movements in general, have rarely threatened the ultimate set of power relationships within the game, and indeed in many cases have never really sought to do so. Fans know that for 'their' club to be successful the economics of the modern game demands that it find a small number of individuals with lots of money. Most fans have thus tended to seek consultation rather than take the levers of power. By the mid-1990s, a combination of good commercial sense on the part of directors and officials and effective spectator pressure had ensured that football fans were less likely to be taken for granted than had often been the case before. However, in terms of the critical decisions that govern the sport, football was still a long way from being 'the people's game'.

Conclusion

THE WORDS 'continuity' and 'change' have always loomed large in the historian's vocabulary, although just how helpful they are is uncertain. The rate and significance of historical change is very much in the eye of the beholder, as much historiographical debate testifies. However, it would be a little cowardly not to attempt an assessment of the main patterns of change that have occurred over the century and a quarter from 1863.

Clearly, the most dramatic changes arose at the beginning and end of the period. Both the game and its social and organisational structure altered markedly between the 1860s and the late 1880s, while the last thirty years, and especially the last ten, have also seen significant changes. While football and its culture was hardly static in the long intervening period between 1885 and 1961, it was marked by certain constant features. It was a sport which drew heavily on a male, working-class constituency whose interest was rooted in an often intense loyalty to a particular locality. The game was played at set times and the media, although hugely important, was decidedly the junior partner in its relationship with sport. Financial rewards for those playing and running the game were generally modest, its commercial element kept under fairly tight control.

Much of this pattern is still recognisable in the late twentieth century, but it has altered in significant ways. Crowds are less overtly working class than was previously the case, although admittedly this may have more to do with changing patterns of social mobility and the decline of manufacturing industry than any major appropriation of the football ground by the 'traditional' middle classes. Women are still in a fairly marginal position, but their attendance levels appear to be rising and the football industry's attitude to women spectators has become ever more positive. Loyalty to place and region is still one of the game's central dynamics and, indeed, football remains arguably the key element in the symbolic conflict between north and south, provinces and metropolis, that remains a potent feature of English culture. However, especially among younger fans, local patriotism increasingly takes second place to support of a small number of successful Premiership clubs. While supporters of

Crewe Alexandra or Torquay United invariably have some link with the local community, those expressing allegiance to Manchester United and Liverpool can be found in every corner of the country.

There can be no denying the extent of the economic changes within the game. All players obviously receive far greater financial rewards than those who laboured under the maximum wage, while an elite group of Premiership players earn more in a few weeks than their predecessors received in a career. Similarly, the game has become far more commercially attuned in the last decade, with clubs enthusiastically turning to sponsorship deals and merchandising ventures as a major source of income generation. The media, and television in particular, has as both sponsor and publicist exerted enormous influence here.

The game itself has most certainly changed since the 1950s, both in terms of the way it is played and the way it is prepared for and managed. The last thirty years have not seen a single transforming influence or defining moment equivalent to the development of the passing game in the 1870s and 1880s or the change to the offside rule in 1925. However, they have witnessed a constant process of tactical innovation, a process further enhanced by the arrival of lighter balls and kit. The outcome has been too varied to allow for easy generalisation, particularly in terms of tactical formations and styles, but the key elements include a remarkable increase in the pace at which the English game is now played and the use of systems of play designed both to deny opponents space and place a premium on maintaining possession. In order to operate such systems, which demand high work-rates and considerable flexibility, players are far more highly trained and fitter and far more in thrall to managers and coaches than has ever been the case. Comparison between players of different generations is notoriously hazardous and the old cliché that the greatest players of previous generations would have been great at any time carries much truth. Suffice it to say that, in their marriage of tactical knowledge, physical fitness and technical skill, the very best players of the post-1960 era have taken their profession to hitherto unparalleled heights.

This book has set out to assess not simply patterns of change but the wider relationship between football and English society. Most social historians have preferred to see this relationship as essentially one-dimensional and have concentrated on the impact that society has exerted upon football. Fishwick, for example, argues that historians of the period from 1910 to 1950 can 'learn more about English society by asking not what effect football had on society but what effect society had on football.'[1] In many senses, this argument is highly convincing, for the football world has so clearly borne the imprint of social and economic forces at every stage of its development. However, such an approach is rather limiting. At the very least it would be strange if such a vital cultural form as soccer did not exert some impact on attitudes and behaviour, even if only in the sense of legitimising and reinforcing existing values and beliefs. Indeed, the football ground has been an important arena within which individuals can learn lessons about social and political roles and identities which are then carried 'back' into other aspects of daily life. Moreover, football-related activity has sometimes actually shaped events and attitudes. To give a very simple example, contemporary outbreaks of 'hooliganism' have had a quite profound impact on the way in which the general public has used city centres and other public places on match days. Again, *representations* of the game and its followers on offer in various media forms do not just reinforce views but actually shape them. To use a grossly simplified model, middle-class England has decided much about its working-class equivalent from images derived from the football pitch and terrace. Obviously, this type of discussion over causality can descend to a fairly sterile semantic debate, involving as it does rather too many 'reflecting' chickens and 'reinforcing and constructing' eggs. Nevertheless, we should acknowledge a little more circularity in the relationship between social and economic base and sporting superstructure, and football's capacity to engender social change. Football, like all cultural forms, must always be allowed a certain autonomy.

Whatever the exact mechanism between football and society, it is tempting to conclude that football did little to challenge the political and social *status quo* at any time from the late nineteenth century. Obviously, definitive judgment on this matter is neither possible nor desirable: sporting culture is capable of the same latitude of interpretation as any other form of culture. Although football had the capacity to frighten sections of society, only rarely – such as in the conflicts over amateurism and professionalism in the 1880s – is it possible to glimpse any sense of it posing a significant challenge to established social and political groups. For all the sense of popular 'ownership' of the game that stems from passionate, committed support and the more sophisticated forms of participatory democracy that have emerged since 1985, the game has always been controlled by sections of various male elites and sub-elites. This is not to view the game as a deliberate ruling-class conspiracy designed to hold the working class in political bondage; it is merely to acknowledge social reality. It may well have been the case, however, that fans' involvement in the game limited the time, space and energy that they had available for political activity and thought. If this was the case, then the game's de-radicalising function was the result of choice and not manipulation. As Richard Holt has argued, 'if football was an opiate, it was a democratic one – of the people, by the people, for the people.'[2]

Football's position within the wider national culture has always been a barometer of elite attitudes towards both popular culture in general and the political and moral health of the working class in particular. For much of the late nineteenth and early twentieth century, the game found both supporters and detractors within the ranks of the propertied classes, some seeing the game as anything from a healthy recreation to a necessary safety valve, others as a trivial distraction from some other more significant area of life and/or one which encouraged gambling and other unhealthy habits. By the inter-war period, the good behaviour of fans and the arrival of mass democracy gave football a protective veneer and, in fact, terrace culture became a synonym for a populist version of good-natured Englishness which was to survive until well into the 1960s. From that point, as 'hooliganism' gained ever more attention and became ever more costly, a nation very far from being at ease with itself often found football a convenient scapegoat for deeper-seated fears about its well-being. At key moments, especially in the early and mid-1980s, when so many institutions associated with working-class culture were under attack from neo-liberal economic and political ideologies, the privileged position that football had held for so long in the national culture came under threat. The game's rise in public esteem in recent years can also be situated in this long-standing relationship between, crudely stated, elite and popular cultures. Reform from within the game and the powerful influence of the media have been central to this process of recovery, but as ever, the attitudes of those in influential social and political positions have proved important. Football has clearly been perceived as less of a threat, and criticism of it gained less purchase, in an age of diminished working-class militancy. Moreover, at a time when the leisure industry has been viewed as a leading route to economic salvation, football as consumer cornucopia sits well with much current economic philosophy.

Re-packaged and partially re-invented like so many other contemporary cultural products with roots in Victorian society, the extent of the game's recovery since its nadir in 1985 has been remarkable. Even the briefest sketch reveals the extent of football's rejuvenation. Attendances at Football League and Premiership matches rose by 25 per cent between 1985–86 and 1994–95. In one week in October 1995, someone who possessed only terrestrial television could watch over 13 hours of football-related programmes, including three that dealt with aspects of the game's history. Football literature continues to multiply on the shelves of high street bookshops, while Fantasy Football League has become one of the most popular cultural phenomena of the decade and a major source of good publicity for the 'proper' game. A combination of greater racial awareness and commercial good sense has led to belated but serious attempts being made to attract supporters and players from minority ethnic groups, especially those from south Asian communities.[3] Similarly, both the women's game itself and women's wider interest and presence within the men's game have received growing recognition and endorsement. Highlights of the women's cup final were shown on national television (by Channel Four) for the first time in 1989, while by the mid-1990s, the WFA's Julie Hemsley had become the first woman member of the FA Council.[4] Again, while the fictional *Manageress* occupied television screens in 1990, 23-year-old Karren Brady became football's first woman managing director at Birmingham in March 1993, and a new generation of women journalists, most notably Charlotte Nicol and Eleana Oldroyd (building on the earlier pioneering work of print journalists such as Julie Welch and Cynthia Bateman) have made radio and TV reporting a little less of a male preserve. Some, of course, would read this as evidence of tokenism and some of these developments and personalities have proved controversial. Nevertheless, some real achievements have been made.

Beneath this confident picture, however, there is a sense that the foundations of football's recovery may be less than secure. One cannot escape the feeling that, whereas the game originally flourished in a highly distinctive, largely settled culture constrained by limits on its choice and opportunity, its recent revival and growth in a far more complex and fluid society is partly a fashion statement, a product of a particularly powerful media campaign. Two possible dangers present themselves. On the one hand, soccer could be oversold. Indeed, some already think it has been; Nick Hornby has argued that televised football has become 'like music. It's on all the time, and you can tune in or not. And most of it isn't any good.'[5] The revolution in television technology, especially the arrival of digital TV, which will make many more channels available, certainly increases the risk of over-exposure. Alternatively, a spell of poor publicity for the game could weaken its symbiotic relationship with the media. Its intrinsic appeal and deep roots should protect it against the challenge of other skilfully marketed sports such as rugby, but football's leadership can no longer afford to take the game's status for granted. Irrespective of what does happen – and subsequent events often make historians look foolish when they speculate in this way – football now exists in a changed social context. Until as late as the 1950s, a local football club absorbed some of the energies of a remarkably large number of the local male community and, as such, served as a 'natural' community focus. That position no longer appertains and future gains will have to be earned and not assumed.

Whatever the social and cultural significance the game may have had over the period from 1863 and whatever its place in the future, it has undoubtedly been the source of immense social, aesthetic and emotional pleasure (and not a little pain) to its numerous devotees. Very few modern cultural forms have stirred the passions of quite so many individuals as football. Those who underestimate or deride the game's power and significance are guilty of the worst kind of narrow-mindedness; they are also missing a rich experience.

Notes to the Text

Introduction

1. For a valuable overview of writing on football history, see T. Mason, 'Football and the historians', *International Journal of the History of Sport*, 5, 1 (1988), pp. 136–41. Percy Young, a musicologist, was a key writer in the 1950s.
2. A substantially revised version entitled *The People's Game. The History of Football Revisited*, was published by Mainstream Press, Edinburgh, in 1994.
3. I have not made detailed reference to sociological and other models in this book, although that it is not to say that I have not been influenced by them. For an excellent introduction, see G. Jarvie and J. Maguire (eds), *Sport and Leisure in Social Thought* (Leicester, 1994).
4. Wales, if only by virtue of having six clubs which have enjoyed Football League membership, does receive more consideration than Ireland and Scotland. Some of the very best sports history has emanated from research into activity in these three countries. For soccer, see, for example, B. Crampsey, *The Scottish Footballer* (Edinburgh, 1978) and *The Scottish Football League: The First One Hundred Years* (Glasgow, 1991); B. Murray, *The Old Firm* (Edinburgh, 1984); M. Brodie, *One Hundred Years of Irish Football* (Belfast, 1980); J. Sugden and A. Bairner, *Sport, Sectarianism and Society in a Divided Ireland* (Leicester, 1993). For a synthesis of the game's history on the broadest canvass, see the excellent B. Murray, *Football: A History of the World Game* (Alsershots, 1994).

Chapter 1

1. F. P. Magoun, Jr, *History of Football From the Beginning to 1871* (Cologne, 1871); J. Walvin, *The People's Game. The History of Football Revisited* (Edinburgh, 1994), pp. 11–31.
2. A. Delves, 'Popular recreation and social conflict in Derby, 1800–1850', in E. and S. Yeo (eds), *Popular Culture and Class Conflict, 1590–1914* (Brighton, 1981), pp. 89–127.
3. R. W. Malcolmson, *Popular Recreations and English Society, 1700–1850* (Cambridge, 1973), pp. 34–5; E. Dunning and K. Sheard, *Barbarians, Gentlemen and Players* (New York, 1979), pp. 21–45.
4. Delves 'Derby', p. 105.
5. Malcolmson, *Popular Recreations*, pp. 138–42; Delves, 'Derby', pp. 89–91, 107–8.
6. R. Holt, 'Football and the urban way of life in nineteenth-century Britain', in J. A. Mangan (ed.), *Pleasure, Profit and Proselytism* (London, 1988), pp. 71–2.
7. Malcolmson, *Popular Recreations*, p. 141; *Morning Chronicle*, 3 March 1851, cited in D. A. Reid, 'Folk-football, the aristocracy and cultural change: A critique of Dunning and

Sheard', *International Journal of the History of Sport*, 5, 1 (1988), p. 230.
8. Reid, 'Folk Football', p. 227.
9. Dunning and Sheard, *Barbarians*, pp. 46–62.
10. B. Haley, *The Healthy Body and Victorian Culture* (Cambridge, MA, 1978); J. A. Mangan, *Athleticism in the Victorian and Edwardian Public School* (Cambridge, 1981).
11. Obviously, this is a very broad generalisation given the complexities of the games. W. J. Baker, 'The making of a working class football culture in Victorian England', *Journal of Social History*, 13, 2 (1977), p. 242.
12. P. Young, *Football in Sheffield* (1981), pp. 16–19; Dunning and Sheard, *Barbarians*, pp. 109–10. Football matches had been played by a 'Sheffield side' since 1855, but the club was not placed on a permanent footing until 1857.
13. Dunning & Sheard, *Barbarians* p. 106.
14. C. W. Alcock, *Association Football* (London, 1906), pp. 2–12; G. Green, *The History of the Football Association* (London, 1953), pp. 19–33.
15. T. Mason, *Association Football and English Society, 1863–1915* (Brighton, 1980), p. 31.
16. Young, *Sheffield*, p. 31; M. Barak, *A Century of Rugby at Sale* (1963), pp. 7–11; G. Williams, *The Code War. English Football Under the Historical Spotlight* (Harefield, Middlesex, 1994), p. 52.
17. Information taken from the club directory in C. W. Alcock (ed.), *The Football Annual, 1880*.
18. A. Metcalfe, 'Football in the mining communities of east Northumberland, 1882–1914', *International Journal of the History of Sport*, 5, 3 (1988), pp. 267–91; the exploits of these three sides briefly graced the pages of the *Accrington Times* in the early 1880s.
19. K. Farnsworth, *Wednesday* (Sheffield, 1982), p. 19; C. E. Sutcliffe and F. Hargreaves, *History of the Lancashire Football Association, 1878–1928* (Blackburn, 1928), pp. 50–1.
20. C. Andrew, '1883 Cup Final. "Patricians" *v.* "Plebians"', *History Today* (May 1983), pp. 21–4. *The Times* seemed to think he was called Crossley.
21. Metcalfe, 'Mining communities', shows that a dense network of junior clubs lay well outside of elite control; *Preston Herald*, 24 March 1888.
22. M. A. Bienefeld, *Working Hours in British Industry. An Economic History* (London, 1972), pp. 82, 106–18; D. A. Reid, 'The decline of Saint Monday, 1766–1876', *Past and Present*, 71 (1976), pp. 76–101.
23. The popularity of rugby in the city was another factor here. T. Mason, *The Blues and the Reds. A History of Liverpool and Everton Football Clubs*, Historic Society of Lancashire and Cheshire (Liverpool, 1985), p. 1: M. Speak, 'Social stratification and participation in sport in mid-Victorian England', in Mangan (ed.), *Pleasure, Profit*, p. 62.
24. H. Cunningham, 'Leisure', in J. Benson (ed.), *The Working Class in England, 1875–1914* (Beckenham, 1985), p. 137; J. Benson, *The Working Class in Britain, 1850–1939* (London, 1989), pp. 39–71.
25. J. K. Walton, 'The demand for working-class seaside holidays in Victorian England', *Economic History Review*, xxxiv, 2 (1981), pp. 249–65.
26. Walvin, *People's Game*, pp. 59–60.
27. Holt, 'Urban way of life'. pp. 73–4.
28. S. Wagg, *The Football World. A Social History* (Brighton, 1984), p. 4.
29. P. Bailey, *Leisure and Class in Victorian England* (London, 1978).
30. C. P. Korr, 'West Ham United and

the beginnings of professional football in east London, 1895–1914', *Journal of Contemporary History*, 13 (1978), pp. 215–16.
31. Bailey, *Leisure*, p. 139.
32. Anon., *Bolton Wanderers F.C.* (Bolton, 1926), p. 2; A. Ward, *The Manchester City Story* (Manchester, 1984), p. 5. In this latter case it must be said that the church initiated the rupture.
33. Bailey, *Leisure*, p. 139.
34. R. Holt, *Sport and the British* (Oxford, 1989), pp. 159–79.
35. For an extended treatment of what follows below, see D. Russell, '"Sporadic and curious". The emergence of rugby and soccer zones in Yorkshire and Lancashire, *c.* 1860–1914', *International Journal of the History of Sport*, 5, 2 (1988), pp. 185–205.
36. *The Times*, 12 November 1880.
37. Dunning and Sheard, *Barbarians*, p. 137.
38. *The Times*, 12 November 1880.
39. Sutcliffe and Hargreaves, *Lancashire Football Association*, p. 29.
40. H. Berry and G. Allman, *One Hundred Years at Deepdale* (Preston, 1982), p. 16; D. Wiseman, *Up the Clarets. The Story of Burnley Football Club* (Burnley, 1973), pp. 13–14.
41. Rev. F. Marshall, *Football: The Rugby Union Game* (London, 1982), pp. 381–2.
42. Russell, 'Sporadic', pp. 194–5. This logic, of course, does not explain the persistence of rugby in and around south-west Lancashire in the late nineteenth century and *soccer's* failure to gain a significant foothold at senior level in this area.
43. S. Edgell and D. Jary, 'Football: A sociological eulogy', in M. Smith, S. Parker and C. Smith (eds), *Leisure and Society in Britain* (London, 1973), pp. 214–29.
44. *The Times*, 12 November 1880.
45. Sutcliffe and Hargreaves, *Lancashire Football Association*, p. 17.
46. Alcock (ed.), *Football Annual, 1880*, p. 10; Alcock, *Association Football*, pp. 33–7.
47. F. Wall, *Fifty Years in Football* (London, 1935), p. 25.
48. Walvin, *People's Game*, pp. 76–7.
49. Alcock, *Association Football*, pp. 32–3.
50. Heading may have been a feature of the early Sheffield game, but its popularisation is often seen as the particular contribution of the Royal Engineers player of the early 1870s, Lt Sims. Players presumably either ducked or shielded their faces when faced with fast moving, head-height balls before this time. Williams, *Code War*, p. 45. For a complaint about its overuse by one-time England captain, N. C. Bailey, see Alcock (ed.), *Football Annual, 1885*.
51. Dunning and Sheard, *Barbarians*, p. 122.
52. *FA Yearbook, 1955–6* (London), pp. 44–7.
53. Williams, *Code War*, p. 63.
54. S. Tischler, *Footballers and Businessmen. The Origins of Professional Soccer in England* (New York, 1981), p. 52.
55. W. Bennett, *The History of Burnley*, part 4 (Burnley, 1951), p. 227; Berry and Allmann, *Deepdale*, pp. 25, 20. Scottish imports were far less frequent in other areas at this stage. See Williams, *Code War*, p. 93.
56. Bailey, *Leisure*, pp. 129–36.
57. Quoted in Tischler, *Footballers*, p. 44.
58. *Manchester Guardian*, 30 November 1884.
59. S. Yeo, *Religion and Voluntary Organisations in Crisis* (Beckenham, 1976), pp. 189–91.
60. Wall, *Fifty Years*, pp. 34–5; Alcock (ed.), *Football Annual, 1883*, p. 67.
61. N. L. 'Pa' Jackson, *Sporting Days and Sporting Ways* (London, 1932),

p. 46; *Preston Herald*, 23 December 1885, 9 January 1889.
62. *Preston Guardian*, 30 Jan 1884; Williams, *Code War*, pp. 89–90.
63. *The Times*, 21 July 1885.
64. Tischler, *Footballers*, p. 48.
65. L. Allison, 'Batsman and bowler: the key social relation of Victorian England', *Journal of Sports History*, 7, 2 (1980), pp. 5–20; R. Sissons, *The Players. A Social History of the Professional Cricketer* (London, 1988).
66. Mason, *Association*, p. 76.
67. This rule was rescinded in 1903. Wall, *Fifty Years*, pp. 118–19.
68. Mason, *Association*, p. 75.
69. Williams, *Code War*, pp. 90, 94.
70. At least 9 of the 21 individuals comprising the FA's officers and executive committee in summer 1885 had attended public schools. *The Times*, 1 September 1885.
71. Dunning and Sheard, *Barbarians*, pp. 175–200.

Chapter 2

1. W. Vamplew, *Pay up and Play the Game. Professional Sport in Britain, 1875–1914* (Cambridge, 1988), p. 63.
2. *The Sports Trader* was a monthly trade journal founded in 1907.
3. T. Mason, *Association Football and English Society* (Brighton, 1981), pp. 188–91.
4. The nets were invented by J. A. Brodie, the Liverpool City Engineer. F. Wall, *My Fifty Years in Football* (London, 1935), pp. 42–3.
5. Referees appear to have first used whistles from about 1878. P. Soar, *The Hamlyn A–Z of British Football Records* (1985), p. 172.
6. T. Mason, 'The introduction of the penalty kick in football', paper presented to British Society of Sports History 14th Annual Conference, Huddersfield, July 1995. Mason also stressed the importance of the changes relating to referees in this paper. B. Dobbs, *Edwardians at Play* (London, 1973), pp. 60–1.
7. Mason, *Association*, p. 211. He was also granted the right to wear a distinguishing jersey from 1909.
8. C. W. Alcock, *Association Football* (London, 1906), p. 39.
9. I am heavily reliant for much of what follows here on the excellent S. Inglis, *League Football and the Men who Made It* (London, 1988).
10. Inglis, *League Football*, p. 13; *Preston Herald*, 10 October 1888.
11. *Daily News* quoted in *Preston Herald*, 3 April 1889.
12. The initial 12 had grown to 14 in 1891.
13. Vamplew, *Pay up*, p. 136.
14. *Staffordshire Sentinel*, 15 June 1907, 4, 6, 12, 17, 19, 22 June 1908.
15. *Yorkshire Observer Budget*, 24 February 1894. For greater detail see D. Russell, '"Sporadic and curious". The emergence of soccer and rugby zones in Yorkshire and Lancashire, *c.* 1860–1914', *International Journal of the History of Sport*, 5, 2 (1988), pp. 185–205.
16. *Brighouse Echo*, 31 August 1906; *Yorkshire Daily Observer*, 8 April 1907.
17. The English Schools Football Association was founded in 1904.
18. On the sporting press, see T. Mason, 'Sporting News, 1860–1914', in M. Harris and A. Lee (eds), *The Press and English Society for the Seventeenth to the Nineteenth Centuries* (London, 1986), pp. 168–86.
19. A. Gibson and W. Pickford (eds), *Association Football and the Men Who Made It* (1906), vol. II, pp. 102–5, vol. III, pp. 33–96. Generally, southern football has been far less heavily researched than the northern game.
20. Many attendance figures at this

stage were only estimates, but we can gain some sense of comparative sizes. In the first three months of the 1905–6 season, for example, Fulham drew crowds of between 14,000 and 30,000 for Southern League games. On a January Saturday in 1900, a Southern League match between New Brompton and Queens Park Rangers drew 2,000, while a First Division match between Preston and Stoke attracted only 4,000 and a Second Division match featuring Burslem Port Vale and Arsenal only 800. *Middlesex Advertiser and Chelsea Mail*; *Football Echo and Sports Gazette* (Bournemouth and Southampton), 13 January 1900. The weather in the north was admittedly very bad on the day in question.

21. Official Football League attendance statistics are only available as from 1925. However, as with the Southern League figures, estimates based on press reports and club records give a reasonable indication. Information on League attendances is drawn from Brian Tabner's indispensable *Through the Turnstiles* (Harefield, Middlesex, 1992).
22. Vamplew, *Pay up*, p. 128.
23. C. Buchan, *A Lifetime in Football* (London, 1955), pp. 79–80.
24. Wall, *Fifty Years*, p. 66.
25. Inglis, *League Football*, pp. 28–9, 34–7, 50, 63–5, 103–11, 387–92.
26. G. Green, *History of the Football Association* (London, 1953), pp. 194–5; Gibson and Pickford (eds), *Association Football*, vol. III, pp. 129–216.
27. D. Birley, *Land of Sport and Glory. Sport and British Society, 1887–1910* (Manchester, 1995), p. 36.
28. W. E. Greenland, *The History of the Amateur Football Alliance* (Harwich, 1966), pp. 17–57; Green, *Football Association*, pp. 203–28. See also J. Lowerson, *Sport and the English Middle Classes, 1870–1914* (Manchester, 1993), pp. 181–6. The title Amateur Football Alliance was adopted in 1934.
29. *Northampton Football Echo*, 12 February 1921.
30. Mason, *Association*, pp. 35–41; S. Tischler, *Footballers and Businessmen. The Origins of Professional Soccer in England* (New York, 1981), pp. 69–87; Vamplew, *Pay up*, pp. 154–73.
31. Vamplew, *Pay up*, pp. 161, 166–8.
32. Lack of space prevents the term 'local elite' from coming under closer scrutiny here. There is a need, though, for greater consideration of exactly which groups were represented in boardrooms.
33. Wall, *Fifty Years*, pp. 112–13.
34. Vamplew, *Pay up*, pp. 86–7.
35. Their companies could bid, however. Vamplew, *Pay up* p. 172–3.
36. Tischler, *Footballers*, p. 78.
37. *Preston Herald*, 13 April 1895. See also Inglis, *League Football*, pp. 28–30.
38. Tischler, *Footballers*, p. 138; H. Glasper, *Middlesbrough. A Complete Record, 1876–1989* (Derby, 1989), pp. 22–3. For further examples of political usages, see Mason, *Association*, p. 48.
39. Tischler, *Footballers*, p. 72; E. Dunning and K. Sheard, *Barbarians, Gentlemen and Players* (New York, 1979), p. 215.
40. J. Golby and A. W. Purdue, *The Civilisation of the Crowd* (London, 1984), pp. 192–3. For a general consideration of socialist attitudes to popular culture, see C. Waters, *British Socialists and the Politics of Popular Culture, 1884–1914* (Manchester, 1990).
41. J. Walvin, *The People's Game. The History of Football Revisited* (Edinburgh, 1994), p. 85.
42. Mason, *Association*, p. 92.
43. J. Harding, *For the Good of the Game. The Official History of the*

Professional Footballers' Association (London, 1991), pp. 3–5; Vamplew, *Pay up*, pp. 126–8.
44. Mason, *Association*, p. 96.
45. C. Edwardes, 'The new football mania', *Nineteenth Century*, October 1892.
46. Harding, *Good of the Game*, pp. 27–28; Vamplew, *Pay up*, pp. 129–35.
47. Inglis, *League Football*, pp. 56–7.
48. A. Bennett, *The Card* (1911), p. 268.
49. C. W. Alcock (ed.), *The Football Annual, 1896*, pp. 80–5.
50. *Athletic News*, 22 September 1922.
51. Mason, *Association*, pp. 121–2. For an overview of the lot of the retired sportsman, Vamplew, *Pay up*, pp. 227–38.
52. This section is based on B. Dabscheck, 'Defensive Manchester', in R. Cashman and M. Mackernan, *Sport in History* (St Lucia, 1979); Harding, *Good of the Game*, pp. 6–115; Vamplew, *Pay up*, pp. 239–53.
53. C. Ehrlich, *The Music Profession in Britain Since the Eighteenth Century. A Social History* (Oxford, 1985), pp. 164–85.
54. Harding, *Good of the Game*, pp. 95–104.
55. Harding, *Good of the Game*, p. 115.
56. The reformed union took on the name Association Football Players' and Trainers' Union in 1919.
57. Vamplew, *Pay up*, p. 252.
58. Inglis, *League Football*, pp. 43–4.
59. Three clubs, Walsall, Lincoln and Doncaster, were voted out on two separate occasions.
60. Harding, *Good of the Game*, p. 34; Vamplew, *Pay up*, p. 119. Vamplew provides some stimulating material on the issue of playing records, pp. 124–38.
61. Overall, Villa won 6 championships and 4 FA Cups. Sunderland were champions in 1892, 1893, 1895, 1902 and 1913. Amazingly, they had to wait until 1973 to win the Cup.
62. Both these figures are for the 'county borough'.

Chapter 3

1. B. Tabner, *Through the Turnstiles* (Harefield, Middlesex, 1992), pp. 69, 73.
2. R. Holt, 'Football and the urban way of life in nineteenth-century Britain', in J. A. Mangan (ed.), *Pleasure, Profit and Proselytism* (London, 1988), p. 78.
3. R. Taylor, *Football and its Fans. Supporters and their Relations with the Game, 1885–1992* (Leicester, 1992), p. 13.
4. T. Mason, *Association Football and English Society, 1863–1915* (Brighton, 1980), pp. 152–7.
5. Music hall admission prices often rose after 1900 as entrepreneurs sought an ever more 'respectable' audience.
6. W. Vamplew, *Pay up and Play the Game. Professional Sport in Britain, 1875–1914* (Cambridge, 1988), p. 82; Mason, *Association*, p. 152. Some clubs did continue with an annual 'Ladies Day', when, presumably, prices were lowered or waived. See report of Leeds City *v.* Bradford P.A., *Athletic News*, 18 March 1912.
7. C. Buchan, *A Lifetime in Football* (London, 1955), pp. 9–12.
8. Mason, *Association*, p. 153.
9. *West Middlesex Advertiser and Chelsea Mail*, 1 September 1905.
10. E. Dunning, P. Murphy and J. Williams, *The Roots of Football Hooliganism* (London, 1988), p. 234; *Bradford Daily Telegraph*, 13 March 1911.
11. On working-class women's leisure, see A. Davies, *Leisure, Gender and Poverty* (Buckingham, 1992).
12. *Preston Herald*, 23 September 1891;

Yorkshire Observer Budget, 11 March 1911.
13. *Bradford Daily Telegraph*, 11 March 1911. The terraces were probably at their most colourful and vibrant for local derbies or cup ties.
14. S. Kelly, *You'll Never Walk Alone* (1987), p. 22.
15. R. Palmer (ed.), 'The minstrel of Quarry Bank: reminiscences of George Dunn', *Oral History*, xi (1983), p. 66; *Southampton Football Echo*, 24 February 1902.
16. D. Canter, M. Comber and D. Uzzell, *Football in its Place. An Environmental Psychology of Football Grounds* (London, 1989).
17. T. Ambrosen, *The Illustrated Footballer* (Derby, 1989); E. Krieger, *Good Old Soccer. The Golden Age of the Football Picture Postcards* (London, 1983).
18. D. Russell, *Popular Music in England, 1840–1914. A Social History* (Manchester, 1987), p. 235.
19. G. Pearson, *Hooligan. A History of Respectable Fears* (London, 1983).
20. *Preston Herald*, 13 May 1885; Mason, *Association*, p. 166.
21. Mason, *Association*, p. 167.
22. W. Vamplew, 'Ungentlemanly conduct. The control of soccer-crowd behaviour in England, 1880–1914', in T. Smout (ed.), *The Search for Wealth and Stability* (London, 1979) pp. 139–154.
23. E. Dunning, P. Murphy, J. Williams and J. Maguire, 'Football hooliganism in Britain before the First World War', *International Journal of the Sociology of Sport*, 19 (1984), p. 225.
24. Dunning *et al.*, 'Hooliganism', pp. 225–9.
25. Their ideas are explored a little more in Chapter 8 below.
26. *Yorkshire Observer Budget*, 11 March 1911; *Bradford Daily Telegraph*, 11, 13 March 1911.
27. *Bradford Observer*, 4 October 1890.
28. R. Holt, *Sport and the British. A Modern History* (Oxford, 1989), p. 8.
29. M. Amis, *London Fields* (London, 1990), p. 90.
30. P. G. Hutchins, 'Sport and regional pride: Association Football and the north-east of England, 1919–61' (Unpublished PhD thesis, University of Sussex, 1990); P. Joyce, *Visions of the People. Industrial England and the Question of Class, 1840–1914* (Cambridge, 1991); J. Richards, *Stars in Their Eyes* (Preston, 1994); D. Russell, 'Sport and identity: the case of Yorkshire County Cricket Club, 1890–1939', *Twentieth Century British History* (forthcoming, 1996).
31. Mason, *Association*, p. 234; J. Bale, 'Playing at home: British Football and a sense of place', in J. Williams and S. Wagg (eds), *British Football and Social Change* (Leicester, 1991), pp. 135–6.
32. Holt, *Sport*, p. 172. The whole section on civic pride, pp. 159–79, is obligatory reading.
33. J. Hill, 'Cup finals and community in the North of England', in J. Hill and J. Williams (eds), *Sport and Identity in the North of England* (Keele, 1996) pp. 85–111.
34. *Accrington Times*, 7 April 1883.
35. *Preston Herald*, 27 November 1895.
36. T. Mason, *The Blues and the Reds. A History of the Liverpool and Everton Football Clubs*, History Society of Lancashire and Cheshire (Liverpool, 1985), pp. 3–5. If there *was* any social or political element in the split, it related to the concern of some members over the club's close links with the brewing trade.
37. Mason, *Blues and Reds*, pp. 17–19. There is some evidence that Everton's recruitment of a number of players from the Irish Republic after 1950 may have given a sectarian flavour to local football in the eyes of a minority of supporters.

38. Kelly, *Walk Alone*, p. 22.
39. *Yorkshire Observer*, 21 April 1928.
40. At this stage, international soccer was probably not sufficiently developed for local ties to play a role in the building of national consciousness. See, though, Hill, 'Cup finals'.
41. *Pall Mall Gazette*, 31 March 1884
42. F. Wall, *Fifty Years of Football* (London, 1935), p. 38.
43. Holt, *Sport*, p. 175.
44. Hutchins, 'Sport and regional pride', pp. 242–3; Buchan, *Lifetime*, p. 32; Russell, 'Sport and identity'.
45. *Southern Daily Echo*, 3 February 1900.
46. J-M. Brohm, *Sport. A Prison of Borrowed Time* (London, 1978), p. 180.
47. S. Tischler, *Footballers and Businessmen. The Origins of Professional Soccer in England* (New York, 1981), pp. 136, 137.
48. S. Jones, *Sport, Politics and the Working Class* (Manchester, 1988), pp. 11, 25–6.
49. J. Hargreaves, *Sport, Power and Culture* (Cambridge 1986), p. 67.
50. J. Maguire 'Conceptual and methodological confusion in the analysis of nineteenth-century leisure. The case for historical sociology', in J. Mangan and R. Small (eds), *Sport, Power and Culture. International and Sociological Perspectives* (London, 1986), p. 41.
51. Mason, *Association*, p. 235.
52. N. Fishwick, *English Football and Society 1910–1950* (Manchester, 1989), p. 143.
53. *Southern Daily Echo*, 10 February 1900.
54. Quoted in Tischler, *Footballers*, p. 130.
55. 'New football mania', p. 627. The article is reprinted in I. Hamilton, *The Faber Book of Soccer* (London, 1992), pp. 6–11.
56. 'New football mania', p. 629.
57. This supposed maxim was noted by Blackburn Rovers director, John Lewis, in 1914. Tischler, *Footballers*, p. 127.
58. *Bradford Weekly Telegraph*, 1 May 1914.
59. *Yorkshire Post*, 15 April 1944.
60. Quoted in Fishwick, *English*, p. 145; Kelly, *Walk Alone*, pp. 28–9.

Chapter 4

1. S. Constantine, *Unemployment in Britain Between the Wars* (London, 1980), pp. 1–44; S. Jones, *Workers at Play* (London, 1986), pp. 9–61.
2. It was expanded to 22 clubs in 1923–4. In 1921 the previous year's 'Third Division' was re-named the Third Division South. Only the champions of each division were promoted.
3. S. Jones, *Sport, Politics and the Working Class* (Manchester, 1988), p. 45; N. Fishwick, *English Football and Society, 1910–1950* (Manchester, 1989), p. 1; A. J. P. Taylor, *English History, 1914–1945* (London, 1976), p. 392.
4. Cardiff, Merthyr, Newport, Swansea (1920), Aberdare and Wrexham (1921).
5. Fishwick, *English*, pp. 26, 27, 147.
6. Leicester were relegated in 1935 and 1939, Villa in 1936 and Birmingham, whose average placing between 1930 and 1939 was 15th, in 1939.
7. All unemployment figures are drawn from the Ministry of Labour, *Local Unemployment Index* and represent an average across the period September 1932 to April 1933. I am extremely grateful to my colleague Rex Pope for his help on this. Middlesbrough's problems may have been compounded by the exceptionally high levels of unemployment in some of the

surrounding towns and villages. *Lancashire Daily Post*, 9 May 1932; Gate books, Football League, Lytham, 1932–33; Fishwick, *English*, p. 50. See also, S. G. Jones, 'The economic aspects of Association Football in England, 1918–1939', *British Journal of Sports History*, 1, 3 (1984), pp. 286–99.

8. *Football Echo*, 22 October 1932. Sunderland's gates fell by almost 6,000 the next year as the economic climate worsened still further, but Wednesday's gates still remained smaller.
9. C. Buchan, *A Lifetime in Football* (London, 1955), pp. 29–30.
10. Buchan, *Lifetime*, pp. 91–2. Buchan claimed that he instigated the system, used before but far less systematically, at Arsenal, following a 7–0 defeat at Newcastle. F. N. S. Creek, *Association Football* (London, 1937), provides a good contemporary guide to these and other related developments.
11. For figures on the period from 1888–1955, see *FA Yearbook, 1955–56*, pp. 48–9.
12. *Charles Buchan's Football Monthly*, February 1961, p. 20; Creek, *Association*, pp. 156–9
13. *FA Yearbook, 1953–54*, pp. 95–6.
14. *Athletic News*, 22 September 1924.
15. Fishwick, *English*, p. 84.
16. *Lancashire Daily Post*, 23 October, 20 December 1926.
17. C. Bastin with B. Glanville, *Cliff Bastin Remembers* (London, 1950), p. 97.
18. FA Disciplinary Committee minutes, September 1936–26 June 1937.
19. *Yorkshire Observer*, 4 March 1920, 10 January 1921.
20. S. Wagg, *The Football World. A Social History* (London, 1984), pp. 44–59; S. Studd, *Herbert Chapman. Football Emperor. A Study in the Origins of Modern Soccer* (London, 1981). T. Say, 'Herbert Chapman: Football Revoluntionary?', *The Sports Historian*, 16 (1996), pp. 81–98. On the history of management in general, see D. Turner and A. White, *The Breedon Book of Football Managers* (Derby, 1993).
21. Fishwick, *English*, pp. 37–8. 'Report of a Commission, "The Arsenal Football Club"', Football Association minutes, August 1927.
22. Bastin, *Remembers*, p. 107.
23. Posthumously published as *Herbert Chapman on Football* (London, 1934).
24. Wagg, *Football World*, p. 58.
25. G. Allison, *Allison Calling* (London, 1948).
26. Wagg, *Football World*, p. 57.
27. S. Rous, *Football Worlds* (1978).
28. F. Wall, *Fifty Years of Football* (London, 1935), p. 144; *Charles Buchan's Football Monthly*, February 1961, p. 21; *Football Monthly Digest*, October 1973, p. 111.
29. M. Amos, 'The Crook Town affair', in B. Hunt, *Northern Goalfields* (1989), pp. 417–23. Most of the bans were lifted in autumn 1928.
30. This indeed continued until well after the Second World War.
31. Fishwick, *English*, p. 77; *Lancashire Daily Post*, 8 June 1929; Studd, *Herbert Chapman*, p. 94.
32. Most of what follows is drawn from Fishwick, *English*, pp. 70–93.
33. Fishwick, *English*, p. 79.
34. Fishwick, *English*, p. 86.
35. *British Labour Statistics* (HMSO, 1971), Table 9, pp. 40–1.
36. For an informative history of the women's game, see D. Williamson, *Belles of the Ball* (Exeter, 1991). See also J. Williams and J. Woodhouse, 'Can play, will play? Women and football in Britain', in J. Williams and S. Wagg (eds), *British Football and Social Change* (Leicester, 1991), pp. 85–108.

37. G. J. Newsham, *In a League of their Own* (Chorley, Lancs, 1994), provides an informative account of the club's history.
38. Williamson, *Belles*, p. 31.
39. Williamson, *Belles*, p. 34.
40. Williamson, *Belles*, pp. 68–9; Newsham, *League*, pp. 59–64.
41. Wall, *Fifty Years*, p. 15.
42. Newsham, *League*, p. 63.
43. On women and war, see G. Braybon and P. Summerfield, *Out of the Cage* (London, 1987).
44. Newsham, *League*, pp. 18, 23–4, 64–5.
45. T. Mason, *Association Football and English Society, 1863–1915* (Brighton, 1980), p. 157; S. Inglis, *League Football and the Men who Made It* (1988), p. 99; A. Davies, *Leisure, Gender and Poverty* (Buckingham, 1992), p. 38.
46. (Northampton) *Football Echo*, 12 February 1921, noted Reading offering half-price admission on production of labour exchange cards.
47. *Sunderland Football Echo*, 2 October 1932; Fishwick, *English*, p. 50.
48. Davies, *Leisure*, p. 44.
49. Williams and Woodhouse, 'Can play', p. 94.
50. *Yorkshire Observer*, 21 April 1928.
51. *Yorkshire Observer*, 24 April 1928; *Lancashire Daily Post*, 3 May 1938.
52. *Bradford Daily Telegraph*, 24 September 1921; *Yorkshire Observer*, 20 April 1928.
53. *Football Favourite*, 5 and 12 February 1927. The songs were intended for dinner queue and other locations, beside the terrace, in this age of intense interest in community singing.
54. Fishwick, *English*, p. 62.
55. *Yorkshire Observer*, 28 February 1921.
56. S. Jones, *Sport, Politics and the Working Class* (Manchester, 1988), p. 60.
57. *Bradford Daily Telegraph*, 2 May 1921; Fishwick, *English*, p. 61
58. P. Murphy, J. Williams and E. Dunning (eds), *Football on Trial. Spectator Violence and Development in the Football World* (London, 1990), pp. 73–6.
59. Fishwick, *English*, p. 65.
60. R. Taylor, *Football and its Fans. Supporters and their Relations with the Game, 1885–1985* (Leicester, 1992), p. 44.
61. Taylor, *Fans*, pp. 25–8.
62. *Yorkshire Sports*, 18 March 1922.
63. Taylor, *Fans*, p. 50.
64. Fishwick, *English*, p. 57.

Chapter 5

1. N. Fishwick, *English Football and Society, 1910–1950* (Manchester, 1989), p. 169. The following section draws extensively on pp. 94–106 of this work.
2. Fishwick, *English*, pp. 100–1.
3. Fishwick, *English*, p. 106.
4. Fishwick, *English*, p. 103.
5. *Preston Herald*, 26 September 1930
6. *Lancashire Daily Post*, 30 April 1937.
7. M. Clapson, *A Bit of a Flutter. Popular Gambling and English Society, c. 1823–1961* (Manchester, 1992), especially, pp. 162–86.
8. J. Walvin, *The People's Game. The History of Football Revisited* (Edinburgh, 1994), p. 127.
9. S. Inglis, *League Football and the Men who made It* (London, 1988), pp. 145–57.
10. M. Pegg, *Broadcasting and Society, 1918–1939* (London, 1983), p. 7.
11. Fishwick, *English*, p. 107; *Radio Times*, 4 March 1927. The games were at West Bromwich, Everton, Stoke and Swindon.
12. G. Allison, *Allison Calling* (London, 1948), p. 37; Fishwick, *English*, p. 107.
13. Allison, *Allison*, pp. 52–3.

14. Allison, *Allison*, p. 40. MacCullough also poured Allison port, 'to relieve an aching throat'.
15. P. Soar, *Hamlyn A–Z of British Football Records* (1985), p. 14.
16. P. Scannell and D. Cardiff, *A Social History of Broadcasting*, vol. 1 (Oxford, 1991), pp. 277–303.
17. C. Bastin with B. Glanville, *Cliff Bastin Remembers* (London, 1950), p. 141. For an outline and sympathetic analysis, see J. Richards, *The Age of the Dream Palace* (London 1984), pp. 305–6; Allison, *Allison*, pp. 180–2.
18. A. Bennett, *The Card* (1911); J. B. Priestley, *The Good Companions* (1929).
19. J. Richards, *Happiest Days. The Public School in English Fiction* (Manchester, 1989): J. Richards (ed.), *Imperialism and Juvenile Fiction* (Manchester, 1989); J. Bristow, *Empire Boys* (London, 1991).
20. The launch title was *Football Favourite* with the longer title being adopted in April 1921. In March 1929 it became *Boy's Football Favourite*. The 'Sport's Library' series was extensively advertised in the *Favourite* and shared many authors and even some characters.
21. E. S. Turner, *Boys Will be Boys* (London, 1975), p. 275.
22. *Football and Sports Library*, no. 11 (1922), p. 2.
23. *Football and Sports Favourite*, 23 April 1927.
24. S. Nelson, *Nell O' Newcastle* (London, 1922), pp. 4, 55.
25. For example, see J. Radford (ed.), *The Progress of Romance. The Politics of Popular Fiction* (London, 1986).
26. Fishwick, *English*, p. 149.
27. G. Orwell, *The Road to Wigan Pier* (1963), p. 80.
28. *Yorkshire Observer*, 23 April 1927.
29. *Yorkshire Observer*, 1 May 1922.
30. *Yorkshire Observer*, 25 April 1927.
31. J. Hill, 'Cup finals and community in the North of England', in J. Hill and J. Williams (eds), *Sport and Identity in the North of England* (Keele, 1996) pp. 85–111.
32. H. F. Moorhouse, 'Scotland against England: Football and popular culture', *International Journal of the History of Sport*, 4, 2 (1987), pp. 189–202, and 'Repressed nationalism and professional football: Scotland versus England', in J. A. Mangan and R. B. Small (eds), *Sport, Power and Culture. International and Sociological Perspectives* (London, 1986), pp. 52–9.
33. Moorhouse, 'Football and popular culture', p. 199.
34. *Football Echo*, 29 October 1932
35. *Daily Mail*, 13 November 1934.
36. C. Buchan, *A Lifetime in Football* (London, 1955), p. 93.
37. *Lancashire Daily Post*, 19 April 1938.
38. D. Read, *The English Provinces, c. 1760–1914. A Study in Influence* (London, 1964), pp. 231–2.
39. C. Korr, 'A different type of success: West Ham United and the creation of tradition and community', in R. Holt (ed.), *Sport and the Working Class in Modern Britain* (Manchester, 1990), p. 152.
40. J. Hargreaves, *Sport, Power and Culture* (Cambridge, 1986), pp. 100–9.
41. Fishwick, *English*, pp. 107, 127–8.
42. Logbooks of St Luke's (SM Pr. 25/5) and St Marks (SM Pr 26/2) Lancashire County Record Office, Preston. I am grateful to Carol Angharad for these references.
43. *Yorkshire Observer*, 2 February 1933.
44. T. Mason, 'Stanley Matthews', in Holt (ed.), *Sport and the Working Class*, pp. 162–6.
45. Large numbers had been mobilised when the club nearly folded in 1908, but this campaign was far more deeply rooted.

46. Fishwick, *English*, pp. 145–6.
47. J. Richards, 'Football and the crisis of national identity', unpublished paper supplied by author.
48. *Yorkshire Observer*, 1 May 1923.
49. Richards, *Dream Palace*, pp. 175–6.
50. Richards, 'National identity', pp. 13–14; P. Joyce, *Visions of the People. Industrial England and the Question of Class, 1840–1914* (Cambridge, 1991), p. 159.
    H. Garland, *Henry Francis Lyte and the Story of 'Abide with me'* (Manchester, 1957), pp. 125–9. Pre-match community singing was introduced for the first time in 1927. Some sources claim that the hymn was introduced on the spur of the moment by the organiser, T. P. Ratcliffe, others that it was requested in advance by Queen Mary.
51. *Yorkshire Observer*, 23 April 1928.
52. C. Waters, 'The Americanisation of the masses: cultural criticism, the national heritage and working-class culture in the 1930s', *Social History Curators Group Journal*, 17 (1989–90), pp. 22–6.
53. R. Holt, *Sport and the British* (Oxford, 1989), p. 273.
54. F. Wall, *Fifty Years of Football* (London, 1935), p. 223.
55. S. G. Jones, 'State intervention in sport and leisure in Britain between the wars', *Journal of Contemporary History*, 22 (1987), p. 170.
56. P. Beck, 'England *v.* Germany, 1938', *History Today* (June 1982), pp. 29–34.
57. G. Green, *The History of the Football Association* (London, 1953), p. 496.
58. *Daily Mail*, 16 May 1938.

Chapter 6

1. The following section draws on S. Inglis, *League Football and the Men who Made It* (London, 1988), pp. 165–74 and J. Rollin, *Soccer at War* (London, 1985).
2. Rollin, *War*, p. 57.
3. This includes Premiership titles from 1992–3.
4. S. Wagg, *The Football World. A Contemporary Social History* (Brighton, 1984), pp. 73–100, has shaped much of what follows here.
5. *FA Yearbook, 1972–73*, p. 62.
6. *FA Book for Boys, 1954–55*, p. 88–91.
7. A. Hardaker, *Hardaker of the League* (London, 1977), pp. 115–17. Birmingham City were England's first representatives in a European final, meeting Barcelona in the Inter-Cities Fairs Cup in 1960.
8. E. Dunphy, *A Strange Kind of Glory. Sir Matt Busby and Manchester United* (London, 1991); Wagg, *Football World*, pp. 86–7.
9. Wagg, *Football World*, p. 94.
10. S. Inglis, *The Football Grounds of England and Wales* (London, 1985), p. 31.
11. *FA Yearbook, 1982–3*, p. 9.
12. B. Tabner, *Through the Turnstiles* (Harefield, Middlesex, 1992), is again invaluable here. Unless otherwise stated, all attendance data are drawn from this source.
13. By Cyril Hughes and entitled 'The Mystery of the Missing Millions'.
14. *FA Yearbook, 1948–49*, pp. 112–13; *1955–56*, pp. 48–9.
15. J. Huxley and D. Howes, *Encyclopaedia of Rugby Football* (London, 1980), p. 14; G. Moorhouse, *A People's Game. The Official History of the Rugby League* (London, 1995), p. 269.
16. PEP, 'English professional football', *Planning*, xxxii, 496 (1966), pp. 81–160.
17. A. Marwick, *British Society Since 1945* (London, 1982), p. 121; J. Benson, *The Rise of Consumer Society in Britain, 1880–1980* (London, 1994).

18. J. Burnett, *A Social History of Housing, 1815–1970* (Newton Abbot, 1978), p. 274.
19. Inglis, *League Football*, p. 194.
20. J. Walvin, *The People's Game. The History of Football Revisited* (Edinburgh, 1994), p. 166.
21. *FA Yearbook, 1950–51*, pp. 48–9.
22. Football League gate books, Football League, Lytham. At this time, away supporters would not generally have attended in large enough numbers to influence crowd size significantly.
23. Inglis, *League Football*, p. 197. The first League game to be played under lights was Portsmouth *v.* Newcastle, 22 February 1956.
24. P. Murphy, J. Williams and E. Dunning, *Football on Trial. Spectator Violence and Development in the Football World* (London, 1990), pp. 79–81, 115–16.
25. R. Taylor, *Football and its Fans. Supporters and their Relations with the Game* (Leicester, 1992), pp. 101, 114–16.
26. Inglis, *League Football*, pp. 195–6, 228.
27. Inglis, *League Football*, p. 194.
28. *The People*, 24 August 1958.
29. Inglis, *League Football*, p. 202.
30. R. W. Cox, *Sport in Britain. A Bibliography of Historical Publications* (1988), pp. 203–55.
31. D. Gifford, *Encyclopaedia of Comic Characters* (London, 1985). Roy Race, first introduced in *Tiger* in 1954, was the oldest of these characters, and was to survive until 1993.
32. *Charles Buchan's Football Monthly*, May 1961.
33. C. Bastin with B. Glanville, *Cliff Bastin Remembers* (London, 1950).
34. For illustrations of several of the works submitted, see *FA Yearbook, 1954–55*, pp. 77–82.
35. *FA Yearbook, 1958–59*, pp. 55–8.
36. N. Fishwick, *English Football and Society, 1910–1950* (Manchester, 1989), p. 70.
37. PEP, 'Football', p. 116.
38. *Charles Buchan's Football Monthly*, June 1968, p. 34.
39. F. Taylor, *The Day a Team Died* (London, 1983).
40. Fishwick, *English*; Inglis, *League Football*, pp. 189, 195, 219.
41. *FA Yearbook, 1957–58*, pp. 56–7; Inglis, *League Football*, p. 212.
42. Wagg, *Football World*, p. 105.
43. J. Harding, *For the Good of the Game. The Official History of the Professional Footballers' Association* (London, 1991), pp. 270–3.
44. Harding, *Good of the Game*, p. 269.
45. Harding, *Good of the Game*, p. 255.
46. Harding, *Good of the Game*, p. 250.
47. Harding, *Good of the Game*, p. 259.
48. The following account derives largely from Harding, *Good of the Game*, pp. 256–81; Wagg, *Football World*, pp. 101–20; Inglis, *League Football*, pp. 218–27.
49. Harding, *Good of the Game*, p. 269.
50. Harding, *Good of the Game*, pp. 282–94.
51. Dunphy, *Glory*, pp. 302–3.
52. *Lancashire Daily Post*, June 1961.
53. Inglis, *League Football*, pp. 217–18.
54. Fishwick, *English*, p. 103.
55. H. Berry and G. Allman, *One Hundred Years at Deepdale, 1881–1981* (Preston, 1982), p. 204, *Lancashire Evening Post*, 2 May 1960.
56. T. Finney, *Football Round the World* (London, 1953), pp. 83–6, 98–100; P. Agnew, *Finney: A Football Legend* (Preston, 1989).

Chapter 7

1. S. Inglis, *League Football and the Men who Made It* (London, 1988), pp. 229–31.
2. Many of them, including the introduction of 'play-offs', a reduction in the size of the First

Division and greater attention to marketing and sponsorship, were to be adopted in the years ahead. DES, *Report of the Committee on Football* (HMSO, 1968); Football League, *Report of the Committee of Enquiry into the Structure and Finance of Football* (Lytham, 1983); N. Jennett and P. J. Sloane, 'The future of League football; a critique of the Chester Committee of Enquiry', *Leisure Studies*, 4, 1 (1985), pp. 39–56. Chester's considerable contribution was acknowledged by the establishment of the Sir Norman Chester Centre for Football Research at Leicester University in April 1987.

3. Despite this it was also sometimes hard on particular League clubs. Both Barrow and Southport seem to have been to some extent victims of their poor support and, in Barrow's case, geographical isolation, as much as their footballing record.
4. Rigorous and, arguably, unfair regulations on the suitability of the stadia used by Conference sides severely undermined the pyramid principle in the mid-1990s.
5. The clubs were QPR, Luton, Oldham and Preston. Plastic pitches were invaluable for community-based activity.
6. FA and WFA Joint Consultative Committee minutes, 11 February 1972, Football League, Lancaster Gate.
7. *FA Yearbook 1972–73*, pp. 90–1.
8. A. Hardaker, *Hardaker of the League* (London, 1977), pp. 126–45, while highly subjective, is very informative.
9. PEP, 'English professional football', *Planning*, xxxii, 496 (1966), pp. 103.
10. *FA Yearbook, 1966–67*, pp. 22–3.
11. *FA Yearbook, 1960–61*, pp. 56–8; *The People*, 12 October, 2 and 23 November 1958.
12. *FA Yearbook, 1959–60*, p. 58, offered this definition. The FA launched a strong anti-gamesmanship campaign in the 1958–59 season, believing, among other things, that the prevalence of bad habits in the professional game might drive headteachers to turn to other sports which would offer their pupils better moral and ethical examples. See, for example, *FA News*, October 1958.
13. For a brief period in the 1950s, the FA Disciplinary Committee did keep a list of cautions given for offences allocated to this category. Such precision was rare.
14. *Yorkshire Observer*, 23 April 1928.
15. *FA Yearbook, 1959–60*, pp. 58–62. These are the words of Nottingham Forest manager, W. H. Walker.
16. S. Wagg, *The Football World. A Contemporary Social History* (Brighton, 1984), pp. 149–50.
17. *FA Yearbook, 1959–60*, pp. 58–62.
18. P. Murphy, J. Williams and E. Dunning, *Football on Trial. Spectator Violence and Development in the Football World* (London, 1990), p. 33.
19. Norwich, fractionally north of Birmingham, but hardly situated in a traditional soccer stronghold, should perhaps have their 2 League Cup successes added to this list.
20. Bristol's population had fallen to 388,000 by 1981. However, its population was still comfortably larger than that of the next city, Coventry.
21. Inglis, *League Football*, p. 308.
22. J. Harding, *For the Good of the Game. The Official History of the Professional Footballers' Association* (London, 1991), pp. 347–50. For a critical view, see A. Parker, 'Great expectations: grimness or glamour? The football apprentice in the 1990s', *Sports Historian*, 15 (1995), pp. 107–27.
23. J. Bale, *Sport and Place* (Lincoln, Nebraska, 1982), pp. 32–8.

24. *Rothman's Football Yearbook, 1979–80*, pp. 11–17.
25. R. Jenkins, 'Salvation for the fittest? A West African Sportsman in the age of new imperialism', in J. A. Mangan (ed.), *The Cultural Bond. Sport, Empire and Society* (London, 1992), pp. 47–83; B. Woolnough, *Black Magic. England's Black Footballers* (London, 1983).
26. *Soccer Star*, 5 December 1953; H. Glasper, *Middlesbrough. A Complete Record, 1876–1989* (Derby, 1989), p. 105.
27. Woolnough, *Magic*, p. 5; 'Now rest in peace, Albert Johanneson', *Guardian*, 3 October 1995.
28. 'Waiting for the Asian effect', *Independent on Sunday*, 5 December 1993; 'Asians can't play barrier', *Guardian*, 10 February 1996.
29. J. Maguire, 'Sport, racism and British society: a sociological study of England's elite male Afro/Caribbean soccer and rugby players', in G. Jarvie (ed.), *Sport, Racism and Ethnicity* (London, 1991), pp. 94–123.
30. Harding, *Good of the Game*, pp. 362–3. Atkinson, always picking on merit, has been a significant 'patron' of black players.
31. Harding, *Good of the Game*, pp362–3
32. 'Move to rid football of racism', *Guardian*, 13 August 1993. The initiative was called 'Let's kick racism out of football.'
33. Inglis, *League Football*, pp. 278–82. The clubs had been concerned that this would destroy the transfer system, for, technically, a transfer involved sale of the player's registration document, not the player, and this would obviously hold no value once a player was out of contract. The PFA compromised and agreed that 'compensation' could be paid for a player once out of contract. In common parlance, all player sales continued to be referred to as a 'transfer', but from 1978, the term was really only applicable to the sale of players still in contract.
34. PEP, 'Football', table six, p. 131.
35. A. Clarke and L. Madden, 'The limitations of economic analysis. The case of professional football', *Leisure Studies*, 7, 1 (1988), p. 61, T. Mason, 'Football', in T. Mason (ed.), *Sport in Britain* (Cambridge, 1989), p. 163.
36. E. Dunphy, *A Strange Kind of Glory. Sir Matt Busby and Manchester United* (London, 1991), pp. 302–3.
37. Mason, 'Football', p. 163.
38. J. Walvin, *The People's Game. The History of Football Revisited* (Edinburgh, 1994), p. 182.
39. Wagg, *Football World*, pp. 121–55.
40. S. Inglis, *Soccer in the Dock* (London, 1985).
41. Recounted by Thompson in BBC's *Kicking and Screaming*, 1995.
42. Wagg, *Football World*, p. 141.
43. H. Davies, *The Glory Game* (London, 1985), p. xvi.
44. Harding, *Good of the Game*, p. 314.
45. Bale, *Sport and Place*, pp. 51–3.
46. *Football Digest*, September 1973, pp. 89–92.
47. For example, *Charles Buchan's Football Monthly*, February 1968, p. 47, July 1968, p. 67.

Chapter 8

1. S. Wagg, *The Football World* (Brighton, 1984), p. 121.
2. J. Walvin, *Football and the Decline of Britain* (London, 1985), pp. 9–10.
3. P. Murphy, J. Williams and E. Dunning, *Football on Trial. Spectator Violence and Development in the Football World* (London, 1990), pp. 87–8 for detail.
4. See especially, June 1968, p. 63.

5. Unless stated otherwise, overall figures have been drawn from J. Rollin (ed.), *Rothman's Football Yearbook, 1995–96*, p. 576 and club figures from B. Tabner, *Through the Turnstile* (Harefield, Middlesex, 1992).
6. For a witty and perceptive comment on 'the only subject that can induce a bloke to swank about his fidelity', see H. Pearson, *The Far Corner* (London, 1995), pp. 14–15.
7. E. Dunphy, *A Strange Kind of Glory. Sir Matt Busby and Manchester United* (London, 1991), pp. 298–9, 309.
8. A. Marwick, *Britain Since 1945* (London, 1982), p. 121.
9. On the presentation of TV football, see E. Buscombe (ed.), *Football on Television* (London, 1975).
10. A. Sked and C. Cook, *Post-War Britain. A Political History* (London, 1984), p. 336.
11. Football League gate books, Lytham. A League Cup tie with Swindon drew only 16,566.
12. *FA Yearbook, 1972–73*, pp. 66–8; *Rothman's Football Yearbook, 1983–84*, p. 493. A set minimum admission fee was abandoned in 1981 to allow clubs greater flexibility in coping with the impact of the recession.
13. PEP, 'English professional football', *Planning*, xxxii, 496 (1966), p. 112.
14. Burnley and Chelsea were only two of the most notorious examples of clubs which witnessed this phenomenon.
15. S. Inglis, *League Football and the Men who Made It* (London, 1988), pp. 266, 276.
16. *Football Monthly Digest*, September 1973.
17. *FA Yearbook, 1955–56*, pp. 48–9.
18. D. Canter, M. Comber and D. Uzzell (eds), *Football in its Place. An Environmental Psychology of Football Grounds* (London, 1989), p. 31, state that fear of violence was the biggest single reason given for the declining attendance habit by their sample of spectator interviewees, although they stress that it was only one of a large range of reasons given.
19. First Division attendances continued to fall until 1989–90. Rollin, *Rothman's 1995–96*, p. 576.
20. FA Disciplinary Committee minutes, Lancaster Gate, 4 December 1961; Murphy *et al.*, *Football on Trial*, pp. 116–18.
21. D. Hobbs and D. Robins, 'The boy done good: football violence, changes and continuities', *Sociological Review*, 39, 3 (1990), p. 551. This special edition of the *Sociological Review* contains a number of stimulating pieces reflecting many currents of sociological writing.
22. *Rothman's Football Yearbook, 1987–88*, p. 9. The York incident is a personal recollection. For an excellent study of 'football as nuisance' see J. Bale, *Sports, Space and the City* (London, 1993), pp. 94–133.
23. For a brilliantly observed glimpse of this, see N. Hornby, *Fever Pitch* (London, 1992), pp. 52–8.
24. J. Williams, P. Murphy, E. Dunning (eds), *Hooligans Abroad* (London, 1989).
25. Murphy *et al.*, *Football on Trial*, pp. 88–9. For an interesting challenge to this picture, and particularly the way in which employment data have been used, see G. Armstrong and R. Harris, 'Football hooliganism: theory and evidence', *Sociological Review*, 39, 3 (1991), pp. 452–3.
26. I. Taylor, 'Hooligans: Soccer's resistance movement', *New Society*, 7 August 1969, 'Football mad', in E. Dunning (ed.), *The Sociology of Sport* (London, 1971), pp. 352–7 and

'Soccer consciousness and soccer hooliganism' in S. Cohen (ed.), *Images of Deviance* (London, 1971), pp. 134–64; J. Clarke, 'Football and working-class fans: tradition and change', in R. Ingham (ed.), *Football Hooliganism* (London, 1978). For a helpful survey of Taylor's work, including his important recent output, see R. Haynes, *The Football Imagination. The Rise of Football Fanzine Culture* (Aldershot, 1995), pp. 5–12.

27. I. Taylor 'On the sports violence question – soccer hooliganism revisited', in J. Hargreaves (ed.), *Sport, Culture, Ideology* (1982); S. Hall, 'The treatment of football hooliganism in the press', in R. Ingham (ed.), *Football Hooliganism* (London, 1973), pp. 15–36.
28. See especially, E. Dunning, P. Murphy and J. Williams, *The Roots of Football Hooliganism* (1988).
29. Murphy, *et al.*, *Football on Trial*, p. 13.
30. See especially articles by Armstrong and Harris, and Hobbs and Robins in *Sociological Review*, 39, 3 (1991). For important early anthropological work in this area, see P. Marsh, 'Understanding aggro', *New Society*, 3 April 1975, and *Aggro. The Illusion of Violence* (London, 1978); P. Marsh, E. Rosser and R. Harre, *The Rules of Disorder* (1978). For an interpretation rooted in psychology, see J. H. Kerr, *Understanding Soccer Hooliganism* (Buckingham, 1994). The phrase 'Leicester School' is not intended to imply homogeneity and ideological coherence amongst the sociologists working there: indeed, over the 1990s divisions have become quite pronounced.
31. Hall, 'Football hooliganism'; Murphy *et al.*, *Football on Trial*, pp. 81–6.
32. For example, R. Harris, *Soccer the Hard Way* (London, 1970), pp. 83–8.
33. Again, a personal experience of an intensely irritating procedure, remembered from the late 1970s.
34. Canter *et al.*, *Football in its Place*, p. 17.
35. S. Kelly, *You'll Never Walk Alone* (London, 1987), p. 62.
36. J. Harding, *For the Good of the Game. The Official History of the Professional Footballers' Association* (London, 1991), p. 361. On race and football in Liverpool, see D. Hill, *Out of his Skin. The John Barnes Phenomenon* (London, 1989).
37. Canter *et al.*, *Football in its Place*, pp. 57–85, demonstrates the subtly different flavour of terrace culture at different grounds.
38. P. Soar, *The Hamlyn A–Z of British Football Records* (London, 1985), p. 14. This was the first national programme of this type, although Anglia TV began the first regular broadcasts of highlights in 1962–63.
39. Inglis, *League Football*, p. 247.
40. Inglis, *League Football*, p. 317.
41. Inglis, *League Football*, p. 320. Gates were lower than average for the Friday games.
42. J. Benson, *The Rise of Consumer Society in Britain, 1880–1980* (London, 1994), p. 116.
43. *The Times*, 7 December 1970. I am grateful to Mike Rowland for providing me with material on *The Times* coverage between 1935 and 1970.
44. D. Gifford, *Encyclopaedia of Comic Characters* (London, 1987).
45. *Football Monthly Digest*, September 1973, October 1973, June 1974. The magazine was soon relaunched once again, finally readopting the old *Football Monthly* title in 1980.
46. Inglis, *League Football*, p. 243.
47. *Football League Review*, 20 November 1971, 11 March 1970. The *Review* did not carry a date and

dates given here refer to the date on the programmes in which they were inserted.

48. Harding, *Good of the Game*, p. 315.
49. A. Nickolds and S. Hey, *The Foul Book of Football* (London, 1976).
50. *Charles Buchan's Football Monthly*, September 1968.
51. PEP, 'Professional', pp. 81–8, 120–2.
52. A. Tomlinson, 'North and South: the rivalry of the Football League and the Football Association', in J. Williams and S. Wagg (eds), *British Football and Social Change* (Leicester, 1991), p. 44.
53. *Football League Review*, 30 October 1971; H. Davies, *Glory Game* (1985), p. 92.
54. Inglis, *League Football*, p. 313.
55. *Rothman's Football Yearbook, 1982–83*, p. 13; Inglis, *League Football*, p. 302.
56. Inglis, *League Football*, p. 313. The tournament was later sponsored by Littlewoods (1986–87 to 1989–90), Rumbelows (1990–91 to 1991–92), and Coca Cola (1992–).
57. A. Fynn and L. Guest, *Out of Time. Why Football isn't Working* (London, 1994), p. 22.
58. Inglis, *League Football*, p. 319.
59. W. Keegan, *Mrs Thatcher's Economic Experiment* (London, 1984). The average age of directors in 1964 was 58. PEP, 'Football', pp. 120–2.
60. *Guardian*, 25 June 1976, quoted in Wagg, *Football World*, p. 137.
61. A. Easthope, 'Manchester United and the miners' strike', in H. Lansdown and A. Spillius (eds), *Saturday's Boys. The Football Experience* (London, 1990).
62. *Rothman's Football Yearbook 1984–85*, p. 32.
63. *Rothman's Football Yearbook, 1981–82*, p. 9. On football and place in recent decades, J. Bale, *Sports, Space*, pp. 55–93
64. Liverpool won the championship seven times between 1979–80 and 1989–90, the FA Cup twice, the League Cup four times and the European Cup twice. Everton enjoyed two championship successes, one FA Cup and one European Cup-Winners Cup success.
65. *Rothman's Football Yearbook 1984–85*, p. 8.
66. Walvin, *Decline*, p. vi.
67. *Rothman's Football Yearbook, 1984–85*, p. 8.
68. Cited in Walvin, *Decline*, p. 8; *Sunday Times*, 2 June 1985, cited in Williams *et al.*, *Hooligans Abroad*. See also, I. Taylor, 'Putting the boot into a working-class sport: British soccer after Bradford and Brussels', *Sociology of Sport Journal* (1987), pp. 171–91.

Chapter 9

1. S. Inglis, *League Football and the Men who Made It* (London, 1988), pp. 343–5.
2. Inglis, *League Football*, pp. 322–41; A. Fynn and L. Guest, *The Secret Life of Football* (London, 1989), pp. 148–67.
3. For full details see Inglis, *League Football*, pp. 339–41.
4. For a gripping, insider's view, see A. Fynn and L. Guest, *Out of Time. Why Football Isn't Working* (London, 1994), pp. 30–59. As they argue, the FA eventually conceded much power to the Premiership as a separate organisation, giving the game a tri-partite structure.
5. 72 overseas players were registered with Premier League clubs in November 1995. *Guardian*, 4 November 1995.
6. 'The League's union is doomed even if the confederates lose', *Guardian*, 12 July 1991.
7. Fynn and Guest, *Secret Life*, pp. 130–47.

8. Fynn and Guest, *Secret Life*, p. 136.
9. Fynn and Guest, *Secret Life*, p. 47; Football Trust, *Digest of Football Statistics, 1990–91* (Leicester, 1991), p. 47.
10. The BBC, short of capital and thus excluded from the warfare of 1988–92, supported the satellite deal, buying highlights from BSkyB for £4.5 million.
11. 'Blue Sky B', *Independent on Sunday*, 24 May 1992; Fynn and Guest, *Out of Time*, pp. 60–90.
12. 'ITV snatches the FA Cup', *Guardian*, 29 November 1995; 'Sky wins football', *Guardian*, 7 June 1996
13. Considerable discounts have been offered to those willing to receive all Sky channels. Sport, again, provides ground bait. In June 1995, BSkyB had 4.16 million subscribers in total.
14. *Guardian*, 11 August 1992. This was not enough to sustain the comic beyond 1993.
15. Another, Wycombe Wanderers, left their traditional ground three years before joining the League in 1993.
16. 'Any old iron as Scunthorpe build a ground for optimism', *Guardian*, 18 May 1988.
17. *Independent on Sunday*, 26 November 1995; *Daily Mail*, 1 September 1995. The school shirt cost £8.99 in comparison with a pack of two plain shirts in Newcastle's C&A branch at £5.99.
18. *Guardian*, 12 August 1995.
19. *Guardian*, 2 December 1995.
20. In spring 1996, United launched 'Red Devil' whisky. Much of the information here comes from a detailed, if hostile, study by Hunter Davies. 'A new set of goals', *Guardian*, 4 April 1995. See also 'A world sold on United', *Independent on Sunday*, 9 January 1994.
21. Inglis, *League Football*, p. 345.
22. 'Funny old game, funny new business', *Guardian*, 16 June 1993.
23. 'Alan Sugar's professional foul', *Independent on Sunday*, 24 May 1992.
24. T. Mason, 'Football', in T. Mason (ed.), *Sport in Britain* (Cambridge, 1989), p. 167.
25. *Viz* itself contributed a sometimes very funny send-up of the older style boy's soccer adventure in the 'Billy the Fish' strip.
26. 'Putting the boot in, but not too hard', *Guardian*, 2 October 1995.
27. *Total Football*, cover lead, September 1995.
28. The average price for these monthly journals in 1995–96 was £2.25. *Shoot*, a weekly, cost only 75 pence.
29. *FourFourTwo*, October 1995, pp. 123–5; 'Player pay goes over the top', *Guardian*, 1 August 1995; A. Parker, 'Great expectations: grimness or glamour? The football apprentice in the 1990s', *The Sports Historian*, 15 (1995), p. 125, note 12.
30. *Rothman's Football Yearbook, 1979–80*, p. 12.
31. J. Harding, *For the Good of the Game. The Official History of the Professional Footballers' Association* (London, 1991), pp. 351–53; 'Getting a kick out of work', *Guardian*, 19 August 1995.
32. For a similar case at Leicester City, see P. Murphy *et al.*, *Football on Trial. Spectator Violence and Development in the Football World* (London, 1990), p. 224.
33. H. Richards, 'Soccer socialism', *New Society*, 2 September 1988. See also collection of press cuttings in Halifax Central Library.
34. By 1988, 13 local councils had helped clubs through financial difficulties. Mason 'Football', p. 186, note 51.
35. Rate expenditure at both clubs was actually minimal. The situation was made worse by the 1989 Local Government Act which would have forced competitive tendering onto municipally controlled clubs.

36. 'Can this really be Huddersfield?', *Independent*, 17 August 1994.
37. Inglis, *League Football*, pp. 277–8.
38. *Rothman's Football Yearbook 1983–84*, p. 493.
39. *Carling Report. A Profile of Football Fans in the 1990s* (1994).
40. 'Running the gauntlet at The Den', *Guardian*, 12 April 1996.
41. *Rothman's Football Yearbook, 1987–88*, p. 9; 'Brass tacks' Radio Four, 9 May 1988; '"Exemplary" Luton system has revenue "draw-back"', *Guardian*, 9 January 1989.
42. Inglis, *League Football*, p. 349.
43. *Guardian*, 15 March 1989.
44. S. Redhead (ed.), *The Fashion and the Passion. Football Fandom in the New Europe* (Aldershot, 1993), has a number of helpful essays on post-Heysel fan culture. See also S. Redhead, *Football with Attitude* (Manchester, 1991) and R. Turner, *In Your Blood* (London, 1990).
45. See, for example, R. Taylor and A. Ward, *Three Sides of the Mersey* (London, 1993); S. Kelly, *The Kop* (1993); T. Watt, *The End: 80 Years of Life on Arsenal's North Bank* (Edinburgh, 1993).
46. This was also turned into a successful one-man play and, at the time of writing, a film version is being mooted. Other key works include D. Bull (ed.), *We'll Support You Ever More. Keeping Faith in Football* (London, 1992); N. Hornby (ed.), *My Favourite Year* (London, 1993); H. Pearson, *The Far Corner* (London, 1994).
47. N. Hornby, *Fever Pitch* (1992), pp. 47–51. The book had sold 300,000 copies by early 1996. *Guardian*, 29 April 1996.
48. This is a term of convenience and it is not intended to suggest that the formal organisations and the fanzines, for all their overlaps, should always be viewed and analysed as one and the same thing.
49. R. Taylor, *Football and its Fans. Supporters and their Relations with the Game, 1885–1985* (Leicester, 1992), pp. 71–2. See also Erlend Clouston's interview with Taylor, *Guardian*, 9 January 1989.
50. Rick Everitt, a journalist and the editor of the fanzine, provides a personal view in *The Battle for the Valley* (London, 1992). See also 'A Valley out of the shadow of death', *Guardian*, 5 December 1992, and, for a player's view, G. Nelson, *Left Foot Forward. A Year in the Life of a Journeyman Footballer* (London, 1995), pp. 149–53.
51. Fynn and Guest, *Out of Time*, pp. 105–11.
52. *Independent on Sunday*, 'Q & A', 12 June 1994.
53. R. Haynes, 'Vanguard or vagabond. A history of *When Saturday Comes*', in Redhead (ed.), *Fashion*, pp. 45–54. *Off the Ball* was another important early magazine of similar type.
54. For a well-documented introduction, see D. Jary, J. Horne and T. Bucke, 'Football "fanzines" and football culture: a case of successful "cultural contestation"', *Sociological Review*, 39, 3 (1991), pp. 581–97. For an extended treatment, R. Haynes, *The Football Imagination. The Rise of Football Fanzine Culture* (Aldershot, 1995).
55. Haynes notes that the magazine has a high number of students and ex-students among its readership. 'Vanguard', p. 47.
56. Jary *et al.*, '"Fanzines"', pp. 587–8.
57. *The Football Pink*, 9, spring 1994, editorial.
58. *The Fox* (Leicester City) 43 (May 1994), pp. 17–18. This article provided a very clear case against the loss of standing room.
59. S. Frith, 'Playing with real feeling – jazz and suburbia', in *Music for Pleasure* (Cambridge, 1988), pp. 45–63.

60. 'The silent majority finds its voice', *Independent on Sunday*, 8 March 1992; 'Saturday night fever', *Total Football*, 1 (1995).
61. R. Haynes 'Marching on together', in Redhead (ed.), *Fashion*, p. 26.
62. Jary *et al.* '"Fanzines"', p. 591.
63. H. F. Moorhouse, 'From 'zines like these. Fanzines, tradition and identity in Scottish football', G. Jarvie and G. Walker (eds), *Scottish Sport in the Making of the Nation. Ninety-minute Patriots?* (Leicester, 1994), p. 191.

Conclusion

1. N. Fishwick, *English Football and Society, 1910–1950* (Manchester, 1989), p. 150.
2. R. Holt, 'Football and the urban way of life in nineteenth-century Britain', in J. A. Mangan (ed.), *Pleasure, Profit and Proselytism* (London, 1988), p. 68.
3. Football Trust, *Digest of Football Statistics, 1990–91* (Leicester, 1991), p. 60, notes the work done by Brentford in this direction. Progress is slow, though. 'Asians can't play barrier', *Guardian*, 10 February 1996.
4. *Rothman's Football Yearbook, 1989–90*, p. 22; *FA News*, Autumn 1995; 'Good sport on a learning curve', *Independent on Sunday*, 16 January 1994.
5. 'Pitch Fever', *Guardian*, 29 April 1996.

Bibliography

Place of publication is London, unless otherwise stated.

Primary sources

Unpublished materials

FA Council Minutes, Lancaster Gate
FA Disciplinary Committee Minutes, Lancaster Gate
Football League Gate Books, 1925–1995, Lytham

Reports

Carling Report. A Profile of Football Fans in the Nineties, 1994.
Centre for Contemporary Studies, *Football as a Focus for Disorder*, 1984.
DES, *Report of the Committee on Football*, HMSO, 1968.
Football League, *Blueprint for the Future of Football*, 1991
Football League, *Report of the Committee of Enquiry into Structure and Finance*, Lytham, 1983.
Football Trust, *Digest of Soccer Statistics*, 1985-, Leicester.
PEP, 'English professional football', *Planning*, xxxii, June 1966.
The Hillsborough Stadium Disaster, 15 April 1989. Inquiry by Rt Hon. Lord Justice
Taylor. Final report, Cm. 962, HMSO, 1990.

Newspapers

Athletic News
Bradford Daily Telegraph
Football Echo & Sports Gazette (Southampton)
Football Favourite
Football Field (Bolton)
Football Gazette (South Shields)
Guardian
Halifax Courier
Lancashire Daily Post
Independent on Sunday
Preston Herald
Radio Times
The People

The Times
West Middlesex Advertiser and Chelsea Mail
Yorkshire Observer
Yorkshire Sports

Periodicals and Yearbooks

Charles Buchan's Football Monthly, 1951–1973
FA Book for Boys, 1948–73
FA News 1956–
FA Yearbook, 1948–
Football Annual (ed. C. W. Alcock) 1873–1908
Football and Sports Favourite, 1920–1929
Rothman's Football Yearbook, 1970–
Soccer Star, 1952–1970

Contemporary Studies, Autobiographies, Oral History

Alcock, C., *Association Football* (1906)
Allison, G., *Allison Calling* (1948)
Bastin, C. with B. Glanville, *Cliff Bastin Remembers* (1950)
Buchan, C., *A Lifetime in Football* (1955)
Bull, D., *We'll Support You Evermore* (1992)
Davies, H., *The Glory Game* (1985 edn)
Chapman, H., *Herbert Chapman on Football* (1934)
Chapman, L., *More than a Match. A Player's Story* (1993)
Catton, J. A. H., *Wickets and Goals* (1926)
Dunphy, E., *Only a Game* (1986 edn).
Edwards, L., *The Official Centenary History of the Southern League* (Halesowen, 1993)
Edwardes, C., 'The new football mania', *Nineteenth Century* (October 1892), pp. 622–32
Finney, T., *Football Round the World* (1953)
——, *Tom Finney's Preston North End Scrapbook* (1982)
Fynn, A. and L. Guest, *The Secret Life of Football* (1989)
——, *Out of Time. Why Football Isn't Working* (1994)
Hardaker, A., *Hardaker of the League* (1977)
Hopcraft, A., *The Football Man* (1968)
Hornby, N., *Fever Pitch* (1992)
Gibson, A. and W. Pickford, *Association Football and the Men Who Made it* (1906), 4 vols
Harris, R., *Soccer the Hard Way* (1970)
Lane, N. ('Pa') Jackson, *Sporting Days and Sporting Ways* (1932)
Lansdown, H. and A. Spillius, *Saturday's Boys. The Football Experience* (1990)
Marshall, Rev. F., *Football. The Rugby Union Game* (1892)
Nelson, G., *Left Foot Forward* (1995)
Pearson, H., *The Far Corner* (1995 edn)

Taylor, R. and A. Ward, *Kicking and Screaming. An Oral History of Football in England* (1995)
Rous, S., *Football Worlds* (1978)
Sharpe, I., *40 Years in Football* (1952)
Wall, F., *Fifty Years of Football* (1935)
Watson, P., *My Dear Watson. The Story of a Football Marriage* (1981)

Secondary

Books

Arnold, A. J., *A Game that Would Pay. A Business History of Professional Football in Bradford* (1988)
Bailey, P., *Leisure and Class in Victorian England* (1978)
Bale, J., *Sport and Place; A Geography of Sport in England, Scotland and Wales* (Lincoln, Nebraska, 1982)
——, *Sports, Space and the City* (London, 1993)
Benson, J., *The Rise of Consumer Society in Britain, 1880–1980* (1994)
Berry, H., *Blackburn Rovers Football Club. A Century of Soccer, 1875–1975* (Burnley, 1975)
Berry, H., and G. Allmann, *One Hundred Years at Deepdale, 1881–1981* (Preston, 1982)
Birley, D., *Land of Sport and Glory* (Manchester, 1995)
Buscombe, E. (ed.), *Football on Television* (1975)
Butler, B., *The Football League, 1888–1988* (1988)
Canter, D., M. Comber and D. Uzzell, *Football in its Place. A Social Psychology of Football Grounds* (1989)
Collett, M., *The Guinness Record of the FA Cup* (1993)
Clapson, M., *A Bit of a Flutter. Popular Gambling and English Society, 1823–1961* (Manchester, 1992)
Creek, F. N. S., *A History of the Corinthian Football Club* (1933)
Cunningham, H., *Leisure in the Industrial Revolution* (1980)
Davies, A., *Leisure, Gender and Poverty* (Buckingham, 1992)
Douglas, P., *The Football Industry* (1973)
Dunphy, E., *A Strange Kind of Glory. Sir Matt Busby and Manchester United* (1991)
Dunning, E. and K. Sheard, *Barbarians, Gentlemen and Players* (New York, 1979)
Dunning, E., P. Murphy and J. Williams, *The Roots of Football Hooliganism* (1988)
Farnsworth, K., *Wednesday* (Sheffield, 1982)
Fishwick, N., *English Football and Society, 1910–1950* (Manchester, 1989)
Green, G., *The History of the Football Association* (1953)
Green, G. and A. H. Fabian (eds)., *Association Football* (1960), 4 vols
Greenland, W. E., *The History of the Amateur Football Alliance* (Harwich, 1966)
Gruneau, R. S., *Class, Sport and Social Development* (MA, 1983)

Harding, J., *For the Good of the Game. The Official History of the Professional Footballers' Association* (1991)
Hargreaves, J., *Sport, Power and Culture* (Cambridge, 1986)
Haynes, R., *The Football Imagination. The Rise of Football Fanzine Culture* (Aldershot, 1995)
Hill, D., *Out of his Skin. The John Barnes Phenomenon* (1989)
Hill, J. and Williams, J., *Sport and Identity in the North of England* (Keele, 1996)
Holt, R., *Sport and the British. A Modern History* (Oxford, 1989)
Hunt, B., *Northern Goalfields* (1989)
Inglis, S., *The Football Grounds of England and Wales* (1985)
——, *Soccer in the Dock* (1985)
——, *League Football and the Men who Made it* (1988)
Jarvie, G. and J. Maguire (eds), *Sport and Leisure in Social Thought* (1994)
Jones, S. G., *Workers at Play. A Social and Economic History of Leisure, 1918–1939* (1986)
——, *Sport, Politics and the Working Class* (Manchester, 1988)
Kelly, S., *You'll Never Walk Alone* (1987)
——, *Back Page Football. A Centenary of Newspaper Coverage* (1995 edn)
——, *The Kop* (1993)
Lamming, D., *An England Football Internationalists' Who's Who* (Beverley, 1990)
Lowerson, J. *Sport and the English Middle Classes, 1870–1914* (Manchester, 1993)
Malcolmson, R. *Popular Recreation in English Society, 1700–1850* (Cambridge, 1973)
Marples, M., *A History of Football* (London, 1954)
Marsh, P., E. Rouser and R. Hare, *The Rules of Disorder* (1978)
Mason, T., *Association Football and English Society, 1863–1915*, (Brighton, 1980)
——, *The Blues and the Reds* (Historical Society of Lancashire and Cheshire, Liverpool, 1985)
——, *Sport in Britain* (London, 1988)
—— (ed.), *Sport in Britain. A Social History* (Cambridge, 1989)
Murphy, P., J. Williams and E. Dunning, *Football on Trial. Spectator Violence and Development in the Football World* (1990)
Murray, B., Football: *A History of the World Game* (Aldershot, 1994)
Newsham, G. J., *In a League of Their Own* (Chorley, 1994)
Redhead, S., *Football with Attitude* (Manchester, 1991)
—— (ed.), *The Passion and the Fashion. Football Fandom in the New Europe* (Aldershot, 1993)
Seddon, P., *A Football Compendium. A Comprehensive Guide to the Literature of Football* (1995)
Soar, P., *The Hamlyn A–Z of British Football Records* (1985)
Soar, P. and M. Tyler, *The Story of Football* (1986)
Sutcliffe, C. E. and F. Hargreaves, *History of the Lancashire Football Association, 1878–1928* (1928)
Tabner, B., *Through the Turnstiles* (Harefield, Middlesex, 1992)

Taylor, F., *The Day a Team Died* (1983)
Taylor, R., *Football and its Fans. Supporters and their Relations with the Game, 1885–1985* (Leicester, 1992)
Tischler, S., *Footballers and Businessmen. The Origins of Professional Soccer in England* (New York, 1981)
Turner, D. and A. White (eds), *The Breedon Book of Football Managers* (Derby, 1993)
Wagg, S., *The Football World. A Contemporary Social History* (Brighton, 1984).
Walvin, J., *The People's Game. The History of Football Revisited* (Edinburgh, 1994)
——, *Football and the Decline of Britain* (1986)
Vamplew, W., *Pay up and Play the Game* (Cambridge, 1988)
Williams, G., *The Code War* (Harefield, Middlesex, 1994)
Williams, J., E. Dunning and P. Murphy, *Hooligans Abroad* (1989 edn)
Williams, J. and S. Wagg (eds), *British Football and Social Change* (Leicester, 1991)
Williamson, D., *Belles of the Ball* (Exeter, 1991)
Woolnough, B., *Black Magic. England's Black Footballers* (1983)
Young, P., *A History of British Football* (1968)

Essays and Journal Articles

Armstrong, G. and R. Harris, 'Football hooligans: theory and evidence', *Sociological Review*, 39, 3 (1991), pp. 427–58
Clarke, A. and L. Madden, 'The limitations of economic analysis: the case of professional football', *Leisure Studies*, 7, 1 (1988), pp. 59–74
Critcher, C., 'Football since the war', in J. Clarke, C. Critcher and R. Johnson (eds), *Working-class culture. Studies in Theory and History* (1979), pp. 161–84
Delves, A., 'Popular recreation and social conflict in Derby, 1800–1850', in E. and S. Yeo (eds), *Popular Culture and Class Conflict, 1590–1914* (Brighton, 1981), pp. 89–127
Dunning, E., P. Murphy, J. Williams and J. Maguire, 'Football hooliganism in Britain before the First World War', *International Review of the Sociology of Sport*, 19 (1984), pp. 215–33
Edgell, S. and D. Jary, 'Football: a sociological eulogy', in M. Smith, S. Parker and C. Smith (eds), *Leisure and Society in Britain* (1973), pp. 214–29
Hall, S., 'The treatment of football hooliganism in the press', in R. Ingham *et al.* (eds), *Football Hooliganism: the Wider Context* (1978), pp. 15–36
Holt, R. J., 'Football and the urban way of life in nineteenth-century Britain', in J. A. Mangan (ed.), *Pleasure, Profit and Proselytism* (1988), pp. 67–85
Jacobson, S., 'Chelsea rule – Okay', *New Society* (27 March 1975), pp. 780–3
Jary, D., J. Horne and T. Bucke, 'Football "fanzines" and football culture: a case of successful "cultural contestation"', *Sociological Review*, 39, 3 (1991), pp. 581–97
Jennett, N. and P. J. Sloane, 'The future of League football: a critique of the Chester Committee of Enquiry', *Leisure Studies*, 4, 1 (1985), pp. 39–56

Jones, S. G., 'The economic aspects of Association Football in England, 1918–1939', *British Journal of Sports History*, 1, 3 (1984), pp. 286–99

Korr, C., 'West Ham United Football Club and the beginning of professional football in east London, 1895–1914', *Journal of Contemporary History*, 13, 2 (1978), pp. 211–32

——, 'A different kind of success: West Ham United and the creation of tradition and community', in R. Holt (ed.), *Sport and the Working Class in Modern Britain* (Manchester, 1990), pp. 142–58

Maguire, J., 'Sport, racism and British society: a sociological study of England's elite male Afro/Caribbean soccer and rugby players', in G. Jarvie (ed.), *Sport, Racism and Ethnicity* (1991), pp. 94–123

Mason, T., 'Sporting News, 1860–1914', in M. Harris and A. Lee (eds), *The Press and English Society from the Seventeenth to the Nineteenth Centuries* (1986)

——, 'Football and the historians', *International Journal of the History of Sport*, 5, 1 (1988), pp. 136–41

——, 'Stanley Matthews', in R. Holt (ed.), *Sport and the Working Class in Modern Britain* (Manchester, 1990), pp. 159–78

Metcalfe, A., 'Organised sport in the mining communities of south Northumberland, 1800–1889', *Victorian Studies*, 25, 4 (1982), pp. 469–95

——, 'Football in the mining communities of east Northumberland, 1882–1914', *International Journal of the History of Sport*, 5, 3 (1988), pp. 267–91

Moorhouse, H. F., 'Scotland Against England: Football and popular culture', *International Journal of the History of Sport*, 4, 2 (1987), pp. 189–202

——, 'Shooting stars: Footballers and working-class culture in twentieth-century Scotland', in R. Holt (ed.), *Sport and the Working Class in Modern Britain* (Manchester, 1990), pp. 179–97

——, 'From 'zines like these? Fanzines, tradition and identity in Scottish football', in G. Jarvie and G. Walker (eds), *Scottish Sport in the Making of the Nation* (Leicester, 1994), pp. 173–94

Parker, A., 'Great Expectations. The football apprentice in the 1990s', *The Sports Historian*, 15 (1995), pp. 107–27

Say, T., 'Herbert Chapman: Football Revolutionary?', *The Sports Historian*, 16 (1996), pp. 81–98

Taylor, I., 'Football mad: A speculative sociology of football hooliganism', in E. Dunning (ed.), *The Sociology of Sport* (1971), pp. 352–7

——, 'Soccer consciousness and soccer hooliganism', in S. Cohen (ed.), *Images of Deviance* (1971), pp. 134–64

——, 'On the sports violence question – soccer hooliganism revisited', in J. Hargreaves (ed.), *Sport, Culture, Ideology* (1982), pp. 153–190

Richards, J., 'Football and the crisis of national identity', forthcoming

Williams, G., 'From Grand Slam to grand slump. Economy, society and Rugby football in Wales during the depression', *Welsh History Review*, 11 (1983), pp. 339–57

Theses

R. Lewis, 'The development of football in Lancashire, *c.* 1860–1914 (Unpublished Ph.D. thesis, University of Lancaster, 1994)

P. G. Hutchins, 'Sport and Regional Pride: Association Football and the North East of England, 1919–1961' (Unpublished PhD thesis, University of Sussex, 1990)

Index

Clubs and individuals receiving more than passing mention are included in the index
Page references in **bold** are to illustrations